D0223417

The Velvet Revolution at Work

Hay Library
Western Wyoming Community College

658.3152 SM95V 2013
John Smythe
The Velvet Revolution at Work

The Velvet Revolution at Work

The Rise of Employee Engagement, the Fall of Command and Control

JOHN SMYTHE

GOWER

© John Smythe 2013

All rights reserved. No part of this publication may be reproduced, stored in a retrieval system or transmitted in any form or by any means, electronic, mechanical, photocopying, recording or otherwise without the prior permission of the publisher.

John Smythe has asserted his moral right under the Copyright, Designs and Patents Act, 1988, to be identified as the author of this work.

Published by
Gower Publishing Limited
Wey Court East
Union Road
Farnham
Surrey, GU9 7PT
England

Ashgate Publishing Company
110 Cherry Street
Suite 3-1
Burlington, VT 05401-3818
USA

www.gowerpublishing.com

British Library Cataloguing in Publication Data
A catalogue record for this book is available from the British Library.

Library of Congress Cataloging-in-Publication Data
Smythe, John.
  The velvet revolution at work : the rise of employee engagement, the fall of command and control / by John Smythe.
      pages cm
  Includes bibliographical references and index.
    ISBN 978-1-4094-4324-7 (hardback) -- ISBN 978-1-4094-4325-4 (ebook) -- ISBN 978-1-4724-0057-4 1. Management--Employee participation. 2. Organizational change. 3. Employee motivation. 4. Corporate culture. 5. Industrial relations. I. Title.
  HD5650.S57 2013
  658.3'152--dc23
                                                                              2013006117

ISBN 9781409443247 (pbk)
ISBN 9781409443254 (ebk – PDF)
ISBN 9781472400574 (ebk – ePUB)

Printed in the United Kingdom by Henry Ling Limited, at the Dorset Press, Dorchester, DT1 1HD

Contents

List of Figures   *vii*
List of Tables   *xi*
About the Author   *xiii*
Foreword   *xv*
Acknowledgements   *xvii*

Introduction   1

PART I: WHAT IS THE VELVET REVOLUTION AT WORK?

1   The Velvet Revolution at Work – Why Now?   7

2   Defining Employee Engagement   15

3   Introducing the Primary Levers and
           Supporting Enablers of Engagement   41

**PART II: STRATEGY THROUGH PEOPLE:
                 DELIVERING STRATEGY AND CHANGE
                 THROUGH PARTICIPATIVE INTERVENTIONS
                 THAT ENGAGE THE RIGHT PEOPLE**

4   Getting Started and Negotiating Business Outcomes   57

5   Your Default Approach to Engagement:
           Enabler or Disabler?   71

6   Negotiating Who Should Be Engaged:
      The Power of the Peach   85

7   Designing and Running Engagement Interventions
      That Deliver Fast Commercial and Cultural Results   101

8   Sustaining the Benefits of an Engagement Intervention   131

9   Creative Dynamics that Liberate Breakthrough Ideas   147

PART III: BEYOND THE INTERVENTION:
**   THE ENGAGED ORGANIZATION**

10   The Evidence   171
      Jerome Reback

11   Helping Leaders at Every Level Engage their People –
      Capability   197
      Jerome Reback

12   Brand Needs Engaged Employees to
      Deliver the Customer Promise   215

13   The Impact of Employee Engagement on
      Internal Communication   227

14   Digital Technology Needs the Right Culture to be an
      Enabler of Engagement   243
      John Smythe with Ben Hart and Max Waldron

15   Objections to Employee Engagement   261

16   Epilogue: Employee Engagement –
      Social Movement or Fleeting Fad?   267

References   275
Index   277

List of Figures

1.1	The four approaches to decision making and engagement	8
1.2	The shift towards an equitable employer/employee relationship	13
2.1	Old and new (E) model workplaces – what characterizes your organization?	19
2.2	Three dimensions of engagement	21
2.3	What engages people at work?	27
2.4	Employee engagement and decision making	28
2.5	The fourth level of engagement	29
3.1	The primary and secondary enablers of leader and employee engagement	42
3.2	Brand and reputation	49
3.3	Digital technology as an enabler of engagement	51
II.1	The primary and secondary enablers of leader and employee engagement	54
4.1	Engagement is not a means to an end	66
5.1	What engages people at work?	76
5.2	Diagnosing your patterns of engagement	79
5.3	The big idea	81
5.4	Awareness of my decision making	82
5.5	Awareness of my personal style of interaction	82
5.6	Typology of decision making	83
6.1	The power of the peach	85
6.2	The what down, the bottom up	86
6.3	Communication and engagement	87

6.4	Communication and engagement	88
6.5	Circular decision making	99
7.1	The Express	102
8.1	A simple chart-based approach to show progress against plan	140
9.1	From incremental thinking to breakthrough thinking	156
9.2	The floorplan and choreography of an event	160
9.3	The Zurich Financial Services touring truck	162
III.1	The primary and secondary enablers of leader and employee engagement	168
III.2	The attitudes and systems that support engagement	169
10.1	Net agree score	175
10.2	Are employees engaged?	177
10.3	The implications for organizations that do and do not engage	179
10.4	Are employees engaged with their work?	180
10.5	How the levels of employer engagement have changed	181
10.6	The correlation between power sharing and engagement	182
10.7	Different forms and levels of involvement	183
10.8	Employee involvement in everyday decisions	184
10.9	Work/life balance and engagement	185
10.10	Recognition, development and engagement	186
10.11	Is employee engagement a priority for managers?	187
10.12	How effective are managers as engagers?	187
10.13	Satisfaction with senior managers	188
10.14	Competencies essential for employee engagement	190
10.15	The impact of measuring employee engagement	191
10.16	Board members' perception of engagement	193
10.17	Employee engagement as a factor in performance	193
10.18	Investment expectations in engagement	194
11.1	The shifting nature of leadership	199
11.2	Attributes that drive engagement	200
12.1	Brand – the third influence on an employee's relationship with the organization	216
12.2	The relationship between interaction, experience and brand	219

12.3	The customer journey in a business-to-business context	224
12.4	The consumer customer journey	224
13.1	The flows of communication in an engaged organization	234
13.2	The what down, how up model	235
13.3	The correlation between communication and engagement	239
13.4	The tell-tale signs of the engaged organization	240
14.1	The stairway diagram	247
15.1	A breakdown of statistics on levels of engagement in the UK workforce	266

List of Tables

2.1   How to recognize engagement   24

7.1   Bite-size cases   128

8.1   Who should be onboard?   138

10.1   Engagement and the perception of performance   176
10.2   Competences to drive employee engagement   189

11.1   Competences that drive engagement   201
11.2   Engagement capability – self-assessment test   210
11.3   Developing your employee engagement capability   213
11.4   Diagnosing your leadership engagement skills – three parts   214

13.1   A communicator's development plan   236
13.2   The make-up of a skilled communicator   239

About the Author

John is one of the founding voices of the leader and employee engagement movement and is a partner of Engage for Change (www.engageforchange. com), a consultancy dedicated to advising on engaging leaders and everyone at work to drive change, transform organizations and raise day-to-day business performance.

Before establishing Engage for Change, John had a fixed term as a visiting fellow with McKinsey and Company. In 1989 he co-founded SmytheDorwardLambert, a consultancy which was acknowledged to be the thought leader in organizational communication, change communication/ leadership and change management, and in addition has been an advisor to Neil Kinnock during the latter's reform of the European Commission. He has also held senior corporate communication roles in the oil and energy sectors with the American companies Occidental Petroleum, Bechtel and Marathon.

His last book – *CEO, Chief Engagement Officer: Turning Hierarchy Upside Down to Drive Performance* – was published by Gower in 2007.

Foreword

There are only three fundamental ways to create sustainably successful businesses: to give outstanding customer service, to innovate with new products and services, or to find new ways of doing what we do more efficiently. People are at the heart of all three. Engaged people do these things well and disengaged people walk past the opportunities that occur every day to delight customers, to innovate or to improve productivity. While this is obvious to some, it is paid lip service to by many others. The ones who take it seriously tend to harness much more of the capability and potential of their people than do the others. In so doing, they improve the performance of their organisations and contribute to the growth of our economy. As a nation we simply cannot afford to have so much of our people's capability and potential left unused. We will not grow and we will not successfully compete unless our people care, unless they are engaged, and we cannot sustainably engage people unless we attend to their well-being. If we want our people to offer better customer service, to innovate and to improve productivity, we must attend to their well-being.

As Nita Clarke and I said in our Report to Government, *Engaging for Success*, 'if employee engagement and the principles that lie behind it were more widely understood, if the potential that resides in the country's workforce was more fully unleashed, we could see a step change in workplace performance and employee well-being for the considerable benefit of UK PLC'.

We are pleased that the Prime Minister and Ed Davey launched a task force which seeks to create a movement which will enhance the importance of this topic and offer some insights and best practise to help organizations enhance their own levels of employee engagement. This book offers important and revealing insights, case studies and the evidence to ensure that you are harnessing more of the capability and potential of your people for the benefit of your organization, the country and, indeed, the employees themselves.

David MacLeod
Chairman Employee Engagement Task Force

Acknowledgements

John Smythe would like to acknowledge the contributions of the following:

Mervyn Walker, Group Head of Human Resources, Anglo American

Jim McAuslan, General Secretary, BALPA

Peter Jones, former Communications Director, BUPA and Non-Executive Director of CTN Communications, BUPA

Emma Bryant, Communications Consultant.
Former Head of Executive & Employee Communication at Dresdner Kleinwort, now Commerzbank Corporates & Markets

Andy Harrison, Chief Executive, Whitbread plc. formerly CEO easyJet

Ted Burke, Global Managing Partner, Freshfields Bruckhaus Deringer

General Sir Mike Jackson, former Chief of the General Staff and Head of the British Army

Rob Withecombe, whilst Partner, Head of Tax at Grant Thornton.
Currently at Barclays Wealth, Head of Wealth Advisory

Tony Voller, SVP Talent, InterContinental Hotels Group PLC

Caron Jones, Talent Resourcing Director, EMEA, InterContinental Hotel Group

Geoff Muirhead CBE, CEO, Mark Johnson, Group Business Services Director, Manchester Airport

Julie Armstrong, Customer Services Director, Manchester Airport

Dominic Fry, Director of Communications, Marks & Spencer

Sir John Parker, Chairman, National Grid plc and Anglo American plc

Paul Barron, whilst CEO, NATS

Rachel Reid, Director Corporate, Customer & Environmental Affairs, NATS

Simon Lewis, whilst Director of Communications and the Prime Minister's Official Spokesman at 10 Downing Street.
Currently Association for Financial Markets in Europe (AFME), Chief Executive

Richard Everitt, Chief Executive, POLA

Clive Schlee, CEO, Pret A Manger

Paul Noon, General Secretary, via Jim McAuslan, BALPA, Prospect

Graham Love, ex-CEO of QinetiQ.
Now chairs a number of private equity backed businesses.

Elisabeth Hunka, Director of Personnel, Royal Household

Peter Thomas, formerly Director of Corporate Communications and Public Affairs, RFU

Ronan Dunne, Chief Executive Officer, Telefónica UK Limited

Carol Kavanagh, Group HR Director, Travis Perkins

Steve Bareham, Regional Director, Travis Perkins

Chris Browne, MD, Thomson Airways (TUI)

John Murphy, Director of Flight Operations, Thomson Airways

Also thanks to Lynette Proctor for all her help.

Introduction

This book is for leaders at any level who are curious about the growing employee engagement movement and those who are interested in devising and delivering strategy through people, rather than cascading decisions at people conceived by elites.

The core idea lies in challenging the orthodoxy that command and control, top-down, hierarchical leadership produces the best results for organizations and their workforces. It argues that soon a tipping point will be reached where there will be a sufficient critical mass of employers who have adopted a more inclusive approach to leadership, providing a viable choice for employees between these new model cultures and post-Second World War command and control cultures.

I and others have previously made the business case for employee engagement. In this book I provide more evidence to support the business case and one of the first attempts to make the social case. I also contend that the social case will be a decisive influence in helping to put employee engagement on the leadership agenda.

The theme of *The Velvet Revolution at Work* stems from the democracy-seeking social upheavals of the velvet revolutions of the former Eastern European states and the continuing Arab Spring. I ask if there is a connection between these wider national movements and the desire for workers and employees to have more say at work. I provide practical approaches at the level of the organization to facilitate the engagement of people in the development and execution of organizational renewal initiatives such as strategy and change, emphasizing that effective engagement can only take place within the context of strong leadership. Employee engagement is not a laissez-faire philosophy. Governing it to produce commercial and cultural results requires belief and, above all, discipline.

At the level of the individual, I also provide insight into the capabilities necessary to equip leaders and managers to engage people effectively. These have been validated across UK plc via independent research.

Further Aims

I also aim to build on my previous book, *CEO, Chief Engagement Officer: Turning Hierarchy Upside Down to Drive Performance*, published by Gower in 2007. In this new work, there is much new material derived from more than 45 interviews and pan-UK research conducted independently by UK poll firm YouGov and the consulting work of Engage for Change.

The concept of leader and employee engagement remains ill defined. Most definitions are statements about desirable outcomes rather than 'drivers' or causes. In *The Velvet Revolution at Work*, I will appeal to those who sense that there must be a better way of leadership than the post-Second World War top-down, command and control hierarchical model; I explore emerging myths about employee engagement including:

- that it is no more than incremental top-end or turbo-charged communication,

- that there is not time to engage people as the elite already know what to do,

- and that management are paid to come up with all the answers anyway.

I question the social utility of coercive top-down internal communication designed to align and mobilize people once decisions have been made by an elite, debate whether employee engagement is a valuable concept which will make the workplace better and more productive, or a cynical re-packaging of existing exploitative management models and, finally, explore why engagement is now on the corporate agenda given that the concept has been around for as long as mankind.

Drucker was writing about it in the 1950s and others even earlier like the Victorian-era philanthropists in the UK and the USA. But it was only when the post-Second World War deal of the 'loyalty for security deal' broke down in the 1990s that it began to be an acceptable topic in the boardroom. Ricardo Semmler pioneered it in his engineering firm decades ago in Brazil, a country that was at the time hardly a symbol of new workplace thinking

The Three Parts of the Book

PART I: WHAT IS THE VELVET REVOLUTION AT WORK?

Part I proposes that employee engagement is here to stay, explores what engages people at work and reviews the primary levers and supporting enablers that organizations have at their disposal.

PART II: STRATEGY THROUGH PEOPLE: DELIVERING STRATEGY AND CHANGE THROUGH PARTICIPATIVE INTERVENTIONS THAT ENGAGE THE RIGHT PEOPLE

Part II focuses on interventions that give an organization's people a well-organized role in devising and executing big-ticket business imperatives like purpose, strategy, change and operational renewal.

PART III: BEYOND THE INTERVENTION: THE ENGAGED ORGANIZATION

Part III is about the role of leaders at every level in creating an environment which encourages and invites employees to engage themselves for their own benefit and for that of their organization. It also covers the three supporting enablers; brand, internal communication and digital technology.

PART I

What is the Velvet Revolution at Work?

1

The Velvet Revolution at Work – Why Now?

In the Introduction, I suggested that in addition to a sound business case, social forces would stimulate the emergence of the employee engagement movement.

Looking back at the history of work in the UK since the Industrial Revolution of the eighteenth and nineteenth centuries, it is punctuated by major events such as the migration from the land to the city, the rise of union power to counteract the power of capital, the decline of union power, nationalizations and privatizations, the influence of various management theories and the rise of entrepreneurship.

The leader and employee engagement movement – E theory – may be a defining shift in the way we work, but it is not new.

Employee Engagement is as Old as the Hills

Employee engagement is as old as the hills in the sense that leaders have been practising it ever since mankind emerged as a collaborative social group. Leaders have been making informed judgments about what they alone will decide versus which individuals or groups will add value to decisions on the basis of the specialist knowledge and experience those groups have or because of the power that they hold. The key phrase is 'making informed judgments'.

When I worked on a study with McKinsey & Company in 2004 called 'Boot Camp or Commune' (one of the first studies to look at this topic), we found that nearly every CEO we interviewed made instinctive, automatic and thus irrational judgments about engaging people in decision making. Questions about their thought process about approaches to employee engagement were met with naiveté and the disclosure that consideration of it was typically not part of their decision-making process. This was in contrast to their approach to strategy (or content) formulation, which they reported as being thought through in a more considered way either alone or with a range of people enfranchised for political and quality purposes. In other words, their approach to engaging their people usually attracted little or no thought at all, with the result that 'decide and tell or decide and sell' approaches to strategy origination and execution were the dominant method of decision making.

Figure 1.1 below represents four approaches to decision making and engagement.

The conclusion from that 2004 study was that leaders should make conscious and visible decisions about which approach, in terms of engaging their populations, will add value. By value I mean the quality of decisions and the broad ownership of them by those who must deliver.

What engages people at work?– power sharing

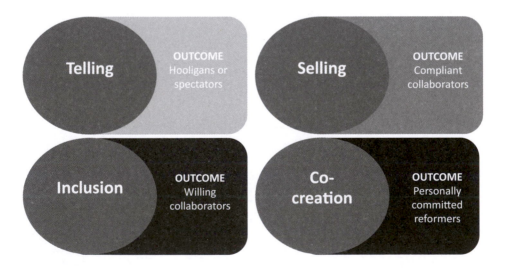

Figure 1.1   The four approaches to decision making and engagement

In a traditional command and control environment, an elite concludes the thinking about the content (the what) and the execution (the how), and then casts about for ways to tell its people what has been decided. This linear approach to decision making inevitably results in a 'tell or sell' mode of engagement which casts recipients as spectators of the process, however apparently engaging or entertaining the communication is. This is a value-destroying approach to decision making, as most of the population have not been invited to challenge and contribute, and thus the outcome is representative of a tiny minority of the collective memory and expertise of the enterprise, added to which those who are relied on to execute a top-down decision feel little ownership of it and are not readily motivated to help.

Under command and control, 'decide and tell and decide and sell' are the default engagement approaches. When people are precluded from challenging and contributing, often through ignorance by leaders of the choices available to them to engage people, it is little wonder that so many organizational initiatives come and go with little impact.

A command and control culture is exposed by its language. Metaphors of the military and religious abound – briefing, front line, vision, mission, mobilize, align, morning prayers and so on. Command and control served well as the postmodern foundation for large, multi-location organizations where it was thought that tight control was the best and only way of standardizing production methods and customer experience.

Whilst there are now many instances and examples of more inclusive and 'engaging' styles of leadership, command and control, in one guise or another, is still the dominant experience for many people at work. Of course, there are many highly successful organizations which seem to thrive on command and control and there may be so for a long time to come.

The Birth of an Alternative to Command and Control

However, we may be at the birth of what is an evolution to the next style of leadership at every level in organizations. This is a protracted birth which will be characterized by as many ups and downs as the Velvet Revolutions that took place across Eastern Europe and now in the Arab world. Peter Drucker's early calls for more inclusive leadership may at last have found their time. What follows is my view of what UK social history has to tell us about the deal between employers and employees. Your country's history and culture will also have a significant bearing on the deal between employees and employers.

I am no historian, but drawing on the accounts of others, it is worth remembering that the history of organized industrial work with massed workforces is barely 250 years old, dating back to the late 1700s. The UK as the cradle of the first Industrial Revolution was the first mover in learning to manage and organize large numbers of workers. If we take a walk back in time in the UK, what do we find?

Among the first vivid images of people at work are the sweat shops of Victorian England brought to us by the paintings of L.S. Lowry or the writing of Charles Dickens and Elizabeth Gaskell. Fast forward to today and these working conditions can still be found in many parts of the world. In the UK people had migrated from the privations of the land to squalor in crowded slums where they found themselves to be the human cogs in the industrial machine. The first capitalist robber barons in the UK and the USA experienced little pressure in the early days of industrialization from the disenfranchised and unrepresented masses for better conditions.

However, amid the gloom emerged social thinkers like Robert Owen writing in the early nineteenth century (*Selected Works of Robert Owen*, William Pickering 1930) and industrialists that brought us Port Sunlight and Bourneville as examples of model industrial towns where workers received a better deal. These individuals were among the first advocates of worker mutuality and engagement.

In the USA, Andrew Carnegie epitomized the idea of social responsibility articulated in his Gospel of Wealth (*North American Review*, June 1889). He said that 'Happier, warmer and healthier' workers produced better results. It was self-interested care, but it was a deal that he claimed was more sustainable than one-sided capitalism. These 'social industrialists' were rewarded with better outcomes and recognition for the way they balanced the needs of workers and capital more equitably.

Soon enough, the benefits of mass output started to benefit the workers and the early seeds of the consumer were planted – after all, without consumption, there is a limit on returns. Consumerism was ultimately to become a brakeon capital in the sense that, without consumer support and demand, profit is limited.

Today this extends to consumers switching away from brands they consider to be misaligned with their own values. Thus, exploiters of child labour have been forced to manufacture with the supply community in mind as well as the consumer. And in the UK in late 2012 the reported underpayment of tax by global businesses resulted in some consumers shunning these companies.

The Engineering Strike in Yarrow Shipyard, Southampton (1897)

In the late nineteenth and early twentieth centuries the struggle between capital and labour spawned the emergence of the union movement which, in its first guise, can take credit for attempting to balance the books in favour of the worker.

The tussle between profit and people included violence. In the USA workers routinely found themselves being policed and killed by fellow workers wearing, among others, the uniform of Pinkerton's private security guards. In the 1877 strike against the Baltimore and Ohio (rail) company, President Rutherford Hayes sent federal troops to quell rioters, who themselves were armed to the teeth under the US Constitution's right to bear arms (see Richard Donkin, *The History of Work* (2010)).

In academia, early theories framed work as a rational machine (*Taylorism, Principles of Scientific Management* (1911)) with workers taking their place as a coerced cog. Taylorism had admirers like Henry Ford and other early proponents of rigidly enforced standardization in which initiative was expressly forbidden.

Taylorism was later characterized as X theory by Douglas McGregor, who countered it with Y (*The Human Side of Enterprise* (1960)) theory that posited that high performance was an outcome of trust and the granting of initiative to workers which drew from Japanese success in driving up quality through collaborative teamwork as demonstrated by Volvo's early successful application to its team-based approach to manufacturing.

The Rise of the State

The periods following the Second World War in the UK witnessed the rise of the state and a rise in the number of state workers. At that time, to be a high-flying civil servant was a glittering career path and many employees in the private and public sectors enjoyed a cradle-to-grave employment promise.

To this day, in the UK the state sector is a well-preserved example of the command and control work place culture. Whilst the rhetoric in the UK state sector may be 'the new model workplace', the reality is a persistent devotion to hierarchy, bureaucracy, protocol, deference and risk aversion.

The rise of the state matters because when it becomes the main employer, as the DNA of work becomes overshadowed by the values and mores of the state institution. In Scotland today the percentage of GDP generated and consumed by the state is around 73%. In Wales and Northern Ireland it is above 60% and is rising. In the south-east of the UK the percentage of GDP deriving from the state sector is 25% and less in Greater London, the engine of Britain (BBC). Following the Second World War, the private sector mirrored the state sector in adopting the leadership model of command and control. People would aim to join and stay with a company or public sector institution for their working life and, by offering their loyalty, would be rewarded with certainty, perks and development.

The deal started to break down as the last millennia came to an end and companies and institutions started to scale back their side of the bargain. The decline of final pension schemes and their generous index linked payouts for life was a major cause of this breakdown. Meanwhile, internal communication in its first guise was a tool of the corporation designed to align its people with its messages and mobilize them into concerted action. It was an adjunct of the top-down leadership style and was the equivalent of a dictator's radio station. Whilst the underlying psychological contract of 'my loyalty for my security' was in force, this was fine. But as that contract fractured, so too would the top-down mode of communication.

Whatever Happened to the 1990s Concept of Employee Empowerment?

In the 1980s and 1990s people became much more mobile and started to demand greater involvement in decisions affecting them at work. The loyalty for security contract was bust. The velvet revolution at work was gaining momentum. It may turn out to be of no surprise that this was occurring at the same time as the spread of democracy across the former Eastern Europe and now in different theatres – social historians will debate whether this is congruence or coincidence.

Figure 1.2 charts the shift from command and control to a more mutual relationship between employer and employee.

Cradle to grave	→	portfolio careers
Loyalty	→	transactional relationship
Dependence	→	independence
'Our human resources'	→	creative talent on loan
Employees	→	citizens
Big institutions	→	my own company
Command and control	→	well governed inclusivity
CEO = GOD	→	CEO = GUIDE
I left the company	→	I left my boss
Local community	→	workplace communities

Figure 1.2   **The shift towards an equitable employer/employee relationship**

The velvet revolution at work is taking place now because command and control is giving way to more inclusive styles of leadership. It is taking place now because people have emerging choices between working for coercive institutions and ones which encourage challenge and contribution. Another reason is because the 'loyalty for security' contract is dead, people are seeing themselves as a unit of one and feel responsible for their own destiny. There is no security anymore, except that which people provide for themselves.

Taylorism hypothesized that people had to be made to work, which explains the prevalence of command and control in the post-Second World War era when this was a commonly held view. Y theory posited that people needed no instruction to work provided that they were doing something they were committed to. You only have to look at vocational pursuits to see the veracity of Y theory. Indeed, you only have to think about the most productive and contented groups of workers in any economy. They are of course the self-employed and those in companies with the greatest discretion over their work.

Developing McGregor's Y theory, Ouchi's Z theory, Drucker's work and others, my colleagues and I suggest that people engage themselves when they are invited to challenge and contribute to decision making that affects them and over which they can have a positive influence. It follows of course that you cannot achieve commitment in a command and control setting; all you can do is to obtain compliance via coercion of a psychological or instrumental nature This is not an environment which is conducive to encouraging challenge and contribution. The command and control culture thus self-limits the creativity of its people. It also treats its people in a parent-child fashion, assuming a noticeable power imbalance between employer and employee. Whilst many of us still experience command and control, like all revolutions, once the velvet revolution takes hold, it will spread at varying speeds. At first there will be movers and bunkers of fierce resistance.

This is of course a UK-centric explanation as to why the velvet revolution at work may now be ripe. Every national workplace culture will be different and will be shaped by its own nation's history of work over the past 250 years or so. They will run at different speeds.

2

Defining Employee Engagement

The concept of employee engagement has become popular rather over-used term. What used to be attributed to communication and relationships is often now packaged as employee engagement. In some enterprises it has even become a defined role with the unenviable responsibility for 'raising levels of engagement', as if this task were adjacent to leadership.

Leaders are still delegating responsibility for engagement to functions within the business or assuming that the engagement survey 'action process' is going to 'fix engagement'. A major part of the problem is poor definition. It is persistently described (as will be seen later in this chapter) in terms of outcomes and claimed benefits, such as 'people providing discretionary effort' (going the extra mile) or 'people getting better connected'.

The actual causes and drivers of engagement remain elusive. Employee engagement is also rather an ugly term more easily associated with the mechanics of moving parts than the delicate ecology of people at work trying to perform at their best. We are probably stuck with it, so the challenge lies in vesting it with a meaning that is of value to people and the enterprises in which they work.

The UK government's Department for Business, Skills & Innovation published its second report on employee engagement (by David MacLeod and Nita Clarke) in late 2012 entitled *Engage for Success* (www.engageforsuccess. org), which will help to legitimize the topic and attract boardroom attention. One of the sponsors, Sir Win Bishoff (currently, Chair of the Lloyds Banking Group) has said that shareholders will soon demand evidence that enterprises are investing in engagement.

Although I run the risk of over-simplification, let's unpack the concept. What does being engaged look like? A child or adult absorbed in a hobby or game is focused, self-organizing, enthusiastic and ambitious for results.

The same can be true for individuals and groups at work. People who have conceived or influenced a goal will self-organize themselves to deliver on it.

To be engaged, people must be invited to influence the goal – the what – rather than just its realization – the how. Organizations should take note as they often dictate goals – the what – and invite some involvement in delivery – the how – and assume that they have engaged people. They have not engaged people unless they have involved them in both the 'what' and the 'how'.

Self-organization is a key indicator of someone or a group being engaged – people need little or no external stimulus or instruction. This truth is also at the heart of employee engagement at work. Creating the conditions in which people feel safe and invited to self organize resonates as a theme throughout the book. The power of self-organization also explains why attempts to coerce people to become engaged usually result in resistance, even anger, or sabotage of the tacit variety.

Yet instruction and coercion are the staple diet of many at work. Leaders, managers and supervisors still think that strong leadership means being bossy. It doesn't – it means bosses who make rational judgements about who will add value to a decision or initiative, and being clear about what is open to others to challenge and contribute to.

Vignette: Environmental Campaign Group

The chief of a well-known environmental campaign group described its culture thus:

> We are a bit like Hotel California, you can check out but you can never really leave – we are an example of an organization that has such incredible sense of purpose and shared ethos that engagement is pretty much automatic. We are a self-organizing group made up of local action groups that can make its presence felt in hundreds if not thousands of locations with minimal direction.

This will chime with anyone involved with a community, religious or other ideologically motivated group, benign and valuable to the greater good at one end of the spectrum, dangerous when motivating zelotry and terrorism at the other end of the spectrum.

The campaign group's insight suggests that having highly engaged people can be brought about simply through shared purpose, vision, values and ethos, with little or no need at all to recourse to surveys and other bureaucracy. This kind of devotion is also evident in start-ups, some of which continue with a compelling sense of mission, and with family-owned businesses that may be many decades old. An example is the confectionary firm Mars. When original or family values are constantly reinforced by the presence of family members an ethos seems to be maintained without too much costly bureaucracy. Barclays bank in the UK was built on Quaker traditions which helped it earn a place as a 'good' bank, a reputation that was badly damaged by the events of 2008 and beyond as those founding values gave way to those of mammon. Values that build reputation are hard to grow and easy to lose.

This chapter covers the following areas:

1. Parallel velvet revolutions in nation states and the workplace – coincidence or congruence?

2. A new model of organizational culture – the shift from Y and Z theories to E theory.

3. What engages people? – The difference between outcomes and causes.

4. Introducing the primary levers of leader and employee engagement.

5. Ruby and Geraldine's contrasting experiences of being engaged in change.

6. Thirteen myths about leader and employee engagement.

1) Parallel Velvet Revolutions in Nation States and the Workplace – Coincidence or Congruence?

Before we turn to the world of work, let us cast our eyes around the world as a reminder about the social context originally, and memorably, marked by uprisings in Soviet Eastern Europe and currently in Africa, the Middle East and perhaps the early beginnings of the end of autocratic socialism in China.

All generations are saying that the impervious, static and often brutal ways of the national despots are over. And workers are saying something similar about the workplace regimes they work in, voting with their feet to find more open, collaborative and liberal regimes. Hopefully brutality does not feature widely at work.

The parallels between social upheavals at the national level and the clamour by workers for more say are intriguing and may be coincidental, but it is possible that the former may well become an engine for the latter. People will hardly throw off political and social oppression and then knuckle back down under autocratic corporate leadership.

In organizations there is a divide emerging between corporations that operate a benign form of control over their people and those that invite challenge and contribution. Employees have been happy to go along with command and control whilst the 'my loyalty in exchange for security' deal held good.

Alongside organizations characterized by command and control are examples of new models of work where the old deal of loyalty in exchange for security has been replaced by a new deal in which people seek freedom of thought and responsibility for their own security and development.

2) A New Model of Organizational Culture – The Shift from Y and Z Theories to E Theory

Employees working in the new model see themselves as being on loan to employers in exchange for the development of career-enhancing skills and for active engagement in day-to-day decision making and in big-ticket change.

In new model E theory enterprises, the leader's role is to provide guidance rather than to be a god with all the answers. Guidance means providing strong leadership on direction and well-governed but widely distributed leadership.

Douglas McGregor invoked the idea of theory X and theory Y organizations. He posited that X organizations are based on a low-trust assumption that employees need to be instructed and controlled – the root of the prevalent post-Second World War top-down, command and control style of leadership.

Autocratic (old)	Distributed leadership/power (new)
Hierarchical	Flatter
Secretive	Transparent/trusting
Monolithic/central planning	Distributed
Adult to child	Adult to adult
Fear culture	Safe to challenge
Status conscious	Achievement oriented
Deference	Candour
Permission culture	Initiative culture
Bullying	Negotiative
Grandeur	Self deprecating
Clubby	Open
Elitist/private	Accessible
Formal	Informal
Serious	Sensitively humorous
Employee	Partner

Figure 2.1   Old and new (E) model workplaces – what characterizes your organization?

The Y leadership style assumes a high level of trust and that people will rise to the occasion and do their best for themselves and the organization with a little direction but lots of room for manoeuvre. William Ouchi added Z theory, drawing from the Japanese quality movement.

E theory is my shorthand for the emergence of the employee engagement movement. As Figure 2.1 makes clear, the old and new (E) models of organization are very different.

Look at Figure 2.1 and consider where your employees might plot the culture of your organization. Would they say it's more on the left side of the diagram or the right? If you were to ask a group of top leaders to do the same it is not unusual for leaders to see their own organizations as far more open and participative than their people do!

It is not a question of left column = bad, right column = good; it is more a question of whether the current state is providing the most compelling employee experience.

The purpose of the shift diagram is to prompt insight about the starting point of your organization or your part in stimulating a shift. If your reflection leads you to believe that your organization is predominantly an old (X) model organization, efforts to create a culture in which people feel safe and enthusiastic to challenge and contribute will require personal resilience and personal risk. The status quo will not wish to relinquish power even though it is these organizations that have much to gain by becoming early adopters of the characteristics of the new mode (theory E) of organization.

What follows should encourage insight about what engages people at work and some of the tools necessary to stimulate it.

3) What Engages People? – The Difference between Outcomes and Causes

There are many definitions of employee engagement, but most are descriptions of desirable outcomes or benefits rather than drivers or causes. Take these UK examples of outcomes presented as causes:

- 'Employee engagement is a process by which an organization increases the intellectual and emotional commitment and contribution of its employees to achieve superior performance' (National School of Government).

- 'Engagement is about creating opportunities for employees to connect with their colleagues, managers and [the] wider organization. It is about creating an environment where employees are motivated to want to connect with their work and really care about doing a good job. It is a concept that places flexibility, change and continuous improvement at the heart of what it means to be an employee and an employer in a twenty-first-century workplace' (Chartered Institute of Personnel and Development).

- 'A positive attitude held by the employee towards the organization and its values. An engaged employee is aware of the business context and works with colleagues to improve performance within the job for the benefit of the employer. The organization must work to develop and nurture environment which requires a two-way relationship between employee and employer' (Institute of Employment Studies).

Figure 2.2   Three dimensions of engagement

Towers Watson, a human resources consultancy, defines employee engagement as the connections people have with their organizations, specifically across three dimensions (see Figure 2.2).

> **Rational (head):** the extent to which employees understand their roles and responsibilities (thinking)

> **Motivational (hand):** employee willingness to invest discretionary effort to perform their roles well (acting)

> **Emotional (heart):** the level of passion that employees bring to their work and organization (feeling)

As you can see, these provide good descriptions of outcomes, but they do not provide the all-important pointer to what brings about or causes engagement.

WHAT DRIVES OR CAUSES ENGAGEMENT?

My view is based on UK-wide research discussed in later chapters, my time as a visiting Fellow of McKinsey & Company (resulting in the 'Boot Camp or Commune' report in 2004) and client work as an advisor to the private and public sectors on 'delivering strategy through people' for many years.

Models abound on the causes or drivers of engagement. The big survey companies attempt to measure the same factors in many clients and offer comparisons. I am dubious about these popular tools. They tick the box and appeal to the egos in the C-suite when all is rosy and they provide functional heads with ammunition to stimulate action. However, the danger is that they lead to 'automated' actions suggested by regression analysis, predicting improvements deduced from reliable data. This syndrome reinforces a C-suite view that the engagement thing can be reduced to a technical task – it can't. Intellectually, it requires a constant act of judgement by leaders about who needs to be engaged in decision making. Emotionally it requires a presence which is emotionally intelligent – employees always remember the emotionally intelligent boss, but they rarely hold fond memories of a 'scientific' workplace.

The engage for change model of engagement has three categories of drivers (causes or influences) of engagement: 'my space', the leadership role model and the organization's compass.

Incidentally, I dislike the term 'driver' as it connotes coercion, but many use it and it has some currency.

THREE CATEGORIES OF 'DRIVERS' OR CAUSES OF ENGAGEMENT

'My space'

- Space and permission to challenge and contribute.

- Involvement with communities, customers and stakeholders.

- Ability to make useful connections and friendships.

- Support and development.

Leadership role model (leaders at every level)

- Skilled in engaging people in decision making.

- Ability to trust others.

- Generosity of spirit.

- Credibility.

- Absolute transparency.

- Consistency across executive team.

The organization's compass

- Moral purpose.

- Distinct business purpose.

- Clear and compelling vision.

- Authentic values and beliefs.

- Believable brand.

- Line of sight between 'my' role and the organization's purpose.

When considering the relationship between the employer and the organization, the local leader's role model is (I believe) the key influence on whether people engage themselves. Local leadership and supervision is the cipher for the relationship between the employee and the organization, and this relationship is always cited as the key determinant of an employee's advocacy, retention and performance. An abbreviated and simpler test of the likely degree of engagement is to ask if the culture provides RAPIC, which stands for:

- Respect.

- Appreciation.

- Personal growth and development.

- Involvement in decision making.

- Community.

PEOPLE ENGAGE THEMSELVES

At our advisory practice Engage for Change, we believe that people engage themselves when they are invited to challenge and contribute to everyday operational decisions and strategy and big-ticket change that affects them and which they can affect.

This idea is expanded in Table 2.1.

Table 2.1   How to recognize engagement

What is employee engagement – how would you recognize it?
You would recognize it when you found people who:
•   Are as creative and productive at work as they are when they are intrinsically motivated pursuing interests outside the work place that they care deeply about. To simulate these conditions at work people need to be given the space and trust to self-organize, and (in groups) to self-discipline and self-reward. In 1971 Edward Deci of Rochester University, USA, found that the highest performing groups in tests were those with no financial incentives offered by management.
•   Had a boss who rewarded trial and risk taking with encouraging feedback that stimulated more self-efficacy. Gabriel Wulf at the University of Nevada conducted tests in which people pitched balls. The groups that were told that they were performing better using a (sham) test actually did perform much better than those who faced no test.
People enjoying these conditions also:
•   Challenge constructively upwards
•   Are willing to drive others' change if they have had a part in it
•   Are more likely to be an advocate of the company outside work
•   Enjoy their work and make other people's work more enjoyable – workers at Manchester Airport (UK) that participate in a scheme in which they can apply for grants to make specific improvements to the customer experience score as highly as senior management in engagement surveys, way ahead of compatriots that do not participate. The first movers recruited more and more colleagues with positive results for the customer and employee wellbeing.

As I have noted elsewhere people engage themselves when they enjoy conditions (described above) in which they are invited to contribute to every day decisions and bigger ticket change that affects them and which they can affect.

We know from our UK-wide YouGov surveys that engagement is also negatively impacted by coercive or charismatic leadership. The primary enabler of engagement is a culture of distributed leadership that enables people to liberate their creativity to deliver good results for their company and themselves.

Creating the conditions in which people engage requires leaders at every level with the generosity, appetite and capability to engage people in the decision-making process – leaders that share some of the power in a well governed way.

THE IMPORTANCE OF SAFETY AND REWARDS

Engagement of people is an outcome of sensibly governed power sharing by leaders at every level in organizations, but people will only engage themselves if they feel they will be safe and rewarded.

The provision of a safe environment in which employees can challenge and contribute, is largely down to the gift of leaders, managers and supervisors. Through their behaviour, they can create the conditions in which people feel safe to challenge and contribute. Rewards for challenging and contributing also rely on managers acknowledging challenge and contributions and providing constructive feedback. Reward is also derived from feelings of pride by individuals who have stepped up to contribute.

WHAT DO LEADERS NEED TO DO TO STIMULATE CHALLENGE AND CONTRIBUTION?

In practical terms, leaders, managers and supervisors need to hit the personal pause button when their instincts are driving them to take a quick decision and align people with it. The momentary pause should be used by leaders to ask themselves the following question: 'Will the outcome of this decision be better if I decide alone or if I first consider who else will add value to the decision if they are involved at the front end?'

Hitting the pause button at decision time is counter-cultural to many people brought up in command and control cultures where they have experienced countless bosses shooting from the hip, thinking that they must show leadership by being the all-knowing hero with all the answers. Hip shooters may also be imbued with the idea that being a leader, manager or supervisor means that leadership involves taking control of the situation and being in sole charge. Ultimately this is correct – leaders at any level must, at the right moment, close down discussion and make the call. The serially indecisive are as bad as the despots. But in the moment or period in between being faced with a call to make and closure, there is also a choice to be made between calling a decision alone it alone and inviting others to challenge and contribute. Pausing to reflect on this choice involves risk – the risk of being seen as hesitant, the risk of being seen as weak and the risk of missing the moment by pausing.

There will always be times when instant action is right in operational settings and sometimes in strategic situations when the leader has assessed that those around have nothing to offer except self-interested delay. But in most situations, the leader will be rewarded if he or she hits the pause button to consider who else will add value before they make the call or at least to rationalize why the engagement of others will add nothing except perilous delay. Pausing not only involves rational risk, taking it also means controlling the chemical activity in our bodies when we are in 'flight or fight' mode. In this mode, our primal instincts kick in hard-wired from when, as hunter-gatherers, we had to outfox sabre-toothed tigers and other predators on the African Savannah. In flight or fight, blood is diverted from cerebral thinking to running away. Transferred into the office, flight or fight mode is often a norm of over-busy people doing more running around than reflecting and thinking.

Risk-taking leaders may also be aware of myths about employee engagement such as 'we know the answers anyway so why engage, we don't have time for this, people just want to get paid and we are paid to take decisions'. At the end of this chapter, there is a catalogue of myths like these and a rebuttal for all of them.

How would you recognize someone who engages other people effectively? What do they do?:

- Risk speaking up to challenge and contribute and are open to the same from others.

- Self-organize – less need for costly supervision.

- Take responsibility for their part in the enterprise.

- Collaborate within and beyond their 'border'.

- Resolve difficulties locally.

- The oxytocin bonus – improving affiliation and performance (by creating conditions in which people work collaboratively, oxytocin levels rise, trust levels rise and better outcomes are achieved).

- Demonstrate awareness of personal limits.

- Are generous – if I look back at (many) successful leaders that have earned the trust of their people they will have been described as being generous in listening and generous in the development. Leaders who are generous in spirit know when to open up decisions and when to close down.

'DOING IT WITH PEOPLE RATHER THAN FOR AND TO THEM'

Fostering a culture of distributed leadership means selecting and developing leaders at every level who have the appetite and capability to engage people in the decision-making and change processes. As the author Charles Leadbeater puts it, doing it 'with people rather than for and to' (TED talk, Edinburgh 2011. TED is a movement started in 1984 designed to encourage thinking about technology, ideas and design). Becoming effective at employee engagement requiresindividual leaders to assess how they have learnt to make decisions and to make conscious choices between the four modes of decision making illustrated in Figure 2.3.

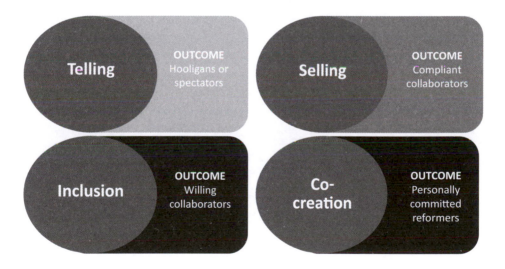

Figure 2.3   What engages people at work?

Employees, for their part, need to take positive steps to get off the fence and volunteer to make things happen. They will do so if they experience the right kind of leadership role model and if they see benefits and rewards for themselves, such as having an influence on decisions which affect them and receiving recognition for doing so. The leader who makes judgements about when to tell, sell, involve and co-create is also much more likely to benefit from employees who become advocates of the enterprise.

Net promoter scores (predicting high levels of advocacy by employees on behalf of their organization) are typically much higher where people are more involved in decision making, as the diagram given in Figure 2.4, developed with our client, Zurich Financial Services, illustrates.

Employee engagement is often presently referred to as a single relationship between employer and employee. At our consultancy Engage for Change, we categorize the relationship as comprising four axes that influence the degree that people engage.

Creating advocacy by inviting your employees who deliver the end result to contribute to decisions, strategy and change.

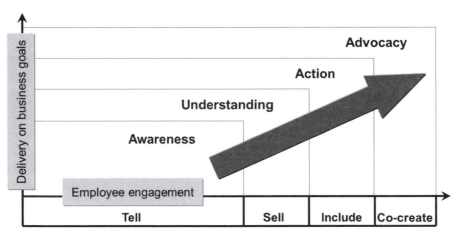

Figure 2.4   Employee engagement and decision making

THE FOURTH RELATIONSHIP IS PROBLEMATIC

People at work engage on four levels – with their job/role, with their team(s), with their organization's brand/ideology and with the organization as a system.

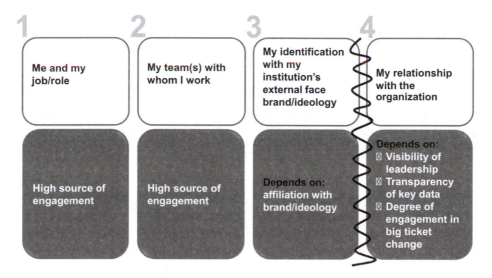

Figure 2.5   The fourth level of engagement

The fourth relationship is impersonal as it is conducted via corporate processes, in contrast to the first two relationships, which are largely conducted on an informal, self-conducted basis. It is largely conducted on a formal and occasional basis. It usually involves the organization doing something to employees like communicating or involving them in change processes and rituals such as performance management.

Thus, the question 'can we manage or change the climate of engagement?' is relevant as the tools and approaches may seem real at HQ, but down on the ground they may be missed or ignored altogether.

What levers or processes are available to influence engagement? There are two levers which I will discuss in the next section of this chapter.

4) Introducing the Primary Levers of Leader and Employee Engagement

Earlier I looked at drivers or causes of engagement. One of the real problems of the concept is that there are potentially many drivers or causes. To attempt to influence them all could become a colossal bureaucratic task.

In this book I have focused on some of the primary 'levers' and supporting enablers that should influence people's level of engagement. These are:

The primary levers:

- Directional, operational and cultural leadership.

- Delivering strategy and change through participative interventions that engage the right people.

- Helping leaders at every level to engage their people – capability, skills and behaviours.

The supporting enablers:

- Brand.

- Internal communication.

- Digital technology.

Participative strategy and change interventions are easier to sell and syndicate because they produce quick commercial results, are popular and are enjoyable.

More and more organizations are experimenting with participative interventions with good results. However all too often execution is not well thought through and the culture slips back from the 'bottom-up' experience of the intervention to the old order of unilateral top down – I will look at this in more detail later.

The following section covers the contrasting stories of Ruby and Geraldine. These illustrate the difference between *participative strategy and change interventions* (Ruby's experience) and *traditional top down, command and control strategy and change* (Geraldine's experience).

5) Ruby and Geraldine's Contrasting Experiences of Being Engaged in Change

In common with many others, I believe that employee engagement is a leadership philosophy as well as a set of practices and processes. As one CEO put it, it is a philosophy first and a set of activities second. Thus, whilst there is much in the way of 'how to' on these pages, effective employee engagement requires bosses to:

- take risks by including some or many people into the space normally occupied by elites;

- create a climate of trust by being absolutely transparent about the state of the business – no hidden bottom draws and progress of execution;

- sanction the creativity necessary to help people see the organization and their role from a different angle;

- govern the process in a rigorous fashion.

Let's start the journey in two other people's shoes – the stories are drawn from real life. Whose shoes would you rather be in: Ruby's or Geraldine's?

RUBY'S SHOES

Ruby receives an invitation to attend a morning meeting called 'Help our recovery'. The invitation confirms recent open communication about the poor performance of all parts of the company and that its parent company is unable to subsidize it, let alone provide more cash for investment. The communication also says that there are no pre-hatched plans and invites Ruby and her colleagues to take ownership (with management) to solve the crisis, recognizing that unpalatable options will have to be on the table. Ruby feels both concerned but flattered that she will be on the inside and so will everyone else. She enters the meeting feeling like a player rather than a spectator.

A three-month timetable is laid out in which Ruby and her colleagues are invited to use their deep local knowledge to slay sacred cows about what cannot be changed and to identify specific and practical plans for efficiencies and cost cutting on the one hand and obvious opportunities for new forms of revenue on the other. Their proposals must be new and not rehashes of plans and ideas already covered by incremental budgets. And they must accord with the SAM mantra: Specific, Actionable and Measurable.

The process is not a free for all. The givens or non-negotiables are clearly identified covering financial outcomes and areas to focus on, including duplicated business unit services, product and service innovation, and cross-company customer and product development collaboration.

Ruby and her colleagues are asked to categorize their proposals into three perspectives:

1. What they would do if they had a free hand from the perspective of their day job?

2. What they would they do if they were a director of the company?

3. What would they do if they had survived a takeover but had been given two months by the acquirer to propose small and radical changes?

Over the next three weeks, they attend three workshops in which they successively adopt the roles above. In a fourth session, they organize the proposals and decide on which quick, medium-term and longer-term wins to propose to the upcoming 'Action for Recovery Strategy Safari' in their part of the business. A Strategy Safari is a low production experience where streams of change and strategy are visited, added to, and challenged – the Safari process is discussed in more detail later on.

GERALDINE'S SHOES

In another company, Geraldine is also invited to a meeting described as a 'cascade briefing'. Rumours have been swirling. Directors have gone to ground and communication from the company is sparse. At the cascade, Geraldine's fears are confirmed when in a PowerPoint presentation the full extent of the dire state of the business is revealed for the first time.

Shock number two then arrives: detailed pre-hatched, top-down plans for re-structuring and efficiencies are revealed. The focus is all on reduction with no hint of 'new business' opportunities. Geraldine feels less like a spectator and more like a victim. To varying degrees, she and her colleagues leave the meeting in shock, in fear and immobile.

Ruby's example resulted in very fast action from a large group of workers who all or nearly all felt that they were driving change where they worked resulting in fast results. Geraldine's experience disenfranchised those who could contribute, resulting in a huge task of execution by an overworked 'change team'. This book is of course promoting the kind of experience enjoyed by Ruby.

As an end to this chapter, I would like to remind readers about one of the best examples of ordinary people tackling complex subjects and making decisions as a self-organizing group. I am referring of course to the system of trial by jury. Employee engagement is a manifestation of the same spirit and confidence in ordinary people to make excellent decisions about topics which can be arcane and technical.

I close with some common myths about leader and employee engagement. I have collected these from executive teams expressing long-held beliefs about the nature of leadership. The purpose of recounting them here is to help the reader address myths that may be expressed to them as reasons not to attempt experiments in leader and employee engagement. It also helps to consider these myths as objections are often made by senior executives who cannot articulate their objection and thus cannot debate it. Armed with these myths readers can draw out objections and debate them rationally.

6) Thirteen Myths About Leader and Employee Engagement

- *Myth 1*: in hard times and crises, employees expect their leaders to take control and make decisive decisions that will help their institutions: that's what they are paid to do and anyway leaders will know more of the context and have the experience to act.

Insight: there are increasing examples of institutions 'turning the hierarchy upside down' and engaging their people in addressing cost, restructuring and efficiency issues as well as engaging people in more positive topics like service improvement, innovation and brand.

- *Myth 2*: most people work to live – many people just want to work to live and do not want to be involved or engaged at work more than they have to.

Insight: in our experience, people become used to a 'parent-child' style of leadership, but when leaders open up decision making in an authentic fashion and govern it well, people respond with courage and creativity. Many are bursting with ideas which they assumed were unwelcome because they are not normally asked.

- *Myth 3*: there's no time to engage people in decisions and change – as the business world speeds up, businesses do not have the luxury of time to engage people.

Insight: leaders are finding that imposed so-called incisive, top-down, command and control decision making often just leads to more failed initiatives and strategies which are easily rejected by a sceptical workforce. The immediate decision seems faster, but the critical phase of execution often fails. Conversely, leaders who minimize the top-down aspects of a decision or change and take time to construct a rational invitation to engage their people are rewarded with the latter's energy and ownership.

- *Myth 4*: communication is the same as engagement – leaders who communicate effectively assume they are effective at engaging people.

Insight: old-style decide-and-tell or decide-and-sell communication may be appropriate in some instances, but, however 'engaging, charming or entertaining' the performance, it is not the same as engaging people in the decision-making process. Old-style communication, by definition, casts recipients as spectators receiving carefully articulated decisions made by others. Effective engagement means making judgements about who will add value if engaged and then managing the discourse.

- *Myth 5*: the front line won't understand strategy, etc. – front-line staff should be focused on operational matters and won't have much to contribute to the bigger picture. Moreover, it is distracting for them to see beyond their silo.

Insight: this displays a shocking arrogance and under-estimation of people who often reserve their intellectual and creative energy simply because they are not respected and included. Most will be inspired by seeing the business case and options and reasons for choices that have been made by management and subsequently may play their part more energetically.

- *Myth 6*: staff don't need to know the whole candid picture – knowing the whole picture will scare people or confuse them.

Insight: people invariably read or sense the whole candid picture or, worse, make up an alternative. The trouble with withholding information is that, as with all deceit, it becomes harder to contain and whispers invariably undermine the credibility of management. Once lost, few leaders can regain trust.

- *Myth 7*: professional groups (train drivers, medical consultants, air traffic experts, etc.) are only loyal to their profession or skill – they do not care who they work for, so why bother to engage them in wider company change?

Insight: this is a firmly held assumption which often leads to a gradual fragmentation of the group concerned – the train drivers, pilots, air traffic controllers, etc. get left out of the loop because they are considered too tricky. In fact, the leader who confronts this assumption will be met with scepticism at first, but if he or she persists, the attitude will change and people will come around and engage. In a train company re-franchise the head of engineering said drivers and others would not be able or interested in contributing. In fact these groups contributed some truly-winning arguments.

- *Myth 8*: our employee satisfaction scores are good, so people must be engaged – our people are happy with their lot according to our measures of satisfaction, so we must be performing optimally as an organization.

Insight: employee satisfaction is a measure of the old security-for-loyalty contract between people at work and their employer. Satisfaction scores essentially measure employee satisfaction with aspects of work. They do so as spectators rating their own satisfaction. The trouble is that about 35–40% of UK plc staff are satisfied but are completely disengaged. They are your hostages who represent an underperforming asset. The measure must change to calibrate real engagement.

- *Myth 9*: we do measure engagement and we do have post-research action processes, so we tick the engagement box.

Insight: yes, many organizations do tick the box in this way, and yet the reality is that many corporate cultures continue remarkably unchanged. Why? Most likely this is because corporations that use this kind of research are by and large the long-established Fortune and FTSE companies which are hard to change; they have been successful, so why change? The box is often window dressing for an old window.

- *Myth 10*: it's only the Y generation that are so keen on asking why and being more involved – the baby boomers and other generations are happy to toe the line.

Insight: from our research, it is true that the Y generation is more demanding, but there is not much in it. All people have given up on the security-for-loyalty contract and will demand an influence, leave or become hostages who cannot afford to leave.

- *Myth 11*: employee engagement may be relevant in the West, but does not fit so easily elsewhere, so we cannot apply it as a global company-wide concept.

Insight: different cultures are interpreting engagement differently, but people are people. And, whether it's the former Eastern Europe or the Far East, demand for personal freedom and influence is rising. The language of leadership and management may require tailoring to fit the local circumstances, but engaging people in their own destiny and day-to-day work is a universal factor.

- *Myth 12*: this is all new thinking.

Insight: it is not – it has been around since mankind started to collaborate to survive. What's new is that in the post-industrial era, we are witnessing the end of the useful life of command and control which took its cues and roots from class control, the military and some 'we know best' religions. Its grip is weakening as the proponents of this style of leadership can no longer keep workers in thrall to them. The breakdown in the contract between capital and employer and the digital age usher in a much more mutual relationship where power is shared with employees and other stakeholders.

- *Myth 13*: my door is open and I get good scores from my people, so I must be good at employee engagement.

Insight: there is a big difference between being an engaging, perhaps even charming leader and being a leader who shares power in a well-governed way. The former helps the latter, but the former alone is likely to be a well-mannered way of maintaining power.

And Finally a Vignette

THE BROMPTON HOSPITAL – AN ISLAND IN THE UK'S NATIONAL HEALTH SERVICE

I interviewed Bob Bell CEO of Brompton Hospital, a genial Canadian from Toronto. There are few non-British CEOs in the NHS; most are a product and appointment of the towering and sprawling NHS, one of the prime bureaucracies in the world. The following covers my thoughts and conclusions from talking with Bob – they are not a representation of his opinions.

The Brompton Hospital is an independent trust which empowers the 3,000 or so staff to run their own ship underneath the NHS umbrella. The virtue of independent trust status is the word 'independence' from as much NHS bureaucracy as possible. With independence, however, comes massive accountability to be the best or among the best.

The job of the CEO is to be accountable for creating world-class standards which attract the best staff so as to appeal to UK customers, who have increasing choice within the NHS, and overseas customers, who have the world to choose from. The UK's fantastic medical pedigree is fast becoming challenged by many other nations, all of whom are eager to learn from its triumphs and mistakes.

At the same time, the trust must be as profitable as it can be to enable it to innovate as, without innovation, a high-tech business like a hospital trust will soon vanish into obscurity or – worse – mediocrity, as is evidenced in many other examples across the UK and is something I witnessed for myself when looking after my mother in a huge south-west London hospital, which would have been quite at home in any Third World country.

Innovation certainly means technology and kit, but much more critical are the skills of all the staff. And this is where the CEO's primary role lies – *to take the risks to improve medical practice which keeps the trust out in front.* Bob likes the analogy of the CEO as football coach, where the coach's job is to enable the best of the best to be individuals who work as a team despite their individual prodigious talents and ambitions. Hard enough with a squad, tougher with hundreds of ace medics. And independent status is a vital part of enabling the trust to take reasonable risk.

In much of the NHS, with many honourable exceptions, CEOs are clearly more restricted both by the NHS machine and the culture resulting in attention to process at the expense of innovation. There is also an element of conforming to the lores of the machine for advancement, status and reward.

As Bob explained, every hospital needs to do well in three spheres and he was the first to admit that the Brompton had plenty to do, especially occupying a building dating back to the days of Prince Albert! The three spheres are as follows:

> *People*: a group of professional people that are among the very best professional service employees in the world – Bob interestingly likes to go beyond the medical world to make comparison with lawyers, accountants, management consultants and the world of sport, which obviously emphasizes and focuses on people winning the race. In the trust's case, this is the race to be the best of the best in cardiac and respiratory care – 'our two super products', as he put it.

> *Ways of working*: methods, processes, techniques, systems, etc.

> *Buildings and technology*: Bob's responses in my conversation with him consistently put the human element first as being the variable that ultimately provided the edge. To emphasize this focus, he talks about the visibility of their *mission* – to be the best cardiac and respiratory centre of excellence; their *vision* – to achieve the mission in world-class facilities; and to *deliver* through service, organizational excellence and productivity.

Everyone's job is conducted and reviewed through theses lenses, whatever their role, and thus there is line of sight with the mission, vision and deliver concepts.

Under the banner of ways of work, Bob makes an interesting point about targets in the NHS where there will be acceptable targets for, say, MRSA – i.e. it's OK to have a few cases. The target or intention at the Brompton Hospital is of course zero, which it may not attain, but to allow for mediocre performance is unacceptable.

The Employee Engagement Connection

Given the theme of constant risk taking to innovate across the vision, mission and deliver concepts, there is a great deal of inclusion and co-creation with those who will be affected by a change and those, where different, who can affect the change at hand. In addition, every consultant knows exactly how profitable they are, which for some readers might suggest creates an irreconcilable conflict between care and profit. The counter-argument is that the consultants (and other staff) understand the business model, they understand their competitors and they understand that being a great medic is a prerequisite, but being profitable means that innovation through joint risk taking keeps them ahead of their competitors, both professionally and institutionally.

The idea that profit and care are conflicting goals is popular, but many businesses can point to a focus on delivering excellence results in profit. As the mission, vision and deliver concepts show, the word 'profit' does not appear – profit is an outcome of delivery. Any group of highly motivated professionals do not want any colleagues to be able to get away with poor performance. However this is not, as I understood it, an issue for the professionals at the Brompton Hospital as it is in many other public sector cultures.

3

Introducing the Primary Levers and Supporting Enablers of Engagement

The focus of this chapter is the introduction of the primary levers and supporting enablers of engagement, which enable people to feel invited, safe and keen to challenge and contribute where they work, both for their own benefit and for the benefit of their institution. The core idea behind the primary levers and the enablers is that engagement is an outcome of well-governed involvement of people in decisions that affect them and which they themselves can affect. The primary levers are prerequisites for creating the conditions which will encourage people to engage themselves. The supporting enablers are important, but without the primary levers may not be relied upon as sufficient to create those conditions.

1. The primary levers are:

   - Directional, operational and cultural leadership.

   - Delivering strategy and change through participative interventions that engage the right people.

   - Helping leaders at every level to engage their people – capability, skills and behaviours.

2.   The supporting enablers are:

   • Brand.

   • Internal communication.

   • Digital technology.

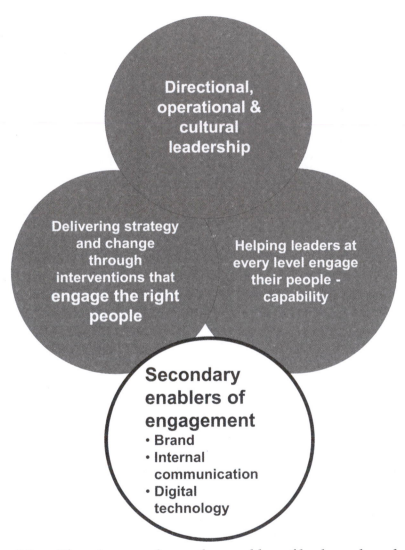

Figure 3.1   **The primary and secondary enablers of leader and employee engagement**

1) The Primary Levers

DIRECTIONAL, OPERATIONAL AND CULTURAL LEADERSHIP

Top leaders are uniquely responsible for directional leadership. Directional leadership means responsibility for the purpose, direction and strategy of businesses and institutions.

The prime role of top management is knowing when to sustain business as usual and when to disrupt. As Jeff Immelt CEO of GE aptly put it … 'we must disrupt our strategy before others disrupt us with theirs'.

It falls to the 'C suite' (CEO, COO, CTO – technology, CMO – marketing, CPO – people etc.) to initiate the process that keeps an eye on the future, whilst others are delegated with operational leadership. Directional and operational leadership are two sides of a coin; neither can operate effectively without the other for long.

The American political scientist Ronald Heifetz (*Leadership without Easy Answers* (2009)) uses the analogy of the balcony and the dance floor, in which the dance floor represents operations from which the horizon can only be glimpsed. The balcony represents a platform above the noise of the dance floor from which to consider new directions. In practice, exercising directional leadership involves leaders making judgements about when to distract other levels (from getting on with operations), to step up to the balcony, not just to glimpse at new horizons but to contribute to the journey.

Under command and control, few are called to be distracted from an operational focus. However, to reap the rewards from engaging more widely requires leaders to design and govern participative strategy and change processes which reach down and across via well-designed interventions which engage people in challenging and contributing to strategy and change.

The answer to the question: 'what are the rewards or incentives for the C suite to switch from top-down, command and control (which is still seen as being quick and efficient by many brought up in its shadow), to broader inclusion in decision making?', lies in the overwhelming evidence (see www.engageforsuccess.org and our own consultancy website www.engageforchange.com) that broader inclusion delivers better commercial and cultural performance. And contrary to myth, broader inclusion does not require more time than top-down approaches.

This book is about improving organizational commercial performance through disciplined leader and employee engagement at the organizational and individual levels. It is also about cultural performance.

CULTURAL LEADERSHIP

In addition to making judgements about when and who to invite up to the balcony (to refresh purpose, direction and strategy), leaders, managers and supervisors at every level need to exercise cultural leadership. This means influencing the everyday experience people endure or enjoy at work in order to make it safe and rewarding to challenge and contribute. The role model of top leadership as individuals is emphasized as a critical part of cultural leadership.

It is said of Paul Barron's time as CEO of the UK's National Air Traffic Service that 'you could not put a cigarette paper between members of the executive group'. Such consistency does not happen by accident; it involves top leadership sponsoring values and culture which help create a good place to work. Whilst culture is influenced, en passant, by running a counter-cultural intervention to drive strategy and change, a values process could be considered as a way to address culture directly.

A global private equity house chose to refresh the attributes that differentiated it from competitors – those being a highly ethical, straight forward approach. The process initially involved one-day workshops in which participants analysed a number of deals to assess where further progress could be made for the firm to claim a real difference over its competitors by creating really high ethical standards. I cite this example because it illustrates a very hard-bitten business culture recognizing that the way it does business is as important as its financial expertise. The presence of the CEO at every meeting across the globe, along with at least two other executive committee members and one non-executive director drove home to everyone that values are a bankable asset. Let's take a slightly closer look at the values concept.

EXPLORING ORGANIZATIONAL VALUES TO ASSIST IN CULTURAL CHANGE

'Values' is a collective term for repetitive assumptions, instincts, beliefs and practices that influence behaviours, experienced and practised by leaders and employees. Employees' experience of values become, in turn, the experience of clients, customers and other external stakeholders.

In some organizations, values may be tacitly absorbed with little or no deliberate socialization, while in other organizations, there may be a conscious and deliberate process which specifies the desired employee and stakeholder experience, which is subsequently inculcated through the rituals of HR internally and marketing/branding externally.

Organizations with a lengthy history will have long-established values that employees and customers implicitly perceive and understand. These are often based on fables and stories bridging generations that bring a particular ethos to the business. The task for established organizations is to ensure that these deep influences on behaviour are still relevant and beneficial. From time to time, it is useful to review whether historical values are supporting or disabling the business. That is what the private equity house, described earlier, did.

Newer organizations or those which emerge as a result of restructures and mergers have a different task. They will need to use the fleeting 'newness of the moment' to articulate values that:

- resonate internally and externally;

- enable the organization to have a clear stance on ways of doing business;

- enable them to differentiate themselves from others;

- are attractive to existing and future employees.

The next primary lever is delivering strategy and change through participative interventions.

DELIVERING STRATEGY AND CHANGE THROUGH PARTICIPATIVE INTERVENTIONS THAT ENGAGE THE RIGHT PEOPLE

Part II of the book is dedicated to helping readers to see how traditional top-down strategy, change and other renewal processes can be partially inverted with much more inclusive bottom-up involvement of leaders and employees, not normally invited to challenge or contribute. If you are in the C suite you will have the influence and possibly the power to enfranchise more of the brain power of the organization by employing a well-designed participative intervention. At the least, you will be able to table a discussion about the relative merits of devising and delivering strategy in more inclusive ways. Too often a top-down approach emerges without due consideration of the choice between top-down and more inclusive approaches.

With Part II you will have all the arguments and the tools to design an intervention that will drive better performance than top down methods.

If you are not a member of the C suite you may be just the person to figure out which member(s) of the C suite might sponsor the idea. You can experiment with smaller interventions perhaps in a function or a change process where there is appetite to change in a different way. If you are an influencer you might want to identify a C suite member who is a little apart from the politics at the centre. Good candidates are those with relatively discrete business areas or territories. Or those who have a major crisis and are willing to experiment (as in the Total case told later).

Designing and running a participative intervention involves the six steps that follow. Each is a discrete chapter.

- Getting started and negotiating business outcomes.

- Identifying whether default approaches to engagement are adding value and speed.

- Deciding who to engage – 'the Power of the Peach'.

- Designing and running bottom-up interventions that deliver fast commercial and cultural results.

- Sustaining the benefits of an inclusive intervention.

- Creative group and crowd dynamics that result in breakthroughs.

The third and last primary lever of engagement is the capability of leaders at every level to create conditions that enable their people to engage themselves.

HELPING LEADERS AT EVERY LEVEL TO ENGAGE THEIR PEOPLE – CAPABILITY

The third part of the book focuses on helping leaders at every level to engage their people.

It provides guidance on helping leaders create a safe and encouraging environment which encourages people to engage themselves for their own benefit and for the benefit of the organization.

I would like to emphasize the idea, mentioned above, of 'people engaging themselves'. Some commentary in opinion-influencing circles could lead to the conclusion that engagement can be done to people. There is the suggestion that 'this programme or that survey' will engage people, in a similar way to how a petrol additive might make a car go faster. To me, the go-faster peddlers are wittingly or unwittingly trying to turn an approach to leadership into a transactional process or, worse, a product. Caveat emptor!

Part III covers findings of UK-wide research into the link between performance and engagement, and the capability and skills for leaders such that they can create conditions that enable people to engage themselves.

It looks at the following areas:

- The evidence for the claim that the right kind of engagement capability drives performance.

- What leaders need to do to enable effective engagement.

- The shifting nature of leadership and new model HR practices.

- Leadership competences that enable effective employee engagement.

- A diagnostic tool to assess (your) engagement skills capability.

Part III of the book also includes the supporting enablers introduced below:

- Brand.

- Internal communication.

- Digital technology.

Brand

Employees do as they are done to, not as the brand script dictates. The employee experience becomes the client/customer experience. It follows that if the reality of the workplace experience and culture is at odds with the brand promise made to customers and others, the brand promise cannot be delivered. The fit between the employee experience and the brand promise takes more than paid-for corporate rhetoric.

Closing the gap between brand promises and the reality of the customer experience is best done inside out. This means working on the employee experience first, using the proposed brand promise as the standard to aim for, before customers' expectations are set. This is a massive challenge to marketers, whose careers more typically ascend by recognition of their work which is externally visible rather than recognition of internal groundwork, which is all but invisible.

The brand and reputation diagram given in Figure 3.2 visualizes how employee and stakeholder experience results from their interactions with the organization. Whilst inter-function politics often intercede to separate the employee experience from the brand, the highest-performing businesses do not allow the separation to perpetuate.

Chapter 12 on brand covers the following points:

- What is brand?

- Dealing with the deficit between brand promise and stakeholders' experience.

- Bringing strategy to life through inside-out brand engagement.

Staff and external stakeholders' experience is the sum of all their interactions with the organisation

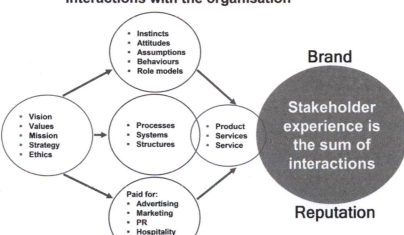

Figure 3.2   Brand and reputation

The retail and food sectors offer the evidence that an engaged workforce does not rely on instrumental factors like pay alone. These sectors may pay above-minimum wages thresholds but not by a lot. The customer experience relies on the sense of a joint mission to deliver a great night out.

In common with brands like Pret a Manger (the UK sandwich chain), Yo! Sushi (a great sushi chain in the UK) hires on attitude. Its assessment centres give hopeful candidates tasks like designing flags, setting up the ideal new nation and other creative challenges. During their probationary period, candidates learn the art of Yo!, where front of house is framed as something of a theatrical role. Their vision is to be an extraordinary employer, which seems to echo the work of Indian business mogul Vineet Nayar, whose recent book is entitled *Employees First, Customers Second*. Yo! aims to engage staff from supplier, to kitchen, to table in order to ensure they have confidence in their knowledge of the product. As the premium hotel chain Intercontinental says, people want to be sold to, they have come out to be looked after, and having staff tempt them with a side order or maybe a digestif makes it easier for the customer to say yes or no – a form of nudging.

The Second Supporting Enabler is Internal Communication

Internal communication lies at a crossroads between being the radio station of the powerful and being a contributor to sustaining a healthy workplace where expression and constructive challenge by employees is encouraged and enabled. In Chapter 13 I argue that internal communication should try to find a balance between the two roles (the radio station and the enabler of challenge and contribution). Presently it seems that many communication functions are being trammelled into being turbo-charged message boards with a primary focus on channel management.

The best internal communicators are in the decision-making circle advising on the consequences of top-level decisions as they are weighed. They also skillfully prioritize and orchestrate communication that engages employees in a dialogue.

Chapter 13 explores the impact of the employee engagement movement on internal communication and covers the following:

- Internal communication at a crossroads.

- What good internal communication looks like.

- The role of internal communication in balancing the top down with the bottom up.

- Implications of the rise in employee engagement on the capabilities of internal communicators.

The Third Supporting Enabler is Digital Technology

There is absolutely no doubt that digital technology has revolutionized communication, collaboration and levels of transparency. It has and will increasingly be a key enabler of engagement. In some organizations it helps to suspend or reduce hierarchy in order to enable the challenges and contributions of the many to influence former elites. Digital technology is on its own journey, as depicted in Figure 3.3.

The right social rewards enable the shift from conscription to volunteering

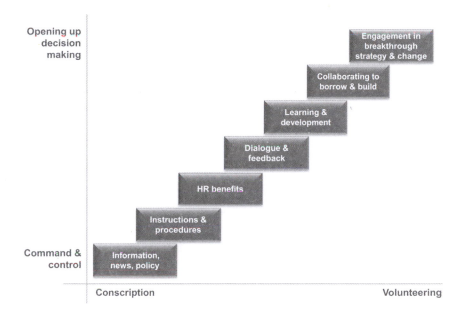

Figure 3.3   **Digital technology as an enabler of engagement**

There are many people much more qualified than me to provide technical and social insight on this topic. However, with my two associates, Ben Hart and Max Waldron, we have tried to focus on topics which will help readers maximize the potential of digital technology to engage people. I see it as a very supportive enabler, not an end in itself.

Chapter 14 covers the following:

- The context – social media offers a new source of social reward, motivating more people to connect with each other.

- Conscription to volunteering – rewarding and enabling employees to volunteer their contributions in a corporate setting.

- Building digital options for engagement into the design of strategy and change interventions.

- Examples of digital engagement.

Strategy through People: Delivering Strategy and Change through Participative Interventions that Engage the Right People

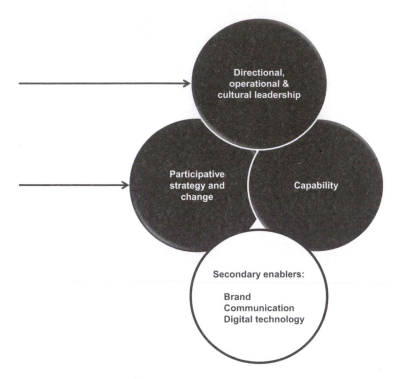

Figure II.1   The primary and secondary enablers of leader and employee engagement

The focus in Part II is on designing and running participative and disruptive leader and employee engagement interventions. These might be to deliver strategy, change and operational improvement programmes and efficiency agendas.

I should explain what I mean by an intervention. Every organization refreshes or transforms itself from time to time, either defensively or offensively. Typically, an elite team or an individual will work out the plan and cascade it down into the organization. This is an intervention, albeit a traditional top-down example where people outside the elite will be told about the plan and their role in delivering it.

Participative, Disruptive Strategy and Change

This part of the book shows how traditional top-down strategy, change and other renewal processes can be inverted with much more inclusive bottom-up involvement of employees not normally invited to challenge or contribute. I will explain how it is possible to engage large numbers of employees (possibly all) in co-creating a plan or strategy or change process resulting in far better business results and widespread support for the plans by employees who feel co-ownership from the outset. This is true even where the plan or strategy to which they are asked to contribute will result in painful results, including job losses. We observe that in these cases, people would rather be part of the diagnosis and remedy than be blind victims of it. Those who leave who have been central to its planning do so with confidence and with valuable experience. And workers at any level must now expect to experience a much more volatile career trajectory with multiple employers, where being equipped to manage organizational and personal disruption provides the best means of self-protection.

Participative strategy and change through people is a series of steps which will reassure those who want to feel that it will be governed in a robust way. These steps are the subject of the next six chapters.

4

Getting Started and Negotiating Business Outcomes

There are seven things to think about to get started on designing participative interventions that engage the right people.

This chapter covers those seven factors:

1.   Getting the sponsor team on board.

2.   Framing the engagement intervention as business strategy or change.

3.   Why labels for strategy processes and change should be considered.

4.   Visible top-level leadership.

5.   The role of an ambassador team.

6.   Articulating simple, communicable business objectives required for the intervention.

7.   The initial plan on a page for the sponsor group.

1) Getting the Sponsor Team on Board

The scenario is as follows – you are a leader with operational responsibility for devising and executing a strategy or a change process, a restructure, an efficiency process or perhaps a customer service programme. You have a sense that the top-down, decide and tell or decide and sell approach is past its sell-by date. Too many initiatives and strategies have failed to live up to hopes. Inevitably this means employees are complaining about the initiative overload of failed measures. This time you have decided to engage your people in the process in a much more inclusive way.

Needless to say, not everyone on the executive or sponsor is keen and some are horrified at the thought of opening a can of worms – you will need to win them over, and the arguments to do so. Chapter 10, which reports on our YouGov UK-wide research into the links between engagement and performance may help with the left-brained argument – it makes a very convincing case and there is now a wealth of research by other institutions on the subject. A notable source of evidence is the UK government's 2012 report into employee engagement – *Engage for Success* by David MacLeod and Nita Clarke (www.engageforsuccess.org), provides a wealth of data and cases to help with the business case.

The left-brained arguments will persuade some, but others will fear that this move will undermine them and they just cannot see how it might work. This is where one or some of the sponsors must take the lead and allow others to step aboard once they see momentum.

I am often asked how to persuade a CEO and others to consider a more inclusive approach to developing strategy or change. I can recommend three techniques: the first is to present evidence that it has worked elsewhere – that there is much you can now to draw on. The second is to connect your CEO or sponsor with another who has successfully executed a leaders' and employee's engagement intervention that has driven performance, and the third is to facilitate your own discussion with the CEO. In it you have two routes to help him or her to gain insight. The first route involves re-telling (by her) the story of the last strategy or change process that was conducted in command and control, decide and tell mode. At the right moment it will be possible to ask if it might have produced more value and moved faster if some or many of those it affected had been offered the chance to influence it before it turned into a cascade from a few to the many. If you make progress his or her next questions will be 'how would it have looked and how do I keep enough control to steer it'. The door is open then to suggest (prepared) options which the next five chapters cover. The other route in the discussion is to ask what kind of legacy he/she would like to be known for. It will be possible to prompt on the kind of internal culture they want to leave.

2) Framing the Engagement Intervention as Business Strategy or Change

I suspect the worst description you can use for these interventions is 'engagement intervention' – it may be interpreted as a functional activity or a programme which is adjacent to real work. In addition, the term 'employee engagement' does not translate well into some other languages, such as German.

The framing needs to be as an integral part of the strategy or change process, which of course assumes that initial ownership is at the highest level; the C-suite. Functional heads can be catalysts, but they need to act as coalition makers in order to get enough power figures on board to make it really happen. They cannot be sole owners except in their own functions.

Time framing is also important psychologically. People need to know how far they have come and how much of the journey is likely to remain.

Framing is psychologically significant at the organizational level, at a business unit level, at a team level and at the level of the individual. In the 'ramp down' period when the UK's RBS (bank) was selling off assets (still in progress at time of writing) such as some overseas businesses, CEO Rory Cullinan and colleagues including Carolyn McAdam and Wendela Currie wanted to ensure that employees, essential to successful sell offs, were retained and motivated.

As the bank is temporarily owned by the British taxpayer it could not rely on handing out bonuses to retain people. One of the key success factors in keeping people was giving them reasonable certainty on how long they could expect to be employed. In many such financial institutions there is no such certainty, especially since the 2008 financial meltdown. In return for reasonable expectations about their length of tenure, many have been retained and enjoyed 'seeing the job through'. Another key factor in retention was much closer relations of employees with their line manager.

In the Total case the framing was Survive, Recover, Thrive. The MD would book-end every significant communication with a reminder about which phase the company was in and where it was in that phase.

Effective leaders know that people react well to framing of past and the future. British Wartime Prime Minister, Winston Churchill, said after the British victory over the German Africa Korp at El Alemain in Egypt in 1942, 'Now is not the end. It is not even the beginning of the end. But it is, perhaps the end of the beginning'.

This illustrates how he set the frame in a way that clearly signalled to the British people that progress was finally being made.

Rhetoric by corporate leaders is something of a lost art. Leaders at whatever level can do much to lift people's spirits and move people to act together. It ought to be taught as part of the leaders' tool kit. It need not, and in most cases should not, be an exercise in charisma. The best examples are those of leaders telling it like it is using visual verbal metaphor and associations to past events which trigger positive emotions in the listener.

3) Why Labels for Strategy Processes and Change Should be Considered

Labels mean that the reach-down process may be remembered come success or failure and, in the event of the latter, provide the source of lampooning and satire. But I like labels as they force headlines such as 'Action for Recovery' or 'Vision to Reality' to become a focus for resources and attention. They also put the sponsor group on the line, which helps to focus their attention on their own reputations.

Labels can be trite unless people quickly see that what lies beneath the label is real work that people want to be part of. They can be liabilities when they are used to package top-down change processes and strategies which cast people as spectators as opposed to participants. They also force a common narrative among sponsors and in formal communication.

Religions use labels to punctuate the year with feasts and periods of special worship, for example, Advent, Easter and Pentecost for Christians, Rosh Hashanah and Shavuot for Jewish people, and Ramadan and Thul-Qedah for Muslims to name but a few. They are highlights of the year and for believers they are an opportunity for congregation and community. Switching to the corporation, former Cadbury CEO Todd Stitzer used the term 'convocations' for his leaders' meetings. All communities pepper the year with reasons to congregate – harvest celebrations, country fairs, city festivals and so on. Nature itself has seasons and crops which define the year – in the UK, the short asparagus season runs for a few weeks in spring, then it is the turn of the strawberry and plum seasons and so on.

Religious metaphors may not be to your taste, but the underlying point is that people like their calendar to be signposted and labelled. This is also the case in the corporate setting, where the year may be divided into quarterly reports, planning rounds, awards ceremonies and so on.

It follows that a renewal of strategy, a change process or operational initiative can benefit from an identity with clear and explicit purpose. Renewal ought to be an exciting intervention, but all too often it is burdened with the language of dull processes attracting the minimum effort to get it done.

Ask any individual or group about the best periods in their working life and they will cite the times when they are at the heart of change, where they were entrusted to make a difference. It matters not that the work itself may be mundane; what matters is to frame it as essential to deliver the vision and to make people feel that their role, however small, is key. In the case of QBE, one of Australia's biggest insurers with operations all over the world, the label 'The Big Difference' was chosen. This is a great label as everyone wants to make a big difference. Labels remind people that what they are doing is part of the higher mission rather than a mundane task with no obvious purpose.

Conversely, there are downsides to labels that we should be wary of. Labels are subject to the attention of internal satirists and programme names can become the focus for derision and opposition. The BBC's 2012 programme to drive efficiency and quality entitled *Delivering Quality First* (DQF) was the subject of lampoons. They can also inadvertently confirm people's fears that another initiative is upon them. In the end, the judgement to label or not is a judgment call that should be based on recent history and preferences.

MINI CASE STUDY: CADBURY – 'GO MAD – GO MAKE A DECISION'

Richard and George Cadbury started their business in or around 1824. They were one of the first 'industrialists' to see that business had to be founded on a moral basis and they believed in non-conformism, entrepreneurialism and being a force for good. Fast forward to the period before the Kraft takeover of Cadbury and CEO Todd Stitzer and his team were succeeding in infusing ideals of accountability, adaptability and positive aggression into the culture. Cadbury had for some time confused consensus and purposeful collaboration. The culture became somewhat static and the company lost its edge. It needed what Stitzer described as 'daring greatly', quoting Theodore Roosevelt. It had also become a deferential culture where permission was sought for everything such that the pace of change had become more akin to that of a snail than a racehorse.

I am including this vignette because of the confusion between consensus and purposeful collaboration. Consensus without direction and without robust closure results in politics and mediocrity. As I have said elsewhere in this book, leaders who engage people effectively are super-facilitators – they are guides, not gods, and they:

- are clear about what is up for debate;

- are clear about what is not up for debate;

- have done their homework on who will add value;

- articulate clearly what is up for debate to those to be enfranchised;

- make it safe and exciting for people to think outside the box, challenge and contribute;

- know when to close and when to make a call should it be necessary.

Consensual managers do not do much of the above. There is often a veil of politeness smothering real debate and negotiation, similar to couples who cannot cope with disagreement, and so cast a veil over it. Companies do the same.

The point is not to confuse consensus with purposeful collaboration, which is what Stitzer and his team wanted to build at Cadbury, ending the 'tyranny of consensus'. The themes of their transformation were giving and taking more direction, pace and leveraging the passion of Cadbury. Their programme – Go mad, go make a decision – combined both strategic interventions and leadership capability interventions, the latter involving reaching down the organization to 30 leaders who would be the future of the company. And the whole process was made visible through a thoroughly refreshed communication process under the leadership of Alex Cole. Stitzer spoke of changing the 'cadence' of communication from the slightly formal, post-colonial period to a focus on leader, manager and supervisors stepping up to be local voices of the transformation. Annual 'convocations' – his word – brought the enlightenment to the regions. This and other stories of turnaround seem to combine the logic, pace and discipline which I can only describe as personal fervour.

Many of the mechanisms, symbols (their purple to green programme obviously focusing on fair trade and real environmental improvement beyond tick box CSR – Corporate Social Responsibility), leadership processes and convocations were designed to generate a sense of fervour for the mission. It required men and women who could do the logic and who had fervour for what they do. Of course, fervour is expressed differently in different cultures. Some Americans love emulating the US military where singing whilst marching and opening and closing exercises with a concerted shout of 'oooo raaaa' is a way to signal collective intent. It means that many of them like charismatic events and larger than life bosses. Continental Europeans and many Eastern cultures do not. The British are somewhere in the middle. The right cadence of ritual and communication and choosing the right leadership role model via trial and error is key.

4) Visible Top-Level Leadership

As with any other programme, there will need to be a sponsor group that designs and governs the process of engaging large numbers of leaders and employees in what was the preserve of a few. In the early phases, leadership almost certainly needs to be from the executive committee or a subset of it. In this way, ownership will be cultivated and opposition identified and addressed head-on at an early stage.

CEOs or any other level of leader need to recognize that (paradoxically) they alone may initially need to drive the process through, especially if they are surrounded by managers who want to protect the status quo or simply do not know how to do it. Thus, the leader will need to be ready to put his or her name on the line.

A characteristic of entrepreneurs is that they have a vision, but perhaps little idea of how to bring it about. Execution for them is a process of trial and error. Designing an effective employee engagement intervention fits the trial and error mold in that the sponsors will have a vision about the business outcomes they want to deliver but may not have designed and managed a participative strategy or change process which engages many or perhaps all of their people. They will be familiar with a strategy cascade, but participative strategy and change means inviting challenges and contribution. Cascading is a linear, top-down process; participative strategy and change is circular.

It is often the case that a CEO will be the one to sponsor a more inclusive approach with a team that secretly thinks that he or she has lost his or her mind and is hoping the whole thing will go away.

Having been part of these teams when they are considering moving to a more inclusive approach, I have observed that opposition by those of a more conservative frame of mind is usually not intentional. Generally people will go through something like the six steps involved in participative strategy (Chapters 6–9) and change from participating at an intellectual level and even appearing to concur and commit. Then, when they are required to role model the change and the pressure is on them, they revert to old comfortable behaviours. The trick is to help the group look at themselves critically and gain insight from what actually took place rather than simply what was talked about.

5) The Role of an Ambassador Team

It is also worthwhile enrolling an ambassador team drawn from across the enterprise to adapt the intervention and ensure that it is culturally suitable for all parts of the business. Ideally, the ambassadors should be at an early stage in their careers and close to and trusted by their local management and colleagues on the ground. They should act as the 'chefs de cabinet' and should be responsible for:

- providing a local litmus test – will the plans meet local needs and result in active participation?;

- being the informal eyes and ears – a channel for 'water cooler' feedback, though they need to ensure that it is representative rather than biased towards their personal views;

- cutting through communication – using the ambassadors to fast-track data to their constituencies;

- getting close to local management to create top-level involvement and support;

- providing insight for sponsors into the causes for local opposition;

- Ambassadors may initially feel compromised about finding themselves inbetween their own management and top management. Local management must recognize this anxiety and assure them.

Remember that this may be the first occasion that individuals have been exposed to such innovative ways of addressing strategy and change; they may have been trained in a traditional top-down, command and control culture. Consequently, they may need an introduction to the ideas behind the engaging workplace. Alternatively, they are just as likely to have experienced a laissez-faire culture where there is never closure.

Ambassadors may also be sceptical until they have some momentum. The group will thus need much cosseting and encouragement to be the vanguard of a different way of carrying out strategy and change. Initially they will lack confidence in the role and so involving them in shaping the process will help them to switch from being a sceptical observer to being an implicated advocate. However, once they have the bit between their teeth, there will be no holding them back – all things are possible with people.

So, assuming that these three building blocks are in place – framing the activity as an integral part of the strategy or change process, having the right sponsorship and having a confident ambassador group – it is time to be clear about the business situation or challenge in which you need to engage people.

MINI CASE STUDY: UK-WIDE BUILDING SUPPLIES COMPANY

This is a quote from a branch manager of a UK wide building supplies company:

> Our branch managers are kings and queens of their domain – they are the cultural role models, chosen in part for commercial nouse and in part for their appetite and skill at weaving their store into the local community. We have 1,000 community engagement projects in the

pipeline – they bring the community into the company and the company into the community and our people love it – stores where there is a vibrant community engagement have terrific engagement scores, which of course encourages other stores to get involved with the community programme.

6) Articulating Simple, Communicable Business Objectives Required for the Intervention

Employee engagement is not an end in itself (see Figure 4.1); it is a platform from which to engage everyone in a vision, strategy or change process such that they feel a part of it as opposed to spectators or victims. In fact, it goes beyond 'feeling a part of it' – it means having a meaningful role in it.

As I have said earlier, it is the process of engaging people in decision making that drives up levels of engagement – it is the well-governed sharing and distribution of power. The question, however, is engaged in what?

There are two categories of business situation: operational refinement and big-ticket change.

Figure 4.1   Engagement is not a means to an end

In all likelihood, there will be a number of desirable parallel outcomes. In our experience, engagement interventions work best when the situation or challenge is hard, gritty and real (i.e. a need to reduce costs or drive efficiency to mend the current operating model and devising big-ticket change or strategy).

People engage themselves when they are invited to contribute to everyday operational decisions and big-ticket strategy and change that *affects* them and which they can *affect*.

Clear business objectives need to be negotiated and made clear, simple and relevant to everyone. These are real examples from our consulting experience:

- 'We need cost reductions of xx%' (a UK unit of a continental energy group).

- 'We need to plan revenue growth from €8 to €14 billion by 2018' (a transcontinental retail group).

- 'We need to dramatically raise the number of clients shared across our practices in order to meet our clients' needs for more consistent delivery (a global law practice).

- 'Drive a one-company strategy so that our customers face a single relationship rather than as many relationships as we have business units' (a global medical engineering company).

- 'Time to bring our brands together to reduce duplicated services, drive more cross-firm client relationships and consistency of delivery' (a major global insurer).

Note the singularity of the objective – each encapsulates a strategy in a line or two. Unless you can boil down the objective to a single idea it will be hard to communicate and complex to deliver.

7) The Initial Plan on a Page for the Sponsor Group

The sponsor group needs to negotiate a narrative about the engagement intervention which will be understood at every level in the organization. To deliver the plan on a page convene the sponsor team and facilitate responses to the four questions that follow. This is about negotiating the substance of a change or strategy first, and articulating a shared narrative second.

Q) What is driving this strategy or change?

Is it a market-driven challenge or an internal requirement for change?

Q) Is the engagement intervention underpinned by a defensive strategy or an attack strategy?

Are we in a leading position finding ourselves having to defend (market share, margin, technological supremacy, brand relevance etc.) or are we attacking a more established competitor? Typically market leaders become defenders as others seek to compete. And defensive mindsets are often characterized by incremental, timid responses. A glance at *Forbes'* or *Fortune*'s (US business magazines) listings of the largest companies tells the reader that the shelf life of big companies is shrinking fast. New regions of the world, new sectors and new corporate stars consign past stars to history faster than ever. Defenders will need to risk radical moves to remain winners. Think currently (in 2013) of the possible re-emergence of Nokia and Blackberry, both marques which were one time heroes before slipping to the edge of extinction, and both going all out with 'bet the farm' strategies. Certainly if either had adopted an incremental approach they would be in the corporate museum along with many past corporate stars.

Paradoxically, a strong brand which can help when companies are in attack mode and are growing, can become an inhibitor to change. Think of Cadbury which became stuck.

The defend or attack question is key as the outcome will permeate the risk appetite and result either in timid incremental interventions or bold bids. Incremental can of course be the right call if it has been arrived at considering other bolder options. Facilitators will need to keep the focus on the business challenge to avoid the outcome becoming overly influenced by the personal risk appetites of the actors present. And if the lead sponsor finds herself being sucked into over-cautious positions she will need to assess the moment to move from consensus seeker to decider. As Jeff Immelt, CEO at GE, commented 'we need to disrupt ourselves before others do it to us'.

A team exercise may help

Step one: Divide the group into two. One group should devise the case for a cautious 'steady as she goes' approach, while the other group should devise the case for a radical or disruptive approach. The opposing views enable the team to relax into the topic.

Step two: Mix together the incremental and radical groups into pairs comprising one from the radical group and one from the incremental group. The pairs share their stories and must negotiate their areas of agreement, disagreement and confusion.

Step three: Pairs share in plenary from which the chief sponsor or facilitator can assess the risk appetite and 'nudge' the conversation along or take the lead.

Q) What is the time frame for the intervention?

It is critical for sponsor teams to fix and announce the duration of the intervention. No-one is motivated by a never-ending process. Fixing the term allows everyone to see progress against an end date and provides something for everyone to work towards. I have elaborated on the significance of framing earlier.

Q) What should the legacy be for this intervention?

Next get the sponsor team to write the headlines about the intervention as they might appear a year from now.

What would you want the Financial Times, *the* China Daily *or the* Harvard Business Review *to be saying a year from now?*

When the international press comes to report on the remarkable turnaround/ strategy/change, what fundamentals of the story would you hope that it covers? Before you get carried away with the picture of success, you might also want to reflect on what the story might cover if some of the organization's reactionary instincts kick in – the change that got hijacked by the ghosts of past change patterns. The imagined negative news story will allow the sponsor group to identify potential blockers to success. These may well be the 'unmentionables', which must be mentioned so that subsequent action streams and role models address them before they rise again and impede progress.

In the Next Chapter

Having clarified the business situation, headline outcomes and a picture of success, the group is ready to move on to reviewing the pattern of engagement normally adopted by the enterprise, which forms the next step in designing an engagement intervention.

From the report I produced with McKinsey & Company in 2004 called 'Boot Camp or Commune', it was clear from the 60 organizations interviewed that approaches to engagement were instinctive and heavily guided by past practices. Deciding which approach to engagement will add most value was, and continues to be, haphazard and is a decision that is often merely delegated to functional departments such as Corporate Communication or HR, who are likely simply to revert to previous patterns. The result is much rhetoric but little real conversation. This happens because most strategy and change processes wearily follow a tired, top-down approach. The result is command and control; the few decide and tell or sell to the many, albeit often with bells and whistles attached and masquerading as engagement.

Thus the need to identify the pattern of engagement that normally prevails. Read on!

5

Your Default Approach to Engagement: Enabler or Disabler?

The next step in delivering strategy and change through participative interventions that engage the right people is understanding the default pattern of engagement in your organization. To help you get that understanding, this chapter covers:

- Businesses invest 90% in the 'what' and 10% in the 'how' – no wonder there are so many failed strategies, change programmes and operational initiatives. ·

- Releasing the grip of past patterns of engagement.

- Agreeing approaches to engagement which will produce better content and faster execution.

- People work in small spaces at work – 95% of their engagement is with supervisors, the real leaders at work.

- Mapping current patterns of engagement.

- Why many organization-wide engagement interventions degenerate into tell cascades.

- How organizational approaches to engagement mirror the decision patterns of dominant individuals.

This chapter will help to give you insight into the grip and influence of history and precedent in your institution when it comes to engaging people in strategy, change and day-to-day operations. It will also provide you with ideas on how to loosen that grip to enable you to engage people more productively.

Elites in organizations are the recipients of the majority of organizational activities – leadership development, leadership events and the like. Yet those who really lead the majority of employees, in real terms, are supervisors who typically receive technical training but little, if any, leadership development.

There are four relationships that people have with their organization which influence the degree to which they engage themselves: the relationships with their job/role, with their immediate team, with their organization's brand and reputation, and with the organization as a system and community to which they belong to varying degrees of affinity. The further you are from the core of the organization, the less you will be exposed to the fourth relationship (with the organization) and the more you will feel affinity with your immediate work team who form your day-to-day community. Peoples' distance from the core of their organizations is highly relevant to this chapter in terms of assessing default patterns to engaging people in big-ticket change, strategy and operational improvement. The further you are from the epicentre of change, the less you will be touched by centrally organized efforts to engage you.

This also casts light on senior management's tendency to think that people are more engaged and interested than they really are. An elite is all too often surrounded by people who would rather present good news. Down the line, most people work in small spaces focusing on day-to-day operations, with much of the drama and the comings and goings of the centre passing ethereally above and beyond them.

People Work in Small Communities at Work, However Big the Institution

During times of change and strategy implementation, most people at work will be reached and connected with the change via their immediate manager, regardless of the efforts to reach them via digital and other indirect communication.

It is relatively easy to build momentum for a change process or strategy in those close to the action. For most of the rest, the action will seem like a far-off thunderstorm whose intensity fades to a low rumble once it reaches the outer communities of an organization.

Leadership engagement is key, but much greater effort has to be put into the supervisors – the clergy, clerics, priests and imams of the organization.

The congregation may get occasional missives from the ideological hubs, but in most cases it is the day-to-day community that just gets on with the day job.

In considering what approaches to engaging people in big-ticket change have been used in the past, it is important to distinguish between those groups close to the source of change/strategy and those expected to act on it who are far from the source.

Mini Case: Williams Formula One – A Purist Philosophy: *Racing to Win*

When the executive team of the Australian insurer QBE came for their strategy day to the pleasant environs of the Williams F1 racing team, they initially had operational distractions on their minds. By the end of the session, they had got the wheel change cycle down to eight seconds a good result for a bunch of (now rumpled) suits, albeit in their case, very competitive suits. QBE is the Williams F1 team of global insurance. Mo Kang, a director of QBE European Operations, had devised this as a core part of improving engagement by the team in the team.

The Williams pit change team has the change down to five seconds and is aiming for 4.5 seconds – yes, it's that tight. Imagine being in the pit as the car races directly at you at 60 miles an hour, the speed they leave the track – it's down to trust. What's more, your every move is on global TV – no pressure then! And there's the heat – 400°C off the brakes and 700°C from the engine requires three layers of heat protection, whatever the outside air temperature.

The pit teams are divided into groups of three which are constantly changed to keep everyone on their toes. (Whatever happened yesterday is history; it's always about what will happen today and tomorrow. No-one remembers who came second any more than we recall yesterday's lunch).

As spectators we see the racing, but what the industry is really about is innovation – every car is a rehearsal and every one is out of date the moment that the rubber hits the road. And here is where the Williams philosophy comes in. Unlike many of the other players, Williams listens to the workforce – anyone can propose an idea or a concept and it will be respected and adopted if it makes sense. Most of the industry, rather like the mining sector referred to elsewhere, is run on a command and control basis. With Williams engagement is a philosophy of leadership, not a functional bolt-on. Staff turnover is virtually unknown – they love what they do.

Change Begins with Insight

As with any individual or group habits, self-knowledge and insight are the prerequisites for change. After all, it is not primarily about adopting a set of tools run by a functional department, it is about opening up the 'way decisions are made around here'. The patterns of engagement are probably entrenched and automatic.

Most executive suites, rightly, put a lot of effort into the 'what'. There will be days, weeks and months of time devoted to the content of a strategy or change. There may well be strategy houses involved and it must stand up to board and external scrutiny.

After completion of content comes the proclamation akin to a papal smoke signal – the cardinals have arrived at a decision. And with attendant pomp, great thoughts are revealed. The executive team breathes a sigh of relief that the really important stuff – the policy or content, the what – is completed.

Whilst much is invested into the content of strategy, considerably less effort is invested into actively considering which approach to engagement will drive value to both content and to execution. Few leadership teams stop to consider if people beyond the elite will add value to content, even though we know that diversified generalists can make better decisions than a narrow elite if they are engaged in a well-governed way.

Most 'Engagement' for the Masses is Little More than a Cascade of Pre-Decided Content

If they are fortunate, staff will get the high-level cascaded version of the strategy, perhaps with a roadshow and digitally distributed content. People may also get chapter and verse from their immediate bosses, who will attempt to create a line of sight between their roles and the big idea. Some do the cascade brilliantly, while others will struggle. At the appointed time, progress reports will be made and for some there may be a quarterly, six-monthly or annual leadership meetings to review it all. The patterns are often quite familiar, even predictable. They are mostly a variation of long-term central planning where much of the effort is frontloaded and focused on the content – the what.

At the other extreme are organizations where there is pride taken in having no strategy – Sir Stuart Rose, former head of Britain's Marks & Spencer chain of stores, said the company had a purpose and a vision but no strategy, since retail changed so much on a regular basis that it would become outdated immediately.

Does either approach sound familiar? It is good to know where you and your institution are on the continuum of central planning versus little or no strategy, as past practice will bear a heavy influence on attempts at more participative strategy and change.

There is an additional subtle message to be added here. Central planning cultures will invariably adopt a 'decide and tell' or 'decide and sell' culture – that's what authoritarian institutions and countries do. But this is not to say that zero strategy cultures are more likely to be inclusive – Marks & Spencer under Sir Stuart Rose mirrored his personal decision-making style, as, of course do many family businesses.

Consideration of Engagement is Rarely Part of Up-Front Business Strategy Planning

There is rarely a considered decision about which approach to engagement will add value as part of the strategy or change process – organizations invariably default to previous patterns of engagement.

Typically, the previous pattern of engagement, certainly in command and control cultures, will be decide and tell or decide and sell. The key point here is that both imply a relationship with staff that is instructional and parent/child in transactional analysis terms. The sell may very well be well executed and engaging in a presentational sense and people may well end up with a very clear idea of the overall scheme and their part in it. This is as good as it gets in command and control cultures – everyone is more or less aligned and hopefully mobilized to use the vernacular of command and control.

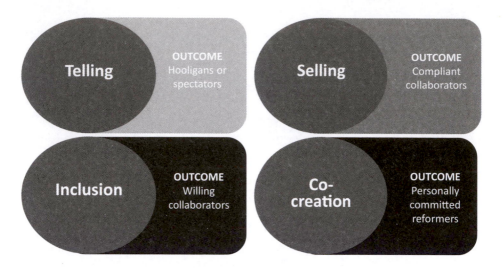

Figure 5.1   What engages people at work?

However, command and control cultures are missing out on the input that staff and other groups can give to the origination of strategy (change, operational plans, etc.) if they are invited to do so. We know this as a fact from our independent research and the many other data sets conducted by others.

Figure 5.1 provides the approaches to engagement diagram from Chapter 1.

Does your organization's approach to engaging people (decide and tell, decide and sell, include or co-create) add value and speed for the company and does it provide your people with the benefits of engagement – being able to contribute, feeling a part of it and enjoying the dynamic and the acknowledgement?

Mini Case Study: The UK's National Air Traffic Service – Personal CEO Brand in a Turnaround

In the National Air Traffic Service (NATS) control centre, the author listens in as Pete works his aircraft. It's a quiet room. All BA flights are called Speedbird – Aer Lingus planes are prefaced with Shamrock [J2], 555 etc.

Between busy moments [J3] I recount my experience of being in the cockpit jump seat (when it was permitted) of a BA Concorde inbound to Heathrow when we were instructed to do a go-around due to a plane on the runway.

As it zoomed up, I overheard the engineer say '15 minutes fuel'. It was a very tight circuit! And it turned out that this was the only occasion that it occurred. When such events do occur the people at NATS have to juggle dozens of planes bearing in mind their fuel reserves.

The story is interrupted by a Midland plane calling a pan, pan, pan call (a medium-level call for assistance). It is vectored straight in. There are, says Pete, around two such calls a day to keep everyone on their toes.

Paul Barron turned NATS around and into a highly successful organization. NATS for many years had the feel of a rather formal public sector organization in which change was a challenge. The air traffic controllers are a group of dedicated individuals in whom we place our trust every day, but they are also a tribe of their own and, perhaps similar to consultants in the NHS, are sometimes sceptical of the motives of management.

One of Paul's insights is that he could not change the organization by dictate from the top. Yes, there had to be a clear vision, but a lot of what he describes is about forging relationships, ripening and bringing opposition out into the open and creating pride in an organization. In his first weeks, he visited all the main sites and held bar-stool conversations with staff in order to probe what was good and what needed to change. His first 90-day plan was heavily influenced by staff – it was unprecedented for them to be engaged in creating a bottom-up vision and strategy. It was a process of creative 'discontinuity'.

Execution was equally inclusive. By involving people in the process of real work, the energy spread. As John Parker, chair of the UK National Grid, reminded me, 'when the best leaders' work is done the people say we did it ourselves'.

Paul also reported that a good 20% of his time was spent online or in direct conversation to the whole organization via his blog – all kinds of challenges were invited and responded to – and those who strongly objected to changes were invited for one-to-one meetings to talk it over. His blog was updated (by Paul, not by a comms person) every night and every query or comment would receive a response – that is some commitment. A total of 77% of staff participated, on average, 18 times each during his 12 week roadshows. Most of his posts would be work-related, but some would be reports from home or business meetings in the community, such as reporting on one occasion that he had been sat between the shoe designer Jimmy Choo and the then UK Chancellor Alistair Darling. The blog also enabled him to put the record straight in the face of union communication which appeared to present a misleading picture. It all added up to a CEO being part of the work community, being seen to be genuinely integrated and accessible at any time of day or night via the blog. Back in the operations area, a staffer tells me that he and many others had never met the previous CEO. "Paul Barron fitted into our schedules by holding meetings on a Sunday shift when we were less busy". The 21 destinations strategy that everyone contributed to had a dramatic impact on performance with average delays to planes falling from 50 seconds in 2008 to 22 seconds in 2009, and an average delay of just four seconds in 2010 [J4].

What is Your Organization's Current Approach to Engaging People in the Decision-Making Process?

You may use the following diagnostic diagram given in Figure 5.2 on your own or in a group. Ask yourself (or individuals in a group) to reflect from an individual perspective on what approach (to engagement *in terms of being told, sold to, involved and co-creating*) they observed and experienced during a recent strategy refresh or change process. The idea is to record in each of the four boxes specific activities which they experienced. Thus, under 'sold to', you might record WebExs, roadshows, conference calls and so on, while on 'co-create' you might record sessions in which you were presented with the problem or opportunity and were invited to solve them. Ask the group to compare experiences and see what dominant pattern of engagement is emerging.

   Earlier in the chapter, I observed that the further people are from the epicentre of change, the more likely that efforts to engage, become little more than cascaded content. Put yourself in the shoes of other levels of workers and predict what specific experiences they received. But beware the pitfalls of positive bias – groups of leaders almost always paint a rosier picture than those on the receiving end. Better still ask other levels of employees to participate in the exercise. You will quickly build up a picture of the current approach to engagement experienced when the institution is going through a process of renewal. And the act of engaging different levels in painting a current picture raises employees' level of knowledge and curiosity such that when you are ready to ask them to contribute, you can refer people back to the foundations of the engagement process.

The pattern of engagement ... what are the specific experiences of different levels of employees

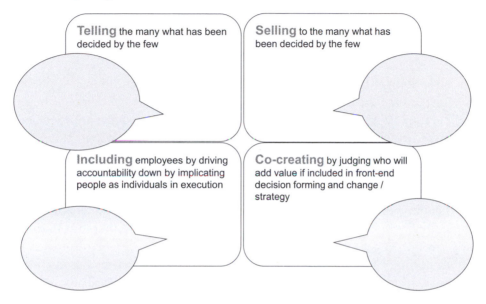

Telling the many what has been decided by the few

Selling to the many what has been decided by the few

Including employees by driving accountability down by implicating people as individuals in execution

Co-creating by judging who will add value if included in front-end decision forming and change / strategy

Figure 5.2   Diagnosing your patterns of engagement

Pay particular attention to which boxes attract the weight of activity, especially from the point of view of those lower down in the organization.

Having completed these exercises, you will have a good idea of current patterns of engagement and will thus be equipped to chair discussions about which approach or mixtures of approach to engagement have been experienced and which shift in approach will add more value and speed to the strategy or change.

I am a great believer in piloting a change of approach to engagement. Choose a stream of activity in a change process or an aspect of next year's strategy and compare results. Or pilot in a business unit or function where there is transformational work to be done and the boss needs to try something different in order to avoid incrementalism.

Is Making a Choice Between Approaches to Engagement Conscious and Rational or Accidental?

CEOs and other decision makers, when asked how considered they are in selecting between approaches to engagement, often conclude that they repeat the same pattern of engagement on autopilot. A conscious choice about which approach will add value is rarely made. Accidental repetition is thus irrational.

Ask yourself the following question. Is your organization's approach to engagement (refer to the four-box model in Figure 5.2 above) chosen deliberately at the outset of the strategy/change/operational improvement process? My guess is that most organizations adopt a previous pattern of engagement without much or any consideration of the risks and rewards of choosing between tell, sell, include and co-create.

Leadership teams focus on the content of strategy and change and typically hand over the execution to others without seeing that the choice of approach to engagement needs to be part of the primary thought process to avoid opting for tell or sell by default. Failing to make a considered choice between approaches to engagement is irrational; a non-choice. The choice of approach to engagement needs to be part of personal and collective decision making.

The Engagement Climate is an Outcome of Individual Approaches to Decision Making

I have focused thus far on collective and organizational decision making which will mirror the patterns of dominant individuals. Let's briefly look at the decision cycles of individuals.

Consider the following diagram given in Figure 5.3. It is the life cycle of any personal (and group) decision-making process in which the individual concerned is asking himself or herself the right questions as he or she forms, closes and propagates a decision.

We developed this diagram at our last firm, 'SmytheDorwardLambert', when working with an investment bank. Each of us has a pattern in the way we go about making decisions, whether they be operational, day-to-day decisions made on the fly or big-ticket change/strategy decisions made by groups.

My process decision making skills - my decision-making map

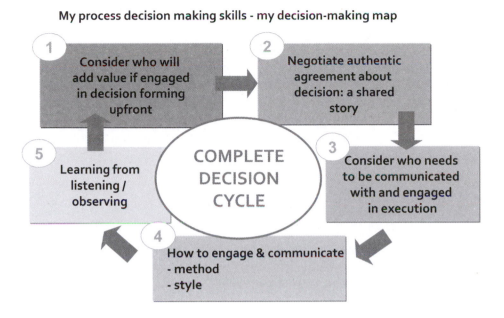

Figure 5.3   The big idea

We determined that managing directors at the investment bank who followed an inclusive pattern like the one above experienced better performance and retention than those who saw managing in this way as a bore and were usually more authoritarian.

An interesting exercise is to complete a picture of your own decision-making cycle as might be reported by your team(s). We know that the leader that 'shares power' in a well-governed way gets better results and colleagues feel well led. This leader is aware that his or her decision-making pattern is made explicit through two processes: awareness of his or her decision-making map and awareness of his or her interpersonal style of interaction. Figures 5.4 and 5.5 will help you test your innate engagement capability.

Personal approaches to decision making and their impact on the choices in terms of mass engagement are explored later.

1. I understand how I make decisions
2. I have insight about how I make decisions
3. I know where the wisdom lies in my people
4. I understand the choices of approach to engaging people in decision making
5. I make rational choices about who to engage in decision making
6. I am clear about the non negotiable aspects and make the invitation to participate clear.

Figure 5.4   Awareness of my decision making

Awareness of my personal style of interaction - God to Guide

1. I facilitate decision making clearly, fairly and do not change the 'goal posts' half way
2. I facilitate to enable people to participate but I know how to close down
3. I am trusted, credible and transparent
4. I listen to respect, encourage and build
5. I disclose my own feelings, doubts and ignorance
6. I make it safe for others to challenge, feedback and disclose
7. I exercise pastoral care & hard love.

Figure 5.5   Awareness of my personal style of interaction

Engagement is the Engine of Origination and Delivery

We should view engagement as the process of both origination (of content – the what) and delivery (the how) – it is not an option, it is a must-have if organizations want to execute well and thoroughly on their ambitions. Increasingly, your competition will do so and will reap the commercial and cultural benefits.

If you conclude that you want to change the approach to engaging people, what can you do to begin the change? You should agree what the present approach is in terms of the four-box model in Figure 5.2, and the DIY diagnostics suggested earlier. You should do this in the context of the last strategy cycle or change process and agree where the process worked well and where, by virtue of the choice of approach to engagement, it underperformed.

Bear in mind if you are in a last millennia organization that the forces of conservatism will be strong. There will be many possible objections to more inclusive approaches, some of which are to be found later.

In reviewing the last strategy/change cycle, you may find our typology of decision making given in Figure 5.6 helpful in working through from *the content – the what, to delivery/execution – the how.*

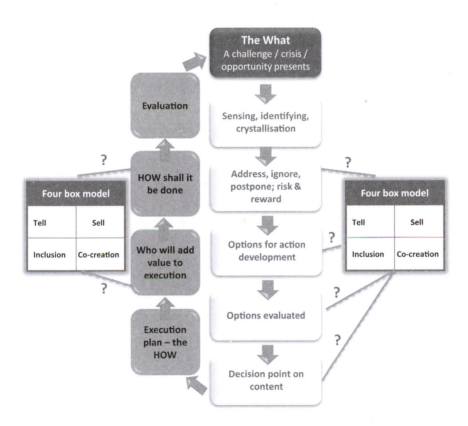

Decisions, large or tiny have a life cycle. Decision makers should make judgements about who will add value to 'the what / content' and the 'how' / execution.

Figure 5.6   Typology of decision making

Having insight into the approaches to engagement in force today provides the basis for determining which approach will add value and speed to the next strategic initiative or change. In the following chapter, I look at the 'Power of the Peach', in which the stone in the peach represents the 'givens or non-negotiables' which must be determined. Chapter 6 will also serve to remind us that there will always be some aspects which will remain pre-decided by a few. And, rightly too, it also explores the balance between the top-down and bottom-up approaches, a balance which energizes and liberates the creativity of the people without turning the office into Speakers' Corner.

6

Negotiating Who Should Be Engaged: The Power of the Peach

Figure 6.1   The power of the peach

Source: http://www.istockphoto.com/stock-photo-14790340-peaches.php?st=b15eb24, Anna Kucherova, photomaru.

The next step in delivering strategy and change through participative interventions that engage the right people lies in negotiating who should be engaged – which is where the power of the peach comes in.

This chapter covers:

1. The meaning of the peach metaphor.

2. The demographics of engagement: identifying who will add value if engaged.

3. Cases illustrating the peach process.

1) The Meaning of the Peach Metaphor

Let me first explain the peach. Think of the stone of the peach as the non-negotiables or givens that a leadership team has negotiated and agreed as being not open to challenge by other levels of leadership or employees. In doing so, the team has had to negotiate why some aspects of a strategy or change are in its gift. The members of the team have also explained to themselves their legitimacy to assume their right to take a position and are ready to explain their rationale to others.

In negotiating what is non-negotiable, they will also clarify the invitation to other levels to challenge and contribute. And typically their negotiation will result in the non-negotiables shrinking as team members gain confidence and suggest that others outside the inner group will add value if invited to challenge and contribute.

The process of actively and openly negotiating the non-negotiables or givens transforms what can be an instinctive, even emotional process (often taken by one leader) into a rational process which strengthens the team and provides its members with legitimacy with other levels of leadership and employees in general. Let us also recall that leadership teams are judged by what they say and decide and by how they carry themselves. People read the tea leaves.

The image in Figure 6.2 sums up the spirit of this chapter.

The leadership or change sponsorship team needs to have made conscious and clearly negotiated decisions about what it alone should be held accountable for. As part of that negotiation, it will and must agree the rationale for taking some decisions without input from other levels.

The rationale may be that only the leadership team members have access to information that others cannot have or that they take the explicit view that they know best or that there is no time to engage others.

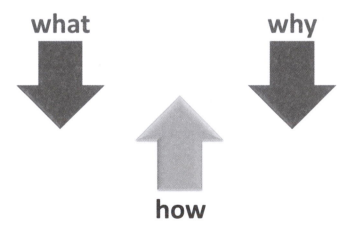

Figure 6.2   The what down, the bottom up

Equally it is possible that these assumptions are delusions of grandeur or a sign of a lack of confidence requiring the appearance of firm leadership.

A conscious pause by the leadership team before they rush into their pattern of decision making at least allows leaders to rationalize what they have deemed to be theirs alone to decide. In so doing, however, they are very likely to challenge themselves and extend the scope for others to contribute or challenge. At the very least, they will have determined whether and how to involve their people in delivering their decisions – the 'what' down and the 'how' up as Allan Leighton put it (a prominent UK business man).

I, of course, contend that the 'what' is not the exclusive preserve of an elite – people on the ground will in very many, and maybe all, circumstances be able to contribute to the 'what' before it becomes set in stone.

Figure 6.3   Communication and engagement

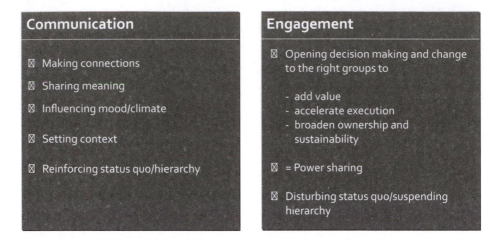

Communication

☒ Making connections

☒ Sharing meaning

☒ Influencing mood/climate

☒ Setting context

☒ Reinforcing status quo/hierarchy

Engagement

☒ Opening decision making and change to the right groups to

- add value
- accelerate execution
- broaden ownership and sustainability

☒ = Power sharing

☒ Disturbing status quo/suspending hierarchy

Figure 6.4   Communication and engagement

Imagine the following situation – the leadership team has decided to reach out and down to invite more people to contribute to solving the business challenges confronting them.

The primary task in designing a leader and employee engagement intervention is to decide what aspects will be handed down as givens and non-negotiables and what is therefore the scope of the invitation to other groups or everyone to contribute to or challenge the process. I use the analogy of the peach – the stone in the middle represents the givens or non-negotiables that the sponsor or leadership team has decided are literally unimpeachable, while the peach flesh is the extent of the invitation to contribute that is open to other groups or everyone.

Determining the givens must be addressed early in the gestation of the strategy or change. If the organization has wittingly or unwittingly elected for decide and tell or decide and sell, this vital exercise is void. And talk by the leadership team of post-decision engagement will become, by default, a communication cascade of pre-decided decisions.

Readers are reminded of the difference between communication and engagement (Figure 6.4).

Most leadership teams, in setting out on a strategy or change process, do not stop to consider which groups might add value if engaged early on in the process. My assumption is that in following this six-step 'Strategy through people' model (Chapters 4–9), you will be considering who will add value by conducting the peach exercise.

The purpose of the peach is to ensure that the leadership team makes good decisions about who to engage.

2) The Demographics of Engagement: Identifying Who Will Add Value if Engaged

The purpose of enfranchising others outside the elite is to add value to the content of programmes and to accelerate delivery because people have been given an intellectual and emotional stake in the process. It is not to 'make people feel involved', which is so often the sinecure of command and control trying to gee people up.

The team should consider the identity of distinct clusters of employees in the organization and what defines their distinctiveness; for example, differentiated clusters could be identified by the following factors:

- hierarchy;

- core business speciality – in an insurance business, for example, the actuaries will be at the top of the list;

- customer/client-facing;

- professional groups (air traffic controllers);

- geography;

- ethnic groups with particular needs.

Ideally the groupings should be confined to as few groups as possible in order to avoid over-complexity, which means tough negotiating about real distinctions between groups. A persona exercise is a device (often undertaken in brand work) that offers a good way to identify who to involve. It involves identifying significant groups of employees by hierarchy, skill set, geography or other criteria (as above).

The following discussion gives an outline of how this exercise should be conducted.

Invite a group of people who know the whole organization well to divide into threes and give them the task of clustering the workforce into distinctly different groups such that representative percentages of each distinct group (or everyone) can be invited to contribute. So, for example, in retail you would expect the clusters to include buyers, merchandisers, procurement, shop staff, administration, functions, etc. Each group of three needs to be able to rationalize its clusters and explain why it chose them on the basis of the nature of the proposed engagement process.

The groups of three present to the other groups of three and negotiate a conclusion on staff clusters for recommendation to the leadership or sponsor team. The process will show whether there is sufficient knowledge of the organization's demographics to base decisions on who to engage. The best group to do this is the leadership team augmented by an ambassador team drawn from across the business. By doing so, the exec becomes more knowledgeable about the demographics of the business and the ambassadors gain the confidence that the exec will support them later when the going gets tough. The demographics exercise can then become a continuous part of engaging and communicating with the organization.

3) Cases Illustrating the Peach Process

There follows one micro case from O2 and two fuller cases in which the executive teams had to determine who beyond the executive team would add value to strategy in the retail case and structure and strategy in QBE's case.

MINI CASE STUDY: O2 – PART OF SPAIN'S TELEFÓNICA – A SMALL STONE AND LOTS OF ROOM FOR UPWARDS IDEAS

MD Ronan Dunne told me:

> 'We have great engagement at the executive level due to continuity of management – the crew are all in the same direction – we spend a lot of time discussing who we are and who we want to be.
>
> I give people permission to make mistakes and make a difference. For example a person rang our customer service desk desperate to get his

Internet back – turns out he was actually a customer of Tiscali, but our people helped him reconfigure his router anyway – he became a customer after that.

We call our customers fans and we call our people fans.

Fanship is about emotion, trust and forgiveness.

Our debt team's job is to make it possible for indebted customers to stay with us.

The idea of freedom is important to O2 – the freedom to move, to challenge, to want to go the extra mile for customers.

We are on a journey from childhood to adolescence – we are already a great mobile company; one day soon we want to be the communication company of choice'.

CASE STUDY: MAJOR FASHION RETAILER

In the case of a fashion retailer, the executive team conducted the 'employee persona cluster exercise' and concluded that they needed to distinguish between the top 100, the top 600, the 1,500 store managers and 35,000 staff – a traditional hierarchical perspective, but a leap for what was a pretty traditional hierarchical organization.

The small executive team members had negotiated amongst themselves what would comprise the non-negotiables, namely their transformational vision, growth targets and six streams of activity as follows:

- Pricing.

- Comparative store growth.

- Property.

- Fashion.

- Online.

- Supply chain.

Whilst these were in part givens, all stream owners (drawn from the eight-strong leadership team) were asked to identify where they wanted challenge and contribution, and how that invitation differed across the organization's distinct groups that they had identified.

How did they do this? Imagine you are in a large room with a long wall. Affixed to the wall at the top is a large reproduction of the agreed vision. Below are six large posters, each devoted to one of the six streams of activity (or strategy if you prefer) that will deliver the vision. Each poster has two sections:

- Who to engage in content (the 'what')?

- Who to engage in delivery (the 'how')?

The leadership team toured the posters and negotiated over who should be invited to contribute to either or both core content (the what) and delivery (the how). By the end of the tour, the invitation for others to contribute had been thorough, well organized and, most important of all, process light and interaction heavy without a PowerPoint in sight.

One of the devices we use in these conversations is to divide the executive into two groups. One group recommends radical engagement options, whilst the other asks the radicals to defend and substantiate their case. This allows people to think outside the box in the knowledge that negotiations with the other side will ensure a realistic outcome. It also injects competition – always a powerful motivator.

The stone in the peach (the givens or non-negotiables) always shrinks in these negotiations as one group will challenge another by observing that, for example, 'the train drivers will have lots to say on how we bid for the franchise', challenging conservative engineers' views that drivers are recluses who don't care who they work for.

Early on, the executive of the European retailer was able to communicate a clear expectation about who would be engaged in which aspects of the transformation, signalling to the top 600 and later everyone that this transformation would not be imposed on them; they would be part of its co-creation within the visible boundaries of the invitation to challenge and contribute communicated to them.

There are other benefits from the stone in the peach approach aside from identifying who will add value and speed. The sponsor or executive group must negotiate and come to definitive agreement over who is to be involved. It is thus a huge spur to teamwork, with the advantage that the group is doing real work rather than an academic 'team dynamics' process in which it is easier for members to appear engaged but in fact not be so. Their 'skin is in the game'. Another outcome is the development of a shared narrative which radiates beyond the sponsor group. In addition, the slightly cartoonish nature of the peach often lifts spirits through associated banter.

The fashion retailer extended the invitation to contribute and challenge to its top 100 and top 600 in separate gatherings. In each, it employed the Engage for Change concept of Strategy Safari,[1] which is explained in more detail in Chapter 9 – the dynamics of creativity. Suffice to say that the experience of being in a tightly choreographed group of 600 broken into small teams of 12–15 is exciting, memorable and energizing. Once again, there was no PowerPoint in sight. With the use of open space wireless technology, the contributions of the 600 in small teams were factored into strategy design within hours, enabling contributions to be acknowledged and challenges to be addressed and learnt from immediately. There was no need for making sense of illegible flip-charts and ponderous board meetings.

Having experienced the engagement intervention, the regions organized their own mirror copies of the intervention for 1,500 store managers, continuing to subsequently enfranchise the 35,000 store staff, who also had much to contribute as a result of their local knowledge. In this way, the process ran through the organization.

This story is all the more remarkable given that the institution is family owned and is prone to secrecy. The idea of asking for a contribution to the forthcoming vision and strategy was almost shocking. But the emergence of a new family head provided the opportunity to change, added to which the former culture of command and control had presided over a period of ponderous performance. The opportunity to change was being seized.

The second example, which follows, features a fast-growing company where the burning platform for change lay in the very cradle of its success.

---

1   Strategy Safari is literally strategy on the move.

CASE STUDY: THE BIG DIFFERENCE – AUSTRALIAN INSURER QBE

QBE is one of Australia's largest insurers with a major and fast-growing presence in Europe, growth fuelled by good performance and acquisitions. Its European strategy had last been updated in 2004 and had served QBE European operations well, delivering good returns year on year.

Some things had to change

QBE is a hard-driving, fact- and evidence-based culture. The traditional stars are the actuaries who book the business and take the risk. They are a no-nonsense crowd. Its operating model had been terrifically successful and people were loathed to question it.

At the outset of this story in 2008, some of the key individuals – John Neal, Steven Burn, Mo Kang and others – sensed that the time was fast approaching when the free roaming period for member companies might be approaching its sell-by date. The telltale signs, in retrospect, were rising costs of duplicated back offices, occasionally inconsistent client service when clients were being dealt with by more than one entity, increasing internal competition as companies began to overlap or spread their wings and so on.

The first challenge was to engage the entrepreneurs, who ran the businesses and who relished their relative freedom, in a dialogue about options for a change to the operating model that would be in everyone's best interests. Everyone being the shareholders, clients, leaders of the business and employees. The essentials of the original operating model were that acquired businesses were encouraged to carry on with minimal interference and bureaucracy, which was popular but had its hidden and not-so-hidden costs too.

The conundrum faced by the management team, familiar to many CEOs, lay in maintaining the balance between an entrepreneurial spirit of the many acquired companies, on the one hand and on the other leveraging the potential to be derived from collaboration where it made trading sense or could provide efficiencies. In other words, how do you bring about a subtle culture shift without throwing the baby out with the bath water?

In late 2007, Mo Kang, Chief Human Resources Officer, asked me to facilitate a discussion with the European CEO and COO about the best way to hold this dialogue with among the 28 or so business unit heads.

We were warned that anything that sounded like a soft engagement or communication exercise would die in seconds!

Strategy refresh – low-key framing

Strategy refresh was chosen as the label of the exercise to engage the wider top team. The approach meant that the 28 or so heads could debate the issue with neutral, external, one-to-one facilitation and so develop their own insight rather than have it unilaterally imposed – an approach unlikely to succeed with a group of independent thinkers.

I interviewed each of them to debate the business case for adjusting the balance between almost complete independence and a measured degree of joint approaches to clients and more internal efficiencies. It was by no means certain that the issue would be seen to be 'ripe' enough to warrant change, but the consensus, by and large, was that this was the time to start creating more of a consistent one-QBE internal and customer experience. This marked the start of a journey that the business is still undergoing today. The idea of ripeness is based on its horticultural analogy. A leader needs to judge how to ripen an issue such that protagonists feel the need to address it. Kotter talks about 'creating a burning platform'. Lyndon 'Bird' Johnson, a right winger himself, deflected calls from the right to send in federal troops to quell the race riots in the US back in the 1960s, electing to wait till 'TVs across the nation were alight with the issue' and states accepted that it was their issue to deal with. He waited till the issue was ripe. As a leader you will have encountered the problem of trying to deal with an issue before it is ripe enough. Often it takes several passes.

One-to-one discussions to ripen the issue

In QBE the one-to-one discovery conversations gave the leaders of the operating companies the space to explore the DNA that had both enabled the extraordinary growth of QBE as well as the risks of continuing with the existing operating model and options for its refinement. The conversations also enabled individuals to develop their own insight and rational ideas for options for change. Had the topic been raised in an open meeting without ripening the issue, the reaction would, in all likelihood, have been emotional rather than rational.

When all the conversations were analysed, there was enough agreement on the need to explore the development of the operating model to bring them altogether and contribute to what became a collectively owned strategy with enough support to allow the CEO and COO to develop and execute the resulting strategy. This was to comprise common support platforms, outsourcing aspects of IT and, perhaps most importantly, seeing clients as shared opportunities rather than the property of business unit fiefdoms.

The discovery conversations formed the basis for the wider Executive team to articulate a refreshment of their European vision and business strategy. An integral part of this was a debate about the public positioning of QBE (European operations) which would represent the underlying strategy to the market once the strategy had started to take root.

Rolling out the 'big difference'

The roll out of 'The Big Difference' – the vehicle that enabled employees to have the same insights as directors – was fronted by directors and internal volunteers acting as strategy ambassadors.

Every Big Difference day was fronted by a director to avoid the possibility of the days becoming trapped by a script. There was indeed a script to convey the non-negotiables, but much of the rest was designed to stimulate challenge and contribution from those who had operational insight. Director facilitators enabled the conversations to be more fluid and thus interesting for both the directors and the participants. They also played a key role in making it safe to be controversial.

As I have remarked earlier, it is very easy for the mass engagement process to reverse back into being a show or cascaded training. The critical difference between engagement and showboating and training is the opportunity for participants to challenge and contribute within a framework where their ideas are not merely welcomed but actually affect the strategy of change. Engagement results in change – cascading and training results in alignment to a preconceived idea.

Once senior sponsors have bought in to the value of engaging people, they usually want it to be as edgy as possible. Reactionary forces may lie in backwards-looking central functions in which the desire to eliminate all risk overrides the need to create creative turbulence.

Employee engagement is supposed to radicalize people via creativity, surprise and humour. The key attributes of a successful intervention are surprise, creativity and an authentic sharing of power – and humour! A room that laughs is infinitely more productive and memorable than a worthy but dull agenda.

In QBE's case, once the top group of 28 was aligned and confident, the decision was taken to engage QBE's entire European staff in 'the big difference' which invited them to:

- understand the changing market conditions and the present customer brand experience;

- identify and celebrate the QBE brand DNA which had propelled strong, profitable growth;

- learn about the capability of other business lines and core support services;

- understand and contribute to the draft vision and action plans;

- draw up team-specific actions to deliver the plans, particularly around the internal and external customer experience: matching reality with brand promise;

- participate in the QBE Big Idea (to make a Big Difference) contest.

After the Big Difference further initiatives continued to execute the business strategy including:

- a focus on the wider European executive team;

- several restructures to further create 'one QBE' from the formerly fragmented, tribal collection of companies;

- outsourcing of services;

- a focus on internal communication;

- programmes to build knowledge of each other's businesses;

- a focus on top-team building;

- developing and measuring employee engagement drivers specific to QBE;

- helping to integrate the latter with personal performance development.

Having worked from the inside out using strategy as the engine of change, QBE Europe raised its brand visibility through a visible marketing campaign, including sponsorship of the English rugby team.

Whilst the European retailer, highlighted earlier, and QBE are completely different business models, they have one key ingredient in common – leadership teams willing to take the risk of opening up decision making beyond the normal boundaries. Both moved forward quickly as a result because their people knew they had been included at the start of the growth agendas, rather than being communicated to after the fact.

I will end this chapter with the idea that traditional top-down command and control is based on a linear model of decision making which then employs a linear model of communication which is mostly top down. It looks a bit like this:

1. Elites deciding.

2. Message forming.

3. Message delivery.

4. Message impact.

5. Reinforcement.

Contrast this top-down mode of decision making with the dynamic at work in the organization that is sharing decision making with employees and which is circular (Figure 6.5).

At the end of this chapter, if you have followed the advice contained, you will be able to shape the invitation for people beyond the leadership team to be engaged, and by doing it with the leadership team, you have strengthened the team and built a shared narrative about the strategy or change you are designing.

The next chapter covers designing a creative intervention to engage your leaders and people.

Engaging people results in decision making becoming circular rather than linear

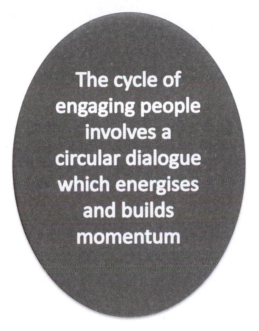

The cycle of engaging people involves a circular dialogue which energises and builds momentum

Figure 6.5   Circular decision making

MINI CASE STUDY: MANCHESTER AIRPORTS (UK) – BOTTOM-UP OPERATIONAL CHANGE

Our customer first teams are self-elected and they can get an investment decision up to £5,000 within three days to create a better customer experience – our aim is to become the world's airports of choice.

Our service teams have engagement scores well above those not participating – give people influence and they will deliver more and enjoy their work more.

People who don't make mistakes don't do anything – we like to focus on converting disengaged hostages to being apostles – the converted are unstoppable.

All our investment is customer-driven, as illustrated by the author's interpretation.

7

Designing and Running Engagement Interventions That Deliver Fast Commercial and Cultural Results

The next step in delivering strategy and change through participative interventions that engage the right people involves designing and running engagement interventions that deliver fast commercial and cultural results.

Think of your organization as an express train (Figure 7.1) (or maybe a plodding country line with too many stops) in which the passengers are your people. The train is racing out of the tunnel and it is only once it has fully emerged that everyone can see the whole train (or, in the case of our analogy, the whole corporate vision).

The purpose of an intervention is to invite those who have insight and experience about a problem or opportunity to contribute to both the 'what' (the content of the strategy/change/operational topic) and to the 'how' (the delivery/execution). There is an important distinction to be made and emphasized between the 'what' and the 'how'. Many leadership teams assume that the 'what' is the preserve of an elite, effectively dividing content from delivery/execution, which explains why so many strategy and change processes look intellectually sound but fail on the ground. Most of the effort is invested into the 'what', with insufficient focus on delivery of the 'how'. If you are setting out on the design of an intervention which challenges the hierarchical pattern, past practices and in particular comfort zones, it is worth thinking about the psychological challenges which sabotage best laid plans.

Figure 7.1   The Express
Source: http://www.istockphoto.com/stock-photo-13553778-steam-train-emerging-from-tunnel.php?st=4d6028b, Gary Martin, tirc83.

An engagement intervention that tries to ride over past cultural patterns without acknowledging the blockages which may emerge from the organization's subconscious when it feels threatened, will stall. People may feel unsafe preventing them from participating. Thus the significance of identifying up front what may impede the intervention. An open discussion on barriers is always fruitful and beneficial to the design and execution of interventions designed to refresh strategy and/or bring about change.

This chapter covers the following areas:

1. What is an authentic participative/disruptive strategy/change intervention?

2. The psychological blockers that may emerge if they are not acknowledged and planned for.

3. Why and when would you use a participative (probably disruptive) strategy or change engagement intervention?

4. Designing and delivering creative employee engagement interventions that deliver fast results.

5. Critical tests of a well-designed intervention – knowing if you have a winning design.

Whilst I do use the term 'engagement intervention', I recommend that you refer to the process as a participative (and possibly disruptive) strategy/change. You need to position what you are doing as the central strategy/change process as opposed to an adjacent 'staff engagement exercise', which may have no credibility or teeth as a functionally led exercise.

1) What is an Authentic Participative/Disruptive Strategy/ Change Intervention?

In the last chapter I suggested that much effort goes into the 'what' of a strategy or change, with little invested in the 'how', the delivery or execution, which is one reason why so many initiatives seem to blossom for a short time before fading – all eruption with no lava flow.

Most strategies and many change processes are presented as done deals – the products of a 'decide and tell or decide and sell' leadership approach. This is what it feels like in a decide and tell or decide and sell culture – a variation of the satirical 'we are like mushrooms; they keep us in the dark and feed us compost'.

The purpose of an intervention is to invite those who have insight and experience about a problem, a challenge or a corporate opportunity to contribute to the 'what' (the content of the strategy/change/operational topic) and to the 'how' (the execution) before decisions are closed by the sponsor team. In Chapter 6 I reviewed ways to help identify which groups of people to enfranchise in the engagement process. It could be targeted groups or everyone.

A strategy or change intervention puts the engaged leader or employee in the decision-making circle, the driving seat; the place normally reserved for an elite – a place where leaders and employees can see options ahead and influence decisions about which options to take.

Interventions can be used in all challenging organizational situations to bring the experience, wisdom and challenge to bear in a well-governed way. These include:

- crises;

- strategy;

- transformation;

- operational improvement;

- vision, purpose, values;

- customers' service experience;

- brand;

- relocation;

- pre- and post-merger.

The intervention can take many creative formats (the cases in this book illustrate some of them and there are more in my previous work – *The CEO; The Chief Engagement Officer*, turning the hierarchy upside down to drive performance, published by Gower in 2007).

Two interventions were described in the previous chapter (Chapter 6) in the case of the retailer and QBE. More detail is provided in Chapter 9 (the dynamics of creativity).

THE TWO FORMS OF STRATEGY AND CHANGE ENGAGEMENT INTERVENTIONS

Strategy and change interventions take two forms – the first is where employees are invited to challenge and contribute from the perspective of their day job. They are literally invited into the center of the strategy or change process and are invited to influence the outcome.

The second involves casting people into other people's (strangers') roles, enabling them to more easily break out of their day job perspective and to look at their institution through the eyes of a stranger. Thus liberated, they suspend the normal filters and prejudices so that they see their world differently potentially becoming, temporary, well-informed 'internal consultants' or change agents.

The stranger's roles includes those below and many more – the choice depends on the nature of the challenge ahead. The trick is to choose roles to cast employees in a way that will best enable them to lift themselves out of their day job so that they can see their world from a broader perspective. In a strategy or change intervention in which leaders and employees are cast with strangers' eyes they will find themselves in a scenario designed to enable them to critique their own organization and role – the 'suspension of disbelief'.

Stranger's roles – being a:

- Start up.

- Competitor.

- Customer.

- Regulator.

- Union.

- Shop floor – if they are not on it.

- Director.

- The change team.

- JV partner.

- Other national cultures – i.e. if we were our French affiliate, how would we react?

Regardless of whether they are invited as themselves or are cast in strangers' roles the invitation is to challenge and contribute rather than just to receive and understand.

EVENTING IS NOT ENGAGING

The events/leadership meetings industry has grown fat on what I call egotainment – leadership events which are too much about selling and aligning people around decisions made by small elites and too little about enfranchising the group by inviting them to challenge and contribute to a strategy or change. The emphasis is also too often on production values, presentation and pomp, when the emphasis should be on low budget creative dynamics that enable and encourage people to challenge and contribute. Chapter 9 elaborates on creative dynamics.

2) The Psychological Blockers That May Emerge if They Are Not Acknowledged and Planned For

Identifying and planning for the psychological blockers that may emerge is an important part of the design of a strategy or change intervention. The blockers that tend to emerge are:

- The realization by some or all on the sponsor group and other influential parties that the intervention will mean less influence for them and more distribution of power to others, which results in subsequent objections.

- Leaders who push too far ahead of their teams (as their teams see it), who then introduce doubts when the leader is vulnerable.

- The lack of readiness of lower levels for the apparent suspension of the pecking order and the possible lack of response to the invitation to contribute induced by apprehension or lack of faith in their own capability.

- A failure to plan for the sustainability of the process into the delivery phase and beyond. This is easily the greatest challenge, especially in can-do cultures that are good at sprinting and operational response but poor at the longer haul. This is exacerbated by a change in leadership unless the new leader has been part of designing the intervention and has ownership. This issue is addressed further in Chapter 8.

ADDRESSING BLOCKAGES

The tricky bit lies in deciding how overt to be about the blockers that may disable the intervention. In some situations, being overt simply gives the reactionaries time to plot. It's a question of being clear about the balance of power between the leader and the team. If the team is being sponsored by one strong leader who must outflank or bring the team along with him or her, you might want to plan this with him or her first. If it is authentically a team effort, then clearly the discussion is with the team from the off. If this sounds manipulative, it is, because setting up the conditions to engage widely is a political process.

Omitting a discussion about potential blockers nearly always leads to unintended outcomes, many of which can be pre-empted. Identifying and dealing with blockers and barriers early means not having those conversations later which go along the following lines:

-I/we had no idea that this would unsettle our culture.

-This is much more risky than I/we thought.

-How do I/we restore normality when it is finished.

When you are confronted by these objections later on in a process, it just goes to show that they should have been on the radar earlier; I've made this mistake myself too many times.

However there is a circumstance in which it may be better to let sleeping dogs lie, when it is wiser not to identify blockers with any or too many others. This is when the team, or some of it, is simply not able to engage in the conversation because its members are too inexperienced – to do so simply lets fear run rife to no purpose. In these circumstances, it may be that the issue needs, in the parlance of US author and academic Ronald Heifetz, to 'ripen' before it can be addressed. This is a judgement call and one which underlines that when you are messing with the established order, these interventions cannot be designed as an off-the-shelf pre-packed product.

3) Why and When Would You Use a Participative (Probably Disruptive) Strategy or Change Engagement Intervention?

The short answer to this question is when the organization identifies or is confronted with a huge challenge or opportunity which requires more than an incremental and traditional response. And when a leader can see ahead that there is a coming challenge or opportunity (that others can't or won't yet see) that requires a disruption to current thinking.

A Leaders' prime role is knowing when to sustain calm waters and when to disrupt. Jeff Immelt CEO of GE: 'Disrupt our strategy before others disrupt us'.

These moments of insight provide the opportunity to seize the day when the normal looks inadequate and the forces of resistance are at their most vulnerable. The scenarios which provide opportunity for participative/ disruptive strategy or change follow.

SCENARIO ONE: IT'S NOT BROKEN, SO WHY FIX IT?

As a leader, you will find yourself dreading the well-worn glove of the organization's change or strategy process. It could be that the leadership team is tired or over-extended to such an extent that the chances are they will vote for incremental rather than deeper change. You, meanwhile, know that the window for change is probably going to be decisive in establishing a growth trajectory or continue a steady downward slide. Past change and strategy processes have served their purpose, but the same formula is beginning to have an ossifying affect and déjà vu is looking over your shoulder. Nobody else around the table is going to risk it except you, because that's what you are there for – the leader is the one who judges when to continue business as usual and when to 'rise above the dance floor' (Heifetz) and disrupt the dance.

SCENARIO TWO: YOU ARE THE NEW CEO ON THE BLOCK OR YOU ARE A MEMBER OF HIS OR HER TEAM (OR A NEW HEAD OF FUNCTION OR BUSINESS UNIT/REGION, ETC.)

You have just been appointed as the boss to continue a business as usual trajectory or disrupt the current strategy. You have six months to signal intent and take action. All eyes are on you, including those internally who might have been expecting to have been given your job. This is the best chance you will get to do it differently – if that is the right thing to do.

Reaching down to include others (beyond the inner embedded and possibly embittered circle) in the process provides the means to reach out directly to those closest to clients and customers – leaders and employees you will need to enfranchise from the start. By so doing, you mitigate the risk of being quietly throttled by the establishment. It's a risk of course, but less so than carrying on with old patterns. Of course you will need to enfranchise the existing leadership team as well. An effective tactic is to enroll them in championing the engagement of their own people and visibly holding them to account for doing so – visible performance drives performance.

SCENARIO THREE: THERE REALLY IS A GOOD CHANCE THAT YOUR COMPANY (OR FUNCTION/BUSINESS UNIT) IS ON SOMEONE'S LUNCH MENU

When fear stalks the corridors generated by the prospect of a big cat coming up from behind, you can fly, fight or lie down and be lunch. As in the animal kingdom, the first few seconds signal which option you have chosen without a word being spoken and whatever your words say.

We have a saying that executive teams think that they are secure behind closed doors from which they can control the narrative, whereas their demeanour says it all without a word being said – employees are fantastic corporate social anthropologists. They sense intention using their eyes in the same way that a dog uses its sense of smell to seek game, to detect illnesses in humans and assess their human's mood via chemical analysis. We, like our animal friends, are tuned to interpret every behavioural hint. In the UK, the talent for satirizing the behaviour of bosses is the worker's way of circumventing the lore of tacit or explicit corporate censorship – the authoritarian regime's method of worker control. Bosses actually live on a stage on which they utter lines of truth or falsehood – if it is the latter, the staff will rewrite the script with satire. It's a great thing to look out for when riding with the workers – if there is a comedy show narrative on the front line, you can be reasonably sure that there is compost being laid down by a blind, dumb or plain bad leadership team. Conversely, a straight leader who can keep his or her ego under control and treats staff as adults and with respect, however tough he or she has to be, will be readily listened to and respected on the front line.

The lesson for leaders with regard to personal 'presence' is to be aware that your inner thoughts are made visible by your behaviour, mood and presence. Be aware of what your body is saying to everyone. Think about your nearest and dearest – they don't need to be told what mood you are in. The same is true at work, except as a senior executive (or manager/supervisor), your inner being is conveyed to teams and multitudes by the formal communication process certainly but, more critically (and quite probably in contradiction to the formal media), by speed of light via the collective sense of the pack.

The fields of social psychology, cognitive psychology and neuroscience are bringing welcome insight into the unconscious mind. Much is unseen and yet it is clear that the unconscious mind is a hugely powerful influence on team and group behaviour. Leonard Mlodinow's book *Subliminal* (2013) provides an excellent window into the 'revolution of the unconscious'. Another good text is *The Moral Molecule* by Paul Zak.

Back in the boardroom when the decision is to fight a takeover, the question is whether you choose to mobilize everyone within your organization or fall back on the capability and resources of the usual core suspects. In the takeover of London's LIFFE financial exchange by the NYSE, the management knew that the takeover was highly likely, but took the opportunity to engage their leaders in the weeks before the transaction. They did so by inviting them to create a united front, to become self-aware of their strengths and challenges, such that there were ready and confident when their new bosses ran the ruler over them. The idea was to fortify them and their teams and to address challenges that had been overlooked but which the acquirer would pounce on. Dealing with the challenges in advance meant that LIFFE had little or less to fear and approached the acquirer with confidence, encouraging a smooth transition, a reduced likelihood of job losses and a sense of confidence both inside the business and for the benefit of the new owners.

People enter mergers as victims or activists depending on the degree of genuine pre- and post-merger engagement rather than any exhortation and grandstanding by leaders who do not recognize that people motivate themselves when they are real players in decision making.

SCENARIO FOUR: MARKETS AND SHAREHOLDERS DEMAND BETTER PERFORMANCE

When the institution comes under external pressure for results and internal incremental measures are not up to the job, you have the perfect cue to create creative turbulence via an engagement intervention.

SCENARIO FIVE: THE EMPLOYEES FEEL THAT THEY HAVE SOMETHING TO OFFER AND ARE BEING IGNORED

A major circle law firm became increasingly concerned that its associate lawyers were becoming disaffected as the number of partner positions reduced as a percentage of associates, whilst other associates were happy not to have to join the partner rat race, but felt under-involved in shaping the firm. One of the answers was a shadow strategy process that enabled associates to influence the firm's actual strategy.

4) Designing and Delivering Creative Employee Engagement Interventions That Deliver Fast Results

There are any number of creative approaches that can be designed and tailored to the business situation and personalities of the sponsor group. In this section I provide five types of intervention which might be freestanding or part of a wider approach:

- *Intervention route one*: reaching down to drive change – delegating the strategy or change mandate.

- *Intervention route two*: make-believe business scenarios which turn the hierarchy upside down.

- *Intervention route three*: Strategy Safari (or Change Safari/Customer Safari).

- *Intervention route four*: hot-house marketplaces.

- *Intervention route five*: employees in customers' shoes.

These are all primarily people-to-people interventions, but they all use technology to some extent. Engagement through digital means is clearly with us and I will examine this in more detail in Chapter 14. And since this work was started three years or so ago the digitalization of engagement has and will gather pace. Just look at how Jive and Yammer have occluded Sharepoint's place in the sun by providing much more accessible and enjoyable experiences.

INTERVENTION ROUTE ONE: REACHING DOWN TO DRIVE CHANGE – DELEGATING THE STRATEGY OR CHANGE MANDATE

It is rarely middle layers that are the cause of delay or stasis in change. The leadership team must bear the weight of responsibility, not because it is deliberately being obstructive but usually because its members are so keen to remain involved that, along with all their other duties, they simply cannot give it the attention and focus that it requires. They may also be anxious not to 'lose control', thinking that they are best suited to lead from the front. In addition, they may be unwittingly wedded to the past, a past they had a hand in creating, and may be reluctant to consider radical alternatives.

Added to this is the observation that the sponsor group are often far removed from execution of the strategy. The solution involves reaching down to layers below the executive – see the case of the global law firm that renewed its strategy with a well-governed mix of the top-down and the bottom-up, later in this chapter.

INTERVENTION ROUTE TWO: BUSINESS SCENARIOS WHICH TURN THE HIERARCHY UPSIDE DOWN

Delegating the change mandate can also be delivered via business scenarios which suspend the hierarchy and put people in the driving seat. In these interventions, people assume a different role or identity and look in on their company as an external analyst might. The scenario has the effect of 'suspending' the status quo and allows people to think what might be unthinkable in their normal role – except around the water cooler.

The key point about all interventions is that they require the sponsors to take the risk of upsetting the old order; without risk, there is certainly no change.

Engage for Change's 'Predator' concept is the collective description for business scenarios which suspend the hierarchy and put people in the driving seat. It was devised in the 1990s at our earlier consulting firm SmytheDorwardLambert. Little did we know that we were engaged in a trial-and-error process that would be impossible under command and control.

People enjoy the competitive nature of scenarios and amazing results can be achieved in a short time. The more realistic the scenario, the better. In one example, the host organization selected the identity of a real potential predator for the scenario as there were some former employees from that organization working for them. They got so under the skin of it that they went on to acquire their adversary who, it turned out, was planning an attack on them – but too late! Fortune favours the brave.

Predator-type scenarios are quite different from old-style brainstorming because they:

- enable people to 'play' safely out of the constraints of their day job;

- involve a stimulating creative scenario;

- are often very competitive;

- are governed and facilitated in a tight/loose fashion;

- are led from the top – the Executive Board will go through it too, but everyone takes part;

- people can see the impact that their ideas are having as part of the governance.

In 'Predator', people are cast in different roles including:

- As a private equity house executives putting the ruler' over their own business and asking the question 'what more could we do with these assets if we were not constrained by structure, outdated operating culture, leadership role models, habit, myths'?

- As themselves when they are poached by an imaginary new or existing competitor and are invited to use their inside knowledge to take business away from their old company.

- As themselves in defender teams (acting as the senior leadership team) in scenarios like those above, but on the home team.

- Roles of other groups who have other conflicting positions to their organization: regulators, unions, joint venture partners and others.

By assuming a different role/identity, people can get remarkably close to the position of the other parties – a corporate game of bridge in which aspects of game theory are harnessed.

Simulations add up to sharing power within a well-governed and usually temporary timeframe, although having done it once and benefited from it, institutions will try it again and then start to figure out how the spirit and practice of leader and employee engagement can be grafted onto their day-to-day culture (see Part III for more).

CASE STUDY: AN EXAMPLE OF PREDATOR

The backdrop is as follows. The leadership group has decided to invite contribution to its business strategy from all colleagues and is kicking off the engagement with a creative intervention that will also equip the top 600 to engage their own people in a four-month harvesting of their ideas to enrich the strategy.

AT THE LEADERSHIP MEETING – STEP INTO THE SHOES OF A DELEGATE

You are one of 600 people who find themselves in groups of about 10–15, some in cross-business sets and others in intra-business sets to allow for a maximum range of outcomes. There is an air of expectation as the pre-meeting note simply said 'we want you to be a contributing partner in co-creating the strategy; let's all bring our imaginations, expertise and insight to bear to help us trash our competition – participate in an experience like no other in this company's history'.

SCENE 1: RED LETTER DAY

You have been poached by an interesting and very well-funded new entrant to the market – a market which most people had assumed was mature with few new angles to create differentiation with the main players. You open the personally addressed envelope to find a welcome letter from the CEO of the start-up competitor.

You are introduced to your colleagues by your team coach who collects your 'old' company (called Heritage) pass, puts it into a box for recycling and hands out a badge with the name of Xanadu – the new company. It feels surreal and exciting – certainly different from sitting in serried rows watching PowerPoint presentations about strategy conceived by others.

SCENE 2: THE PREDATOR APPEARS

The CEO of Xanadu appears on giant screens to spell out the vision for a new company built on superior customer service. She reinforces that the market is undifferentiated, that service built on an efficient platform with a really sexy loyalty programme is the only strategy and that few of the existing players have the right values or leadership to pull it off. With the exception of Heritage, which is why the assembled teams have been poached! As a member of the assembled group, you feel you are part of an exciting venture.

The CEO then reveals that she has obtained a top-secret service dossier from their former employer – 'Heritage' – which elaborates a plan to steal the service crown for itself. She waves the dossier at the crowd and invites people to open their own copy of the dossier. In it are details of Heritage's service innovations and customer loyalty programme. She invites the team leaders to take people through these.

SCENE 3: THE FIRST CHALLENGE – TO KNOCK OUT HERITAGE!

The CEO returns to the screen and invites the teams to draw from their knowledge of Heritage and:

- agree where Heritage will execute well against its own service improvement dossier;
- agree what will slow Heritage down or suffocate them (silos, bureaucracy, etc.) by mapping the Heritage customer journey and analysing the 'cracks in the journey' which damages the experience;
- agree which of the given service innovations in Heritage's 'secret service' Xanadu must prioritize in order to steal a march on Heritage.

Using their attack plan frameworks covering the above, the teams' deliberations are captured on open space wireless technology (with each team provided with a lap top).

SCENE 4: SHORT REVIEW OF SERVICE ATTACK PLANS

The 30 teams are divided into six groups of 100 in which each of the six present their best ideas to each of the other five teams. The combined group takes the best from the six and the final six teams with their composite ideas present briefly to the assembled house – the composite forms the basis for the customer service attack plan. For good measure, the 600 have investment funds to vote on the best, which provides a collaborative but competitive spirit. The sound of 600 people working in constantly changing dynamics is amazing and yet each group is able to tune out and focus on the prize.

As this part comes to an end and a new day beckons, the teams are provided with the next instruction – having analysed Heritage's weak spots, the CEO of Xanadu invites the now fully confident group to outflank Heritage in the context of its weaknesses.

SCENE 5: THE SECOND CHALLENGE – GOING ONE BETTER THAN HERITAGE

The CEO of Xanadu re-appears and congratulates the teams, but notes that the dossier of secret service innovations has come from a few elite top-down Heritage teams.

This next part is based on Engage for Change's 'Borrow, Build, Breakthrough Stairway'. Participating staff will not become radical straight away; they need to work up to Breakthrough mode, building confidence as they go, in much the same way as any sportsperson or other achiever does in their particular field. Many corporate improvement processes involving many people falter because they are asked to go to the top of the mountain immediately.

In this case, employee teams are asked to review the journey of a typical customer and work through the 'Borrow, Build, Breakthrough Stairway'. At each step they are reminded that this is a new company – they can put anything that is specific, measurable, practical and actionable up for consideration.

SCENE 6: REVIEW OF GOING ONE BETTER THAN HERITAGE

Plans to go one better than Heritage are shared in the wider group. And the assault on Heritage is all but complete when their old boss from Heritage appears in person on stage.

SCENE 7: FROM VISION TO REALITY

The CEO welcomes the teams who were poached to join Xanadu back into the fold – Heritage has acquired Xanadu and he invites the teams to make the transition back to Heritage. He explains the process by which their bottom-up ideas will be analysed, accepted and acted upon. Finally, he lays down the challenge to turn their ideas into action.

SCENE 8: TAKING IT HOME TO MAKE IT HAPPEN

Participants are asked for their ideas for how Predator needs to be refined to make it easier for them to run it. To help in this endeavour, everyone is paired up in buddy teams to give them a partner to help them through the process, ideally from another part of Heritage to reinforce the one-company theme.

AFTER PREDATOR

A number of Predator sessions will be professionally run in each part of the business. All the outputs will be analysed in order to determine:

- reaction to the given ideas;
- success so far;
- bottom-up ideas to be approved/rejected.

These will be discussed by each business executive board and then the group-wide executive board in order to:

- determine forward process;
- recognize success;
- approve bottom-up ideas.

INTERVENTION ROUTE THREE: STRATEGY SAFARI

Strategy Safaris are interactive face-to-face experiences that enable an orderly contribution and challenge to a strategy, change, service, brand or any organizational improvement process.

Strategy and change from command and control cultures are typically a product of decide and tell or decide and tell approaches to leadership, in which an elite deliberates behind closed doors and presents the fruit of its (very private) labours to the organization. At best, the inmates, including quite senior levels, are then subject to an information cascade of some sort. At worst, these will be a presentation of an incremental budgetary process probably focusing on performance targets.

They may include charismatic activities which do indeed inspire, provided the audience is OK with being told what to do – but the agenda is still principally top down and will still include the statutory but less inspiring exhortation to 'get on the bus or get off it', a sentiment so beloved of command and control.

By contrast Strategy Safaris are interactive face-to-face experiences in which people are active participants rather than spectators. As a spectator, you might be expecting a relatively dull if informative peroration by the CEO.

As an engaged participant what you experience is quite different. In the retailer's case in Chapter 6, employees were treated to a short presentation by the CEO who built a mind map on four 90-metre screens, filling all four walls in the TV studio – participants were in and surrounded by his thoughts. After a short break, the studio was transformed into three colour zones, each with five strategy stations. In teams of 15, the employees toured the stations with time to receive, challenge and contribute to content. Their experience was one of being contributor and co-creators, rather than idle spectators.

In this case (and typically) Strategy Safari is the first stage in what becomes a bottom-up strategy/change process. The sponsor team will have negotiated the absolute givens/non-negotiables of a strategy/change/operational process using the power of the peach. In so doing, they will have shrunk the peach stone – what is non-negotiable – and articulated the nature of the invitation to others to contribute.

Then there is the question of how to engage each part or layer of the organization in a practical, time-efficient way. If the megaphone and the cascade are the weapons of choice for command and control organizations, how can decision making be opened up without it becoming a commune ?

Here's how it works. The exec or sponsor team work through the peach and determine which groups will add value to the 'what/content' and the 'how/execution'. They also identify where they are most interested in inviting contributions and challenge for each element of the strategy/change.

The exec team are owners of separate parts of the strategy and they are asked to summarize their part and their requests for contribution and challenge. This is always fun. On first pass, they will arrive with a large power point deck. Hours later, when they have bored each other into staring at their BlackBerries and drained the energy away, the penny drops that this is not the way to energize themselves or other groups.

On the next iteration, the exec team will have boiled their parts down to a few coherent power points. The final challenge is into turn these 'stump performances', with their only prompts being a few words, pictures or illustrations which can be easily seen by groups of up to 15. They are now ready to take their positions in a Strategy Safari. The iterations have enabled the exec:

- to boil down their parts of the strategy to essentials – a good story;

- to make it second nature by working hard with the rest of the exec or sponsor team;

- to accept with good grace teasing about their jargon/mumbling and so on!

In the retail example given in the previous chapter, the exec first had to open up to their top 100, which gave them a real rehearsal for a next meeting of 700 which took place in a giant TV studio. As with all these Safaris, the event had the sense of being informal and fun, but behind the scenes it was managed to the second. During the course of the day, all 700 had had a chance to interact with all streams of strategy, contributing and challenging, with their ideas captured electronically to avoid the awful filter of the flip-chart.

Within six months, the entire crew of 40,000 people right down to the shop floor had contributed and so made the process their own. This had been done 'with and not to' them and in so doing had addressed the criticism that widespread engagement takes too long with few obvious benefits. In this case, the benefits of the engagement process were as follows:

- An exec team had negotiated the givens and non-negotiables and the extent of the invitation to others to contribute and challenge.

- An exec team that through this negotiation had made progress as a team and had developed a naturally shared story (rather than a learnt script drafted by someone else).

- Credibility of leadership – the people witnessed them taking a big risk in a confident way and pulling it off.

- Fantastic ideas added to the strategy at all levels.

- Fast execution by people who felt that it had been done with them, not to them.

Strategy Safari does not have to extend throughout the organization – it may in the first instance be used to break the hold of the old command and control central planning mentality and then spread over time. But my experience is that when the process starts with an ambitious CEO and he or she sees it unleashing creativity, he or she wants it everywhere – NOW!

INTERVENTION ROUTE FOUR: HOT-HOUSE MARKETPLACES

The core idea behind Hot-House Marketplaces, as with Strategy Safari, is to drive ideas upwards in the organization in an organized fashion. Hot-House Markets are principally designed to focus energy to identify existing and potential ways to:

- innovate;

- transform; and

- grow profitably.

It can take many forms.

Profitable growth powered by you: one example involved a global financial services organization which had reached a certain plateau but which had to find organic growth to maintain momentum. An open competition was mounted in which leaders were asked to identify the best existing fast growth (or transformation/innovation) ideas judged against clear financial critical tests.

Competitors were pitching for a restricted number of places at a Hot-House Marketplace which was attended by the top 650 leaders. As a delegate, you would have found yourself in California in a giant convention space where there were 40 top-class examples of product and service innovation, each vying for the popular vote. Aided by complex choreography, participants visited many of these.

Having visited and interrogated the aspiring award-winning experiences in deliberately randomized teams, participants rejoined their natural teams to borrow, build and break through with options for creating new and profitable revenue streams.

In an earlier example of an innovation hot house market, £30m in seed money was at stake to fund new product ideas.

INTERVENTION ROUTE FIVE: EMPLOYEES IN CUSTOMERS' SHOES

In the case of the retailer given in the last chapter, leaders visited showcase stores having assumed the identity of a particular type of shopper: a mother with young children, a mother with teenagers, a teenager, a father, grandparents and so on. Schooled in the habits of their adopted customers, they 'experienced' the shopper's experience. In this case, the purpose was to educate the visiting executive with the perspective of the customer. Each team was equipped with voting tablets, enabling net promoter scores to be analysed by the time the teams had returned from their visits, prompting immediate reactions to what they had seen.

Other techniques include employing a customer-centric strategy. In the Predator example given above, employees were asked to construct the customer journey from start to finish, critiquing it from the customer perspective and identifying the fault lines caused by fiefdoms, systems, competitive P&Ls and so forth. Casting groups of employees as analysts serves to help them understand how the 'system' rebels against the customer, to express empathy and propose operational shortcuts that cost little or nothing. It also enables them to suggest big ideas which require cash and it sets an expectation of change which might otherwise have caused fear when dropped in by surprise by an elite.

In this case, the 'elite' had the grace to say that they would not have come up with a better strategy.

5) Critical Tests of a Well-Designed Intervention – Knowing if You Have a Winning Design

The critical tests that I offer are a guideline rather than a checklist.

It is useful to agree your measures of success before you start the actual design of an intervention:

- *Hard business outcomes*: will the intervention deliver the business outcomes agreed at the beginning of this process?

- *Real work*: are the tasks set comprised of real work to deliver real results, rather than a team game?

- *Scope/the peach test*: have sponsors pre-determined the givens/non-negotiables so that participants understand the extent of the invitation open to them? Does the design honour the invitation?

- *Demographics*: is the rationale for the choice of the group invited to participate clearly articulated?

- *Governance*: will participants be able to understand how their ideas will be assessed and utilized? The best solution is where the executive team is asked to do this on the spot. A global medical engineering company took its top 200 to a five-day offsite and cast them into defend and attack teams to devise a breakthrough strategy. The exec group had to make on-the-spot judgements about which ideas to accept or reject without recourse to delay or board meetings further down the line.

- *Feedback*: is there commitment from final decision makers to communicate about ideas which have been adopted or rejected, with the rationale behind these decisions made clear?

- *Surprise*: will the design of the engagement intervention surprise (in a creative sense) participants?

- *Dynamics*: interventions provide multiple opportunities to maximize networking – have the groupings been thought through and are there sufficient randomized exercises?

- *Engaging, not eventing*: will the design provide real opportunity for challenge and contribution or has it receded into being a spectator event?

I think that most of these criteria are exemplified by the next case, although some three years in, the client and I reflect that more could have been done to drive a focus on execution in the later months.

CASE STUDY: THE STORY OF VISION TO REALITY

Bob Charlton became head of DLA's Finance and Projects division in the autumn of 2009, having previously been with Freshfields Bruckhaus Deringer.

DLA Piper is a youngster on the global law firm stage, having come together in its present form in 2005 as a result of the largest merger in the history of the legal profession, although it can trace its roots back to Yorkshire some 200 years ago. Freshfields dates back to 1640 and Linklaters to 1810. However, in that short time, it has shot up the global league tables and has ambitions.

The appointment of Bob came with a mandate to fuel those ambitions from the Finance & Projects (F&P) perspective. Lateral hires to all professional service firms are a challenge for both the host and the new arrival. In common with any new arrival, Bob would need to show progress in a relatively short space of time.

Clearly, the first stop was to review the purpose and direction of F&P. He had a choice to either do this from an elitist, top-down perspective or to adopt a more inclusive approach. He chose the latter.

Law firms are a funny mix of the seemingly consensual and the hierarchical and a cocktail of the meritocratic and deferential. They are also full of very able and very competitive people. For the most part, strategy in law firms is more top-down than bottom-up and for many this is okay as it leaves them to get on and service clients. Up to a point that's good; however, all the evidence from clients of global practices suggests that the days of lawyers acting in siloes are long gone. Global clients want a consistent approach and level of skills in every port of call. They want a one-firm approach where their interests come before the interests of different practices or regions in the firms. To get on the panels of preferred 'suppliers' means living this ideal.

This of course is not new to DLA Piper or its competitors – they are adaptable creatures. If anything, DLA Piper ought to have a bit of edge in this respect as it has less baggage to tow around. Indeed, it already had a 'One DLA Piper' aspiration prior to this strategy intervention.

Bob's instinct was to invite a lot more people than usual to develop a strategy process, sensing that this window would not be open to F&P for too long. So, what did he do? From March 2010 onwards, he invited the partners and then the entire legal staff to co-create F&P's strategy in a series of meetings, including one with 330 employees meeting in Amsterdam in late 2010. The process is ongoing; it is not a 'show and tell', but an experiment in broad-scale engagement. The steps are explained in a little more detail below.

SCRIBE HOTEL, MARCH 2010 – A PLAN ON A PAGE IN A DAY

After a brief period of nosing around, Bob asked location heads and some others to attend a strategy meeting in the Scribe Hotel in Paris in March 2010. Our firm Engage for Change designed and facilitated it. By the end of just one day, the group had participated in a high-speed strategy process which would lay the basis for becoming 'the most relevant F&P practice for our clients, our people and our firm'. The idea of Relevance as a vision took hold.

In Paris the 40 or so attendees found themselves in a constant whirl of changing dynamics characterized by very small teams of twos and threes where intellectual and emotional abstention was impossible (see Chapter 9 for the dynamics of creativity). They moved through five key steps of high-speed strategy development:

- A vision which is different, aspirational but achievable – Relevance.

- Assessing the current reality of the experience for key stakeholders against the vision.

- Assessing the key gaps between the current reality and the vision for key stakeholders.

- Towards a strategy – filling those gaps utilizing Engage for Change's 'Borrow, Build, Breakthrough' methodology, which shifts people's appetite for risky breakthroughs, harnessing, in this case, the group's inherent competitiveness.

- The engagement plan and the programme management plan.

What's so different about that? When Bob arrived at this meeting, he had an idea for vision consisting of one word: Relevance. This wasn't spelt out in advance and nor was any of the work that the 40 people went through pre-decided, aside from the process for the day. It was true co-creation without a single prescriptive power point.

The group, although still highly sceptical, in some quarters, felt that they had created something rather than received something. More significantly the early adopters had a vehicle to drive and Bob had momentum. His task over the six months was to make it a 'We rather than I' process.

GLOBAL PARTNERS MEETING, MAY 2010

By the time of the F&P partners conference in May 2010, the six 'imperatives' of action had been shaped by the Paris 40 and had signed up associates to do the initial work. The six imperatives were as follows:

- The vision – to be the most relevant F&P practice to our clients, our people and our firm. This is being delivered through the following five enabling imperatives.

- Leadership capability.

- I to we.

- Communication.

- Employer of choice.

- Team offerings and knowledge.

LEAD PARTNERS MEETING, GLOBE THEATRE, LONDON, JULY 2010

This meeting was designed to challenge, progress and accelerate progress. Critically it was designed to enable each imperative team to identify where they needed bottom-up challenge and contribution from the wider professional group which would meet en masse in October of the same year in Amsterdam. This was to not to be a dog and pony show, as our American cousins might call it; it was to be face-to-face open source strategy building.

During the months after March 2010, the back story was about the gradual signing-up process from those partners who had been to meetings but had thus far held back from joining . It was not until October that the 'surge' could be said to be in progress. This is a good insight because movements take time and authenticity.

It's no good leaders thinking they can exhort people to join in, especially lawyers who, by and large row their own canoes. The whole point about leader and employee engagement is that people self-implicate rather than comply for the sake of appearances. With command and control, you may achieve surface compliance, but delivery will be far harder work for the leader who is in constant rhetoric mode – leaders with the god complex, as *Financial Times* journalist Tim Harford calls them.

THE CLAN GATHERS IN AMSTERDAM IN OCTOBER 2010

As one of 330 people at a leadership meeting, you might be expecting to spend a good deal of time sitting, watching and listening. But the secret of producing great ideas from large numbers of people gathered in one place is to subdivide them into very small teams of twos and threes in which they will participate, follow instructions and feel mutually supportive. And then once these subteams have ideas to trade and defend, gradually get inter-team negotiation until you might have a group of 100 negotiating on the final contending ideas which in turn will compete with several other groups of 100 – each group of 100 is given a few minutes to explain their (specific, actionable, measurable) ideas in front of the 330 assembled lawyers. A voting process resulted in the best being adopted.

In Amsterdam, the primary aim was to expose the whole legal population to the process that had started in the Scribe hotel in March of that year and provide for this much wider group an opportunity to influence the Relevance strategy using Engage for Change's Strategy Safari, described earlier in this chapter.

Delegates found themselves exploring the six imperatives of the strategy with an invitation to understand, challenge and most importantly, contribute. The use of the Strategy Safari concept requires work-stream leaders to be visible and to compete – it makes strategy visible, pliable and fun.

The cycle of partner meetings continued in February 2011 in Madrid and July 2011 in Manchester, with much of the vision becoming reality.

Insights from the ongoing process include:

- A leader needs to put his or her name on the line and run with it.

- Engagement to drive strategy and change cannot be functionally led.

- It is not an engagement project, it is a way of reaching down to originate and execute strategy and change.

- A lot can and must be done at the first session with sceptical executive/partners teams in order to create momentum.

- A lot must be done in a day, but these are 12–24 month commitments.

- The intervention must be different, bold, creative, active, visible and fun.

- A lot of work must be done to keep the key people on the train, especially at first.

- The prime mover needs an amazing chef de cabinet – Andy Williams in this case. Andy brought his knowledge of the players and the politics into play and worked prodigiously. It is essential to have an Andy to fulfill these roles.

Bob Charlton went on to lead the Asia Pacific region based in Hong Kong and carried out a similar exercise across a rich mixture of cultures.

Bite-Size Cases

Let's close the chapter with a series of short case examples to illustrate the kind of business challenges and opportunities for which an intervention can be helpful.

Table 7.1   Bite-size cases

	Situation	Intervention	Result	Comment
CASE 1 **Bringing disparate divisional heads into one strategy umbrella – 20 people over a day**	Focus a siloed group of business unit heads on identifying a market-based strategy common to them all	Pressurized scenario – what would an equity buyer do differently? Implications for this team's behaviour, strategy, leverage of inter-business unit staff collaborations	Unusual cross-business strategy development, reach-down programme.	People like to work outside their normal groups
CASE 2 **Customer service – six months, 15,000 people**	The holiday company which came back from the brink, scored the highest margins in the sector and then engaged all staff in developing a service strategy		Voted best tour operator and margins improved	
CASE 3 **Engaging the top 200 over one week**	The global engineering company switched from defensive to offensive by reaching down below the executive team to mid-level executives to drive strategy		Middle of the sector to top performer and on the acquisition trail	
CASE 4 **Driving costs down and efficiency up – representative groups**	The public utility which had to drop 40% from its costs base and did so by engaging those who would be affected most in the decision-making process		Cost saving achieved with no strike action and 'many better solutions than management would have thought of'	

Table 7.1   Bite-size cases (*continued*)

	Situation	Intervention	Result	Comment
CASE 5 **Engage to transform: two years, 5,000 people**	The logistics company taking six days to deliver freight from A to B was under threat of outsourcing. Engaging militant shop-floor staff challenged all the norms of command and control leadership		Threat of outsourcing was lifted, ballot of employees resulted in 75% positive vote for change, $400 million investment approved by the board	
CASE 6 **Engage the MDs to retain their people – 30 MDs**	Was it the money? Was it the brand? No, it was the way their MDs engaged engaged their people in decision making		Retention of top-performing teams greatly improved	
CASE 7 **Call centre staff redesign team measurement process**	Turnover in the high 20s. Customer satisfaction plummeting – big impact on business	Staff redesign score card based on their experience of the customer. Take charge of former middle-manager role.	Turnover drops to single digits % Staff engagement and performance rockets	
CASE 8 **European multinational adopts shared services outsource model by engaging countries in the plan**	As part of a global transformation, costs had to be lowered and effectiveness radically improved	In recognition of widely varying industrial relations practices, countries implicated were given a big say within a framework	No industrial action, concluded in half the time expected by the board	
CASE 9 **Airport operator wants to drive margin improvement by improving passenger flow, allowing more discretionary spend**	Airport owner wanted customers to have more shopping time and airport operator wanted to attract passengers/airlines from rival airports	Staff empowered to make operational improvements (customer flow, better customer experience, etc.) competing for budget	Industry-beating low waiting times, discretionary spend up, airport margins up, participating employees engagement scores up from low 40%s to mid-70%s (same as top management)	

In the next chapter I look at sustaining momentum after an intervention has produced breakthrough ideas that have the potential to deliver results and drive performance.

Sustainment is nearly always the weak link – lots of energy is invested into the intervention and too often the execution process is wanting. We have learnt to warn clients that unless the execution process is designed in parallel with the intervention only partial success is likely.

8

Sustaining the Benefits of an Engagement Intervention

The penultimate step in delivering strategy and change through participative interventions that engage the right people focusses on sustaining the Benefits of an Engagement Intervention.

This chapter looks at how the great ideas produced through an intervention can be delivered and built on. Too often you hear that 'nothing happens after the kick off, the intervention, the leadership meetings, the town hall, the webcast and other programmatic activities'. Without follow through, any interventions will be remembered as just another failed initiative or jamboree. Moreover, if people have stepped up, challenged and contributed and then see no benefit, the institution's leadership will lose credibility.

In our commercial practice, Engage for Change, in earlier interventions we observed that all the effort tended to be invested in the intervention, with little or no forethought given to follow through. It is easy, on reflection, to see why. The design and execution of an intervention is a bit like planning and running a children's birthday party. It's great fun and even better when it's all over. Many corporate events share similar attributes – they are often little more than ritualistic diversions which are long on entertainment and short on addressing issues; too often they are 'egotainment' for bosses.

Alternatively, embedding ideas and longer-term thinking may simply not be a part of the psyche of the business, or perhaps of the organization's marketplace, in which case the assumption that this is the right thing to do may be wrong.

The key is to raise the merits of planning a process of embedding ideas up-front to build it into the design of the intervention or deliberately choose not to.

This chapter covers the following areas:

1.   Why interventions stall.

2.   The keys to the sustainability of an intervention – process, conviction, compassion and connection.

3.   What needs to be done as part of the planning process for the intervention to be sustained?

1) Why Interventions Stall

The point of this section is to encourage readers to be aware of possible reasons why an intervention may not have or need an afterlife.

FIRST TIMER?

The intervention may be a first foray into more inclusive approaches to strategy and change, in which case all of the focus and energy will probably be invested in the intervention itself. This is perfectly understandable as the risk taker will be keen to ensure that his or her event is seen to be successful. But a great intervention or event with no follow through soon turns sour for the sponsor, especially if it was highly visible and costly. The advice that should be given to the first timer is to ask whether you need to plan for the post-intervention period at the same time as designing the intervention itself in order to obtain full value on the investment.

THE CYNICISM OF OPENING UP DECISION MAKING FOR A LIMITED TERM

Another explanation for the lack of sustained change may be that the CEO will have decided that what he or she needs is a limited period of turbulence to energize the business followed by a return to command and control, without realizing that a return to command and control may result in the erosion of the benefits of the intervention. The sponsors should ask themselves whether they want to risk demotivating their leaders and staff by opening up and then reverting to type. If they are intending to generate a short, sharp shock, then they should consider being transparent about it.

CEO/SPONSOR SHELF LIFE

The shelf life of the CEO may be an issue – the intervention may be his or her swansong. It's instructive to ask sponsors how far ahead they feel able to plan. If you know them well, this will be very useful in terms of investing effort within the right time frame. It's quite possible that they have not asked themselves the question and will be appreciative of being asked about the legacy they might hope to leave behind.

SHORT OR LONGER-TERM ORGANIZATIONAL CULTURE

Another contributing factor will be the DNA of the organization. A highly flexible and operational culture will say to itself 'job done, let's move on'. This might include retailers and other sectors where the market changes rapidly and unpredictably. Sir Stuart Rose, former head of the UK retailer Marks & Spencer, famously commented that retailers such as M&S don't have long enough time horizons for strategy. Conversely, organizations which are more comfortable with a 'planned approach' (highly capital-intensive industries and those with high risk profiles – insurance, mining, oil and so on) may expect a much longer time horizon.

Being aware of the time horizons of the business will help predict the appetite and value for 'embedding'.

2) The Keys to the Sustainability of an Intervention – Process, Conviction, Compassion and Connection

Process, conviction and compassion are all needed by the sponsors of interventions that turn the norms of top-down strategy and change upside down. A transparent process provides credibility and the necessary governance to convert contributions and challenges into value.

PROCESS

Without the rigour of disciplined and highly visible process and rigorous project management, all you have – and all your people have – are vivid memories of an intervention, a volcanic eruption that quickly cooled and solidified on contact with the cold light of day of the business-as-usual work experience. Vivid eruptions can be a cruel promise for people that are encouraged, fleetingly, to imagine that the intervention they have enthusiastically contributed to will lead to a different and better way of doing business.

Elsewhere I have argued that interventions need to be characterized by surprise and creativity. However, an exaggerated focus on the creative aspects of the intervention may suggest that sponsorship of it has migrated excessively to the creatives in the organization, who are unlikely to be that interested in the business of the completer finisher.

The design or sponsor team needs to comprise catalysts and completer finishers.

VISIBLE CONVICTION – PERFORMANCE MADE VISIBLE DRIVES PERFORMANCE

As I have asserted elsewhere, effective engagement requires strong leadership of the intervention process, particularly maintaining a focus on delivery downstream of an intervention process with visible championing of the project management process. In addition, conviction is exerted and conveyed through the transparency of the intervention's progress via effective formal communication, including acknowledgement by leaders of colleagues' efforts to execute the strategy. Readers should recall the dictum that 'performance made visible drives performance'.

COMPASSION

By compassion I mean staff sensing that their leaders understand that transition to a better place involves living in the old place for a while and tolerating systems that duplicate work, interdepartmental irritations and immediate bosses who may be unsure of their own futures. An example of this is the UK's Royal Bank of Scotland (RBS). Following the public rescue of RBS in 2008, the bank has been selling off billions of pounds in assets via its non-core division under the aegis of CEO, Rory Cullinan. His HR and corporate communication teams asked Engage for Change to help assess engagement levels and to facilitate an appropriate response by the executive team. The bank responded with an industry-leading initiative to engage its people during the 'ramp down' of assets.

Most conventional shutdowns or restructures result in everyone losing their jobs more or less at the same time or through a series of cuts. This was not the case at RBS, where the so called 'ramp down' began in 2010 and (at the time of writing) still has a couple of years to go – or more, depending on buyers being found and suitable prices being obtained. A key objective of its engagement process is to retain core talent whilst preparing people for what lies ahead for them within or outside of the bank.

In this example, a key part of the engagement process lay in the guidance given to front-line managers for designing and running regular one-to-one sessions for their staff, tailoring these according to the personal situations of each of their employees. These managers increasingly found themselves wearing two leadership hats at the same time: one hat being business as usual where their people have a relatively long time period before they work themselves out of a job; and the second being a coaching hat under which their people are just months or weeks away from leaving. Most managers will also be leaving at some stage, so they have their own anxieties to manage.

This intervention was designed to help managers stay close to their people by ensuring absolute transparency about what was known as well as what was still considered to be work in progress. Close connection in times of uncertainty seems to have resulted in greater trust and willingness to 'see the job done'.

SOUND BITE FROM O2

> *Instrumental drivers of engagement quickly run out of traction. Superior engagement is always an outcome of peoples' managers and supervisors knowing how to share decision making with their people, which means a new view on leadership – we have more than 2,000 managers – they are the culture.*

3) What Needs to Be Done as Part of the Planning Process for the Benefits of the Intervention to be Sustained?

- Making it safe to join in – nobody engages without trust and trust requires transparency of information.

- Existing strategy/change process – friend or foe?

- Tactics to help deliver value from the intervention.

MAKING IT SAFE TO JOIN IN – NOBODY ENGAGES WITHOUT TRUST AND TRUST REQUIRES TRANSPARENCY OF INFORMATION

I will use an analogy from family life to explain the idea of a safe environment. If you decide to change the way that decisions are made in your family about certain issues, such as more engagement of children so that they can influence decisions affecting them, you have the choice of just doing it or telling them that you are changing the rules of engagement, explaining why you are doing it and how they should handle their responsibility in order to make it beneficial for them. The child is making the transition to becoming a responsible participant in some decisions affecting him or her – from parent to child to adult to adult.

This is a simple analogy, but if we take ourselves back to the corporate organization, the shift towards a more inclusive approach will, in all likelihood, come as a surprise to the workers. If they work within a command and control culture, people may also be loathed or too distrusting to join in. As with the child, the change to a more inclusive approach to decision making needs to be explained, with the rationales and benefits to the organization and employees clarified. Even then, workers will need to practice and experience it before it becomes a norm. The importance of framing expectations and reassuring people that it is safe to challenge and contribute is vital. If you work for an organization that has been economical or secretive with key information, it will take more than simple assurances to convince you that all is now different; nobody engages without trust and trust requires transparency of information.

In the case of the subsidiary of the European energy company Total in the UK, the new CEO was faced with an organization that was used to top-down, hierarchical approaches to leadership, with characteristic economy on disclosure of business information. The new CEO needed to show, time and time again, that there was no secret archive with data and information that was not being shared. Obviously there will always be some commercially sensitive information that you may be unable to share, but all too often this old excuse is trotted out by reactionary forces to justify secrecy across the board. This usually points to management which is either weak or arrogantly feels that it can just steamroller its people.

In the example given here, the executive committee had, at the outset of the process, agreed a set of guiding principles around engagement and communication which were useful when spurious objections were thrown in to frustrate transparency. These guidelines make up an engagement and communication contract, the objectives of which were 'to retain, engage and motivate colleagues through a period of significant challenge, adversity and uncertainty'. They are reproduced in full in the expanded case study given later.

The engagement and communication contract was measured frequently to focus attention on the people factor in executive meetings.

EXISTING STRATEGY/CHANGE PROCESS – FRIEND OR FOE?

As part of upfront planning, it is also good to agree if the intervention is to be a part of or separate from an existing strategy/change process. Why is this important? The answer is that by reviewing the current approaches to refreshing strategy and change, it will quickly become clear if current approaches/patterns are a part of the problem. The existing strategy cycle may be a barrier because it is incremental and designed to minimize disruption when conscious disruption is exactly what is needed.

If the existing strategy or planning process is tired or discredited, this provides an opportunity to call time on it. On the other hand, there may be political advantage to be gained from using the guise and timetable of the existing process to achieve buy-in from more conservative camps – if there is one and if their opinion counts for much. Good politics if a new CEO/boss needs to head off reactionary forces.

TACTICS TO HELP DELIVER VALUE FROM AN INTERVENTION

There are four tactics to deliver value from an intervention.

- Getting the design team right – syndicating ownership.

- Leaders' physical and emotional footprint.

- Quarterly 'mini eruptions' – rigorous review.

- There is nowhere to hide. Wiki Dashboard League Tables – performance made visible drives performance.

Getting the design team right – syndicating ownership

There is a balance to be struck between the senior sponsor giving enough of himself or herself to the intervention to make it sustainable and the need to allow sufficient space for others to feel ownership and involvement. The secret of syndicating ownership is engaging the right core team from the outset in designing the intervention. In practice, this means thinking at the outset who needs to be on board as you work through the phases of the design of the intervention.

Table 8.1   Who should be onboard?

The design phases	Who needs to be involved?
Who should identify the default approaches to engagement in the organization?	
Which groups need to be involved in negotiating the givens/non-negotiables?	
Who should decide which groups of leaders and staff will be engaged in decision making?	
Who needs to be involved in designing the intervention?	

As the team works through the intervention, you will almost certainly want to add and subtract from the design team, bring people up from the sharp end of the business and cede your own control to other key players.

Leaders' physical and emotional footprint

The eyes of your people throughout will be on the obvious organizational processes of change, but they will also be on the physical and emotional footprint of the sponsors of change.

Leaders are advised to build time into their weeks when they can reflect on progress, ask staff how it is going from their perspective and offer acknowledgement of real achievements. As in the RBS example referred to earlier, staying connected with staff is the best bridge of trust.

Quarterly mini-eruptions – rigorous and visible review

From the outset, the sponsors should set aside quarterly 'mini-eruption' meetings. In DLA's case, this involved the strategy stream leaders reviewing and being reviewed against a consistent framework comprising:

- Have we actually delivered what we said we would by this date?

- Have we communicated what we have delivered?

- What has slipped and why?

- What shall we drop because it no longer makes sense?

- What must be delivered by the next review?

- What can we do to transfer responsibility for execution to younger lawyers and other staff?

- What needs greater visibility?

- Who needs to be acknowledged for executing diligently?

There is nowhere to hide. Wiki dashboard league tables – performance made visible drives performance

A wiki dashboard or similar device, accessible to all, encourages leaders of delivery streams to do just that: deliver. It also creates a level of competition between them which helps drive action. In the Total case departments began to compete on maximizing savings and efficiencies, and the dashboard became a part of the weekly reviews by the exec team. An effective dashboard ensures there is nowhere for any fifth columnists to hide and the entire organization will know who is pulling their weight.

Figure 8.1 illustrates how departments in the Total case study discussed above were compared. Each blue panel is a specific department identified on their UK net site for all to see, with much more detail available on every aspect of performance. The department on the left-hand side went on to achieve well after a slow start.

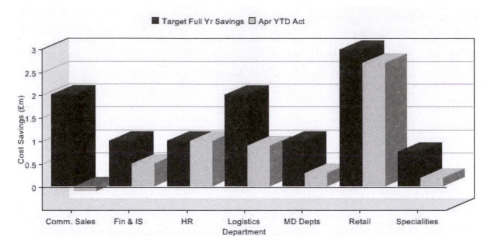

Figure 8.1   A simple chart-based approach to show progress against plan

Action for Recovery – A Case Study Illustrating a Bottom-Up Engagement Intervention

In 2009 Total UK (TUK) was in the eye of a storm afflicting the global economy. It had been a part of the UK oil industry for many years and a part of the community in its many locations around the UK. The perfect storm amounted to losses in all its operating units, an experience that was being repeated across the sector. As the months went by, the storm worsened, as did losses.

Total is a highly successful, indeed iconic, French company which, broadly-speaking, is run on traditional command and control lines from Paris, with varying degrees of local discretion depending on the strength and appetite of local management.

In 2009 new UK managing director, Didier Harel, a Total veteran, surveyed the scene knowing that Total France could not bail out the UK subsidiary due to competing demands for investment. This was a shock for many in the UK; Total had represented a secure career choice with many attractions to its employees. The choice open to Didier was between making the necessary efficiency gains and finding new revenues either through traditional top-down methods or more inclusive approaches.

Didier and I debated the risks and rewards of both approaches, advocating that an inclusive approach would avoid people becoming victims and spectators. The leadership agreed that their people would know as well as managers where the 'bodies were buried'. The management committee comprised a mix of long-serving Brits with a good sprinkling of expatriate French.

After debate, the bottom-up road was chosen on the basis that the size of the challenge was huge and incremental cost-cutting via the traditional planning process was considered unlikely to deliver. The objective was quite simply to return to the black as soon as possible.

'Action for Recovery' was born. The programme was designed to deliver non-budgeted efficiencies and new revenue streams within a year. Some doubted the wisdom of asking staff to undertake what they would have previously expected of managers behind closed doors. However, these concerns were unfounded as it turned out that people would always rather be on the inside of the tent in possession of the facts and be given a real role in addressing the situation, than be cast as passive spectators or victims. Businesses sometime forget that their people manage crises of a financial kind in their own home life and are very adaptable if they are treated as adults.

THE PRINCIPLES OF ACTION FOR RECOVERY

Behind Action for Recovery lay principles which were energetically negotiated by the executive committee and which guided the process:

- 'The need to act is not negotiable, but how we act is wide open to all our people'.

- The business rationale has to be painstakingly explained.

- Our people know as well as, or better than, management where to seek efficiencies and new revenues.

- We need to make it safe to challenge and contribute to the process, particularly in the boss-to-employee relationship.

- We must make performance data available so that everyone is working on a level playing field.

- Transparency of efforts – all businesses will post progress on the Action for Recovery wiki, introducing an element of competition and a reference point for use in the weekly high-speed reviews.

Whilst these principles were implicit, they were supported by an engagement and communication contract which was measured frequently:

- Decision makers will engage relevant colleagues who add value before decisions are closed.

- Clear, consistent and timely communication will accompany business changes.

- Colleagues will hear appropriate news from the company before peers and external sources.

- Managers will receive communications about major decisions immediately prior to the same communication going to all colleagues.

- Colleagues must feel able/safe to question/seek clarification from managers on key decisions.

- A challenge posed to management by an employee results in timely, constructive feedback to the challenger and to anyone else who will be affected.

- Demographics and the communication preferences of colleagues are understood and used to guide communication that people will find accessible.

The objective of the Action for Recovery programme was 'to act as a key driver in helping to retain, engage and motivate our colleagues through a period of significant challenge, adversity and uncertainty'.

WHAT WERE THE KEY ELEMENTS THAT DEFINED THE ACTION FOR RECOVERY INTERVENTION?

Action for Recovery was a complete departure from how such changes would normally be addressed. It required some 'heralding' so that people could be sure that they would not get their 'heads shot off' when they aired ideas which, in many cases, challenged years of accepted practice.

The management committee first negotiated amongst themselves what was non-negotiable using the peach exercise referred to elsewhere. They did this via a Strategy Safari in which the 12 or so management committee members produced their own mini-Safari vantage point – to continue the analogy, a watering hole at which they used non-traditional techniques to present their part of the overall strategy for their fellow management committee members.

You may think that the members of a management group are familiar with all aspects of a strategy, but it is often the case that members are familiar with their individual bit, but not that of others and particularly not with the interconnections between different parts of the business.

No PowerPoint was used in the Strategy Safari. Instead, the process required the group to rotate and explore all parts of the strategy and how they fitted together. The Strategy Safari built confidence between members of the group and enabled them to address the challenge of determining how to design the invitation to all colleagues to propose efficiences and new revenues.

Following the initial Strategy Safari the executive group acted as tour guides to a wider group of 80 managers. This involved each of the tour guides explaining his or her own part of the strategy and inviting challenges and contributions from the 'tourists' in the context of the non-negotiables. The stakes were made clear, namely that if 'we and our people don't fix this, it will be done for us by others'.

Replete with the contributions of the 80 Safari tourists, each business amended its recovery strategy and enfranchised all its own people in a similar exercise, drawing ideas from them to drive efficiencies and new revenues. Throughout it used Engage for Change's Strategy Safari 'Team Size Escalation' technique, in which people start their thinking in pairs and escalate into much larger groups involving an auction of ideas. Only the best and most practical ideas survive – a kind of organized crowd-sourcing. Team Size Escalation involves three stages of escalation: borrowing ideas, building on ideas and incubating breakthrough ideas to enable those involved to increase the level of their involvement at each stage. The breakthrough ideas stage results in ideas that breach formerly untouchable processes such as merging offices, selling parts of the business and so on. People will adopt some initially inconceivable ideas if they are given the time and the space to come to terms with what is needed, hence the 'Borrow, Build and Breakthrough' process.

The results of all 10 of the business units' bottom-up Action for Recovery programmes were combined and made visible through a wiki, with UK Net reporting on weekly management meetings and quarterly Safaris. MD Didier Harel maintained a blog throughout the whole process, which provided a personal perspective on the change and ensured the intimacy of his involvement throughout.

In one sense, the sequence of events is little different from more conventional top-down approaches. The crucial difference is that this was not a cascade of what had the been decided by the few to the many, as is the norm in command and control. Instead, this was the few advising the many that, whilst some elements had been pre-determined, much remained open to their challenges and contributions. What matters is the contract between the elite and the many. In this case it was deliberately co-creational, within a well-governed framework.

OUTCOMES?

The company made double-digit millions of pounds stirling efficiencies and new revenues, within a year, which allowed it to return to making a profit ahead of the deadlines specified by the Action for Recovery programme.

The epilogue to the story involves the retail arm, comprising hundreds of petrol forecourts. These were sold to Gerald Ronson, a well-known UK property entrepreneur who had big plans to build the business as the major oil companies pulled out of what had become the marginally profitable business of petrol retailing.Thanks to Action For Recovery Ronson's company Rontech gained a business in good shape financially and culturally. Having been involved 'on the inside of the tent', Didier's people equipped themselves to deal with whatever the new world would bring. They had become personally implicated and self-empowered. Command and control, converseley, turns people into spectators and victims. Well-governed engagement enables people to be reformers even when this entails short-term personal loss.

There is of course a fine line to be drawn between what Michel Foucault might have described as 'a manipulation of workers' and authentic power sharing. No toolkit will help people strike that balance without a leadership team with a strong sense of fairness.

In the next and final chapter on engagement strategy and change interventions I look at the dynamics of creativity – the choreography of crowds that delivers high performance, not just noise.

9

Creative Dynamics that Liberate Breakthrough Ideas

This chapter concludes Part II on delivering strategy and change through participative interventions that engage the right people.

This chapter offers a practitioner's perspective on practical dynamics that bring the creative best out of groups as small as two and as large as several thousand. The largest live group we have worked with was 2,500 in one location. If you have the space, there is no limit to the size of a creative group.

The difference between a potentially chaotic crowd and a creative group is that the latter is performing collaboratively, accepting clearly signalled prompts, instructions and being sensitive to good facilitation. The trick lies in minimizing controls and inputs whilst sticking to the business agenda to hand.

In this chapter I will try to share some of the experiences I and my colleagues have had of setting the stage for people to contribute to strategy, change and operational plans. We are not alone as a species in being able to self-organize. From ant swarms, bees, termites, flocks of birds, dog packs and migrating whales, we learn, according to Peter Miller's book *Smart Swarm*, that there is often no single active leader. Individuals may take turns to lead (as in a flight of birds), but there is no 'wing commander'. Each of these groups of creatures shows highly developed and effective collaborative behaviours, enabling larger numbers to survive by working collaboratively together.

There are many things that we have in common with the animal kingdom. Packs, herds, shoals, flights and other mass movements by animals are characterized by distributed:

- leadership;

- intelligence;

- collaboration.

Add to this Peter Miller's other ingredients to make a swarm smart and a smart human group:

- competition in the group;

- independence of spirit;

- diversity of opinion;

- individual judgment.

You will see that all four of these ingredients are present in the practical ideas that follow.

This chapter covers the following areas:

- People engage themselves in a trusting environment.

- Getting value from the human pack – what we have learnt about liberating the mind and spirit.

- Finding the right sponsor – characteristics of the early adopter of engagement.

1) People Engage Themselves in a Trusting Environment

Participative strategy and change that deliver great commercial and cultural results is ultimately all about getting the right people involved in a creative trusting environment that encourages them to engage in a collaborative endeavour. You can't coerce people to be engaged; they must elect to do so when they trust you and accept the need to challenge and contribute. The key word is trust. In a relationship where there is trust, people will relax and let down their defences. Fight or flight mode, which channels blood and oxygen to the limbs to enable the individual to escape, needs to be replaced by reflection and insight, enabled by blood and oxygen flooding the brain, leaving the body relaxed and resting. This is the state of mind and body that allows people to step out of their day job and to see, imagine and dream other possibilities. Paul Zak, in his book *The Moral Molecule*, talks about the 'Oxytocin affect'. Oxytocin is the chemical released into the blood when we are calm, reflective and feel trusted in good company. It is credited with encouraging insight and creative thinking.

This chapter explores the choreography of groups of people that produce breakthrough ideas. At our consultancy, Engage for Change, we have stumbled on the dynamics of creativity through trial and error. Neuroscience will unravel the power of creative dynamics that will stimulate great developments in group performance.

Creating the right dynamics is key to enabling people to relax into the creative challenge. People will only adopt a calmer and reflective state of mind if they trust the sponsors of the intervention to which they are being invited to contribute. The invitation to challenge and contribute must seem safe and conducive to let go of natural defences.

It follows that there are two key ingredients of an intervention which result in people letting go – trust and an experience that channels their positive energy to solve the problems and opportunities put to them. The exercises and activities they experience must surprise, stretch and even amuse the players to help them leave their usual preconceptions and prejudices behind and explore how to add value to a strategy or change working through three levels of creative reflection:

1. Borrowing ideas from others that are trusted.

2. Building ideas with others that are trusted.

3. Breaking through with ideas that may demolish or build on previously successful ways of working.

Traditional brainstorming techniques ambush people into trying to engage at the third of these levels before they are equipped to do so, often resulting in incremental thinking rather than breakthrough thinking. This also explains why there are often disappointing results from hasty exercises in strategy, many of which are not much more than tick-the-box breakouts as part of another wise directive meeting or conference. Traditional brainstorming often fails the critical tests of trust and an experience which escalates participants to breakthrough thinking. The worst thing you can do is to kick off creative thinking with an energizing activity. These put people back into flight fight operational mode when you actually need them to be calm and reflective.

I have made all the mistakes of confusing entertainment for engagement – this chapter is designed to shed light on creating trust and experiences that are conducive to enabling people to let their guard down and liberate their creativity.

2) Getting Value From the Human Pack – What We Have Learnt About Liberating the Mind and Spirit

Getting value from the human pack is the holy grail of employee engagement. When people engage themselves, they shift gear and create amazing ideas – they act as if they are working on their favourite hobbies or the causes closest to their heart. On the other hand, to expect people to be constantly in a state of over-performance would be to expect far too much. Most of us can perform at an exceptional level only for limited periods – there's an ebb and flow. Some people are prodigious, most of us are less so.

This section of the book is about interventions which stimulate creative ideas by immersing people in scenarios that are conducive to creativity. Engagement interventions are the equivalent of a long walk, a hot bath or a lovely view which allows the mind to wander. They are about reproducing the dynamics that allow people to be at their most creative as part of a change or strategy process.

Paradoxically, organizations often confuse entertainment of their people and creative thinking. They invite people to spectator events that are 'engaging', entertaining and very temporarily enervating, but that have a half-life of moments. Rowdy spectator events at work tap into fight or flight chemistry, which extracts blood and oxygen from the brain to the body, stimulating action and expression rather than reflection and lateral thought. The problem with staff entertainment is that the creativity is mostly top-down – it is the anti-matter to bottom-up creativity. Most corporate eventing is medication and manipulation. It is often enjoyable and fun at best and boring at worst; it is rarely the stage for reflection and the generation of new ideas. In staff entertainment, people are cast as spectators. Spectators expect to be stimulated with drama.

They are in receipt mode, where much of what they are receiving is in effect a top-down message. In this sense, much corporate eventing is like watching sport – it enervates or disappoints and is quickly forgotten. So when organizations say they have engaged a particular group via traditional eventing, they will have done the opposite of engaging them; they will have asked the group to accept ideas from an elite, which they will be asked to accept as the new 'message' and be sent out to proselytize.

Some decide and sell rituals will make an attempt to involve digital feedback and face-to-face breakouts. Any involvement is better than none, but I would add a word of caution about using traditional breakouts as a route to breakthrough ideas. As a participant, you are asked to switch from being a spectator to an activist in a group, usually at short notice. You are asked to free-think and form a group opinion with little or no warm up. If you do not have good facilitation, this can easily result in small group dynamics where extroverts, mavericks or saboteurs dominate. In this environment, other participants will be pleased to switch off and return to spectator mode.

Creating the right conditions in which people engage requires dynamics that emulate the hot bath, the walk in the country and the stimulating exchange between enthusiasts – the breakout rarely does this. (The digital exchange, on the other hand, may do so if participants have control over timing and freedom of expression.) With that warning in mind, let me share what I have learnt about creating conditions which liberate people to contribute to the business agenda by posing and attempting to answer the most asked about questions on this topic:

- Should the mixture of people be natural or unusual?

- Should the groups be random or assigned?

- What size is an effective breakthrough team?

- Do different backgrounds make a difference to how the dynamics are managed?

- What technology enables creative breakthrough?

- How can you manage the dynamics of hundreds or thousands of people in the same or different places?

- The lightness of being – how important is space and light?

- What does a good exam question look like?

- Who should be the conductors or referees of interventions?

- How do you help those who are reluctant, to engage?

- Should the sponsor team/exec watch from the best seats or should they participate?

My responses to these are an attempt to provide the ingredients for creative dynamics. We should remind ourselves here that the physical experience is the part of the event that people will remember. Will it be a boring repetition of static methods, forced feel-good entertainment or an authentic engagement experience in which it is impossible to hide and which involves real contribution designed to make a difference?

The key to creative dynamics lies in crowd dynamics rather than in event management. Creative dynamics are best set in low budget settings rather than amongst ceremonial and distracting theatrical sets.

SHOULD THE MIXTURE OF PEOPLE BE NATURAL OR UNUSUAL?

Natural work teams (the board, executive committee, function, project team, shift, platoon and so on) are groups that will continue to work together after the intervention. The natural work team can use an intervention to address an *intrinsic* agenda, such as the health of its own dynamics, or an *extrinsic* agenda, such as the refinement or reinvention of the team/business unit/company-wide operating model, vision, values, strategy, change process, service proposition, brand or re-structure. The pro of a natural team is that they will apply the thinking to their team. The con is that a natural work team may not think out of the box.

An unusual team is formed as a result of deliberate thinking about what composition of people will result in exchanges that will be valuable and probably unusual.

The challenge in choosing between the natural and unusual lies in deciding between fairly predictable outcomes for the former and unpredictable outcomes for the latter.

SHOULD THE GROUPS BE RANDOM OR ASSIGNED?

There are arguments in favour of using both random and assigned groups. I like a mixture of both, depending on the desired outcomes of the intervention – if the solution lies in 'hot-housing' a particular group (say two sales teams that have much to gain from more collaboration), this may be an argument for pre-assignation. Employing both random and assigned groups is good, as changing dynamics at the right intervals keeps energy levels and competitiveness up – a key characteristic of creative groups.

There are actually three options:

1.   imposed random;

2.   pre-assigned;

3.   self-organizing.

Imposed random: participants pick a table or group number from a raffle or online auction. This approach prevents the natural factions that exist back in the office from forming – assuming you are looking to satisfy the critical tests of the valuable pack:

- competition in the group;

- independence of spirit;

- diversity of opinion;

- individual judgement.

Imposed random is great if you want to discombobulate the group by disrupting comfort zones to generate creative turbulence. I tend to prefer using it at the beginning of a process where invariably you are trying to shake things up by disrupting a well-normed group with strangers from different business units, departments and countries.

Pre-assigned: this can be useful in many situations, although you have to be watchful of the control freak who wants to impose his or her order on everything. Situations which warrant pre-assignation might include:

- pre- or post-merger mixing of the two side's teams;

- internal re-structurings when people have to meld;

- after an exercise with randomly assigned teams when it is time to apply the learning back into natural work teams;

- when part of the population has more insight and knowledge than another and you want a fast migration of that knowledge into the less experienced group.

Self-organizing: in registering for the process, participants are asked to make some decisions about preferences and choices for each part of the intervention in which they will take part. Thus, if you were given in advance first, second and third choices about which elements of a strategy you were most interested in contributing to or challenging, these would be reproduced on your 'boarding card' for that part of the meeting. Your job would be to find a quorum of like-minded people before the maximum group number was exceeded, which means you would need to find a second choice of subject group, and so on, until you can 'board'. This makes the group formation process much more considered and competitive, and observes many of the characteristics of creative groups:

- competition in the group;

- independence of spirit;

- diversity of opinion;

- individual judgement.

Moreover, no-one can accuse the organization of fixing the dynamics – the self-organizing choice is probably the most enervating even before the work starts. It is also the choice most in keeping with the spirit of employee engagement. It is worth noting that it can get somewhat competitive; an active referee may be required!

Another route to creating self-organizing groups is to lay down some membership tests, such as:

- locate yourself in a group where you know no-one;

- locate yourself in a group where there is no more than one person from each country;

- locate yourself in a group where there is no more than one person from each department.

WHAT SIZE IS AN EFFECTIVE BREAKTHROUGH TEAM?

The easy answer to this question is small to begin with, which can be a bit of a problem when you've got 700–1,000 people in a room and 100,000 outside it. But never let size of the overall group be an issue – the principles are the same. Some sponsors start having nightmares at the thought of hundreds of people turning into a mob. It's never happened to us. In fact, big groups are a wonderful experience – people get caught up in the collective mood and noise and commotion. In addition, it raises the bar for future gatherings, challenging the group to extract even more value next time.

Our solution to the question 'what size of group will result in breakthrough thinking?' lies in our methodology of *team size escalation*. Before I describe 'team size escalation' bear with me whilst I explain the conditions necessary to prepare people to do breakthrough thinking. In the first instance people need to be asked to respond to a task on their own. A favorite solo exercise of mine is to ask individuals what the difference is between incremental and disruptive (strategy or change etc). They are given a brief window of perhaps 15 minutes to prepare a 90 second response. The purpose of the solo exercise is to draw people away from operational concerns, which they will arrive at the meeting with at the front of mind, towards more celestial matters. It is also to get people to form their own view about the topic to hand – it is causes individuals to listen to themselves before they react to other people's views. By so doing individuals will slow down and become more reflective. Their heart rates will slow and they will relax a little.

The next figure illustrates this process:

Getting people into the breakthrough zone

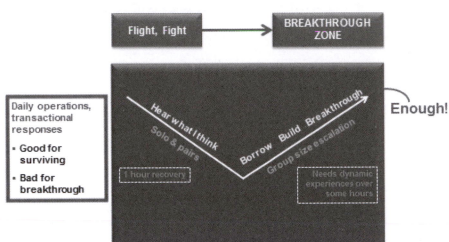

Figure 9.1   From incremental thinking to breakthrough thinking

In the early phases of working with groups on difficult problems and opportunities, we escalate from solo challenges to small groups; pairs, then trios. Pairs and trios are too intimate to opt out of and it's a number in which it feels safe to challenge and contribute. It's also too small for anyone to dominate, except the odd corporate psychopath. A pair is best at the very beginning of a process when people may be wary in a larger group – in a pair, you really have nowhere to hide. Also, it's a familiar social dynamic.

Small groups also exploit social identity theory, which explores the ability of small groups to influence larger groups. If you feel safe and in a self-supportive group, you will negotiate and develop a strong view which you are confident to support in a larger group later.

In *team size escalation*, group size is escalated by joining pairs and trios together to negotiate an agreed position. We regularly escalate from teams of two up to 100 where the best of the 'swarm's' ideas quickly meld into a formidable proposition, solution or set of options backed by the 'hives' behind the ideas. The key to managing this creative process is second-by-second time management with a simple, crystal-clear written 'flight plan' which is contained in participants' 'flight logs'. The paraphernalia like personal flight logs, though cheap, add the sense of being lifted out of the day-to-day.

The full answer to the question 'what is the most effective team size?' is actually *all team sizes.* You need to escalate into larger sizes as fast as the teams can manage, without burning them out too quickly. If it is too slow, people get bored and the BlackBerries appear. If it is too fast, people get irritated with the process. So, whilst the flight plan is timed to the second, the *conductor of the process* is constantly slowing down, accelerating, taking steps out or improvising new ones.

As indicated in the figure we have found that about an hour is required in small groups to bring people down with a maximum of five subsequent hours in groups escalating in size. After around five hours, creativity declines.

DO DIFFERENT BACKGROUNDS (OF INDIVIDUALS) MAKE A DIFFERENCE TO HOW THE DYNAMICS ARE MANAGED?

The answer to this question is very much so – engaging people in an intervention requires thinking and planning for different dynamics for people with different backgrounds and levels of experience. This is not training, this is creating environments in which people feel safe and confident to challenge their own assumptions, challenge the cultural barriers to radical improvements and contribute specific and valuable ideas.

The speed at which you can escalate people's engagement is heavily influenced by their past experience, disposition and professional background:

- Their experience of hot housing – the more experience they have, the greater the need for fast and sophisticated changes in dynamics, though this is also in conflict with the next but one point about people with high opportunity costs.

- Rookies will need to be made comfortable but will be very eager to contribute.

- People with high opportunity costs (boards, exec teams, partners in professional service firms, traders, etc.) actually need to be slowed down to get them out of transaction/instant judgement mode. These people spend much of their life in 'fight or flight' mode, which channels the blood to extremities of the body to equip the person for an extreme physical reaction. The problem with this is that with blood and oxygen channeled to the body's extremities, there's not much left for reflection and exploration – hence the need to design dynamics that slow them down.

HOW DO YOU JUDGE WHEN TO CHANGE TEAM SIZES AND COMPOSITION?

Team size and team composition are different concepts. Taking composition, there is value from team bonding – trust and humour proliferate. However, if this goes too far, the team may become over-bonded to their ideas. The judgement to be made is at what point are their ideas at their freshest and best before they become positions to which they become over-attached and protective? You need to give individuals long enough to open up, challenge themselves and break the mould.

The way to lessen 'position taking' is to force groups to negotiate with other groups using techniques like team size escalation and the careful choice about the teams with which they have to negotiate. Changing group size is also a good way to change the dynamic.

WHAT TECHNOLOGY ENABLES CREATIVE BREAKTHROUGH?

I will focus on a reminder of some of the simple applications that help in the running of engagement intervention. Technology means that more people in more places can be enfranchised in a physical gathering. These will be familiar to many of you, so I'll keep the discussion of this to a minimum (see also Chapter 14).

Wireless laptop technology which, for those who have not experienced it, allows a small group to negotiate agreement (on, say, a challenge to a strategy) and commit their response to the server. Other teams around them respond to the same challenge, allowing facilitators, team leaders or C-suite figures to watch the stream of responses and drill down, choosing from the responses. It also means that the whole record can be instantly shared with teams assigned to take things forward. Groups may also be in different locations if you have the benefit of this technology.

- The humble text can be used in similar ways to generate challenge or contribution.

- Open up behind-closed-door meetings: Open up key gatherings to the rest of the organization or selected groups using webcam and the Internet before, during and after.

- Sidebar conversations: Twitter can be used to generate challenges and contributions, with messages being projected onscreen or to facilitators and presenters who may choose to respond to or acknowledge them.

HOW CAN YOU MANAGE THE DYNAMICS OF HUNDREDS OR THOUSANDS OF PEOPLE IN THE SAME OR DIFFERENT PLACES?

In Chapter 6 I relayed the story of engagement in a large retailer. If you had been a participant at one of the retailer's strategy breakthrough interventions, you would have had your boarding pass with precise logistical details for every leg of the journey. No boarding pass, no boarding – delegates as responsible citizens have to take responsibility for their own logistics as they do when they go on vacation.

Let me describe the choreography involved in governing the movement of 600 or so people. In the retailer's scenario, there were 18 stations, one for each of the six areas of the strategy, each repeated three times so that three simultaneous identical Strategy Safaris took place in the same room with 16 people per team. At each station, the group was split into teams of four for more detailed work and debate in accordance with the small group rule discussed earlier. Input from each team to each strategy station was provided with the open space technology. In the case of DLA, presented in the last chapter, the choreography was different and looked on paper like the example given in Figure 9.2.

The secret, as with most things, is meticulous preparation and the ability to improvise if things go pear-shaped.

In summary on the topic of big groups, we thoroughly recommend them as a way to get mass input from large numbers quickly and creatively – and with no PowerPoint, no-one falls asleep!

Floor-plan

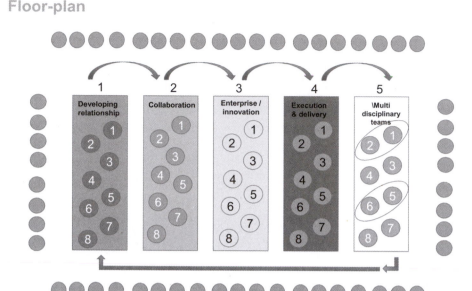

Figure 9.2   The floorplan and choreography of an event

THE LIGHTNESS OF BEING – HOW IMPORTANT IS SPACE AND LIGHT?

The architecture of the workplace sets the tone for the work to be done. The background environment has a big impact on the fleeting moments when groups and crowds gather to reflect, learn and reinvent. We have all been to offsite meetings and left uplifted. On the other hand, I expect at some point of your time at work, you have sat as an audience member in a bad seat in serried rows, often over-heated and in poor lighting. Moreover, there are usually no windows; the place is drab and the food execrable.

Despite the benefit of experience, organizations still overlook the impact of the venue on the success of their leadership development or strategy, or the exciting launch of a change process. The setting for an intervention that is intended to change the course or re-affirm one is subliminally key to the mood and disposition to *reflect, challenge and contribute*. Whether it is a meeting for 10 or 1,000, place and light are symbols and enablers of purpose. I want to look out of a window and say 'wow, look at that green and pleasant land, or seascape or bustling city'. With many notable exceptions, hotels are the kiss of death for creative dynamics. You will all have breathtaking exceptions of course, especially if you throw money at it. But many, if not most hotels are places of detention. I have seen thousands and have despaired at the impact on people who arrive upbeat only to be mugged by visual mediocrity and then bored by PowerPoint.

You don't have to spend vast sums. Unusual is the key word – there are lots of creative spaces out there:

- Magnificent spaces in local art galleries where a little revenue goes a long way.

- Local theatres struggling to make a living – stages are particularly suitable (e.g. the Globe Theatre in London).

- School facilities.

- Charity premises.

- Empty office floors/warehouses that can be made to be fantastic with a little imagination.

- TV studios when there is no filming scheduled.

- Aircraft hangers.

- Pop-up venues.

- Giant trucks.

- The great outdoors with nothing but the heavens above to allow people to flow with the landscape.

- Anywhere but a windowless hotel room!

Zurich Financial Services opted for a touring truck (see Figure 9.3) for their employee engagement intervention called 'Look Out', which was designed as the first part of a process to raise levels of customer service.

Figure 9.3   The Zurich Financial Services touring truck

With a highly dispersed workforce around the UK, bringing staff to large centers was unworkable as service would have been put at risk. So it was decided to take the 'Look Out' experience to the staff. The mobile experience opened up into a multi-space venue. Staffed by their own employees, 'Look Out' was designed to enable staff to literally look out at what service levels were like in their industry, other industries and in their own daily lives.

In the first instance, groups analysed their own favourite service experiences in retailers, banks, the NHS, holiday companies and many others. Thus suitably engaged in the topic, the groups moved to the next space, in which they explored the service experience of top-performing brands in financial services and beyond. With the context well and truly established, the third space involved an analysis of Zurich's own service experience using customer interviews and mystery shopping data. Finally, the groups were ready to challenge themselves and contribute specific, actionable and measurable ideas for service improvement. It was a dramatic and novel way of getting people involved – better than any mediocre hotel space and, with no travel time, an economically effective solution.

WHAT DOES A GOOD EXAM QUESTION LOOK LIKE?

Any group discussion starts with a question or questions, the clarity of which will determine the quality of the response. We will all recall providing brilliant answers to a misread exam question. But we can all be excused for being misled by unclear questions. Groups of any size can only do great work if the 'exam questions' are crystal clear and reflect the desired outcomes of the process.

The problem is usually manifested in woolly and unclear tasks. Taking a real example, in an exercise designed to invite people to offer ideas to enhance a part of a business strategy, the early draft of the question for participants read: 'Given your understanding of this part of the strategy, what ideas do you have to extend the franchise of the X range of women's clothing?' The final wording appearing on the wireless laptop 'exam question' was: 'Given your understanding of this part of the strategy, what *specific, deliverable, potentially profitable recommendations* do you have to extend the franchise of the X range of women's clothing?'. The slightly revised question helped the groups to critique and reject ideas that were conceptually interesting but when written down were not actionable.

The critical tests of effective exam questions are as follows:

- Do they focus people precisely on one clearly articulated business challenge (in the above case, the extension of the clothing franchise)?

- Have the sponsors made a distinct choice between asking a question which is deliberately conceptual in nature (to open people up) or deliberately focused on specific, actionable, measurable solutions? The mistake often made is to mix the conceptual with the specific.

- Are the exam questions geared to the attendees such that they feel confident about participating?

A lawyer or a sub-editor's mind is required to hone questions for group exercises. Getting them razor sharp will energize people much more than racy production values because the energy comes from within participants keen to engage rather than from staged entertainment.

In addition, people have very limited memory for verbally announced instructions. Verbal announcements go right over people's heads – all instructions must be repeated in written or digital form such that the exam question (or questions) is always there in front of the group. This is not rocket science, as any teacher will corroborate, but it is key to tapping into the creativity of any group, be they schoolchildren or employees. Nobody can be creative if they are struggling to recall the exam question because it is not in front of them or because it is badly articulated. This is especially true of groups of people in unusual surroundings, where there are many distractions.

Air traffic controllers require pilots to repeat back instructions – pilots always jot down instructions knowing full well that they may not recall accurately from memory or in their case confuse flight levels with exciting results. And because they must repeat them back word for word to ATC. We also know now that, presented with partial information, our subliminal selves will fill in gaps, often unconsciously – hence the absolute need for clarity of questions/tasks and instructions.

WHO SHOULD BE THE CONDUCTORS OR REFEREES OF INTERVENTIONS?

Think of this role as the stage director or conductor. He or she will have the blow-by-blow route of the intervention (be it a day or a six-month intervention) mapped out in detail. The golden rule is that the conductor should have designed the creative dynamics from the ground up such that when it goes live, the conductor has little need to refer to the journey, except when things go wrong. The conductor needs to do more than 'follow the score' – he or she will have to constantly accelerate or slow the pace to engage people productively as an orchestral conductor does. This role is not to be confused with the role of sponsor or leader.

HOW DO YOU HELP PEOPLE WHO ARE RELUCTANT TO ENGAGE TO DO SO?

The creative dynamics described earlier should take care of most of these problems. Engaging people in very small groups at the beginning of an exercise causes people to invest in the process early on. The trouble with traditional breakouts of, say, 10 people is that at least three are going to observe others and may never really engage. If they do that at the beginning of an intervention, they may remain spectators or, worse, may become obstructive – they literally disengage.

SHOULD THE SPONSOR/LEADERSHIP TEAMS WATCH FROM THE BEST SEATS OR SHOULD THEY PARTICIPATE?

They must participate as participants. Doing so provides a great opportunity for them to listen and appreciate other people's ideas. Peeling off presents an image of detachment.

In the case of QBE directors aided by facilitators ran every single intervention.

In another recent example a global private equity house had determined that its values were its best source of market differentiation. Day long immersion sessions were all fronted by the CEO, at least two other leadership team members and one non-executive director who typically brought powerful stories from their portfolio of other NED positions.

NEDs are underused in internal engagement processes – they provide terrific critical endorsement and attendance by them improves their knowledge of the business and their ability to advise.

3) Finding the Right Sponsor – Characteristics of the Early Adopter of Engagement

Let's end the chapter with a brief reminder of the characteristics of the early adopter of engagement – those people we must look out for to sponsor an intervention. I have touched on this throughout this chapter, but to serve as a summary in one place, I offer the following advice.

SPOTTING THE EARLY ADOPTER IN THEIR NATURAL HABITAT – WHAT TO LOOK FOR

The following are signs of how to spot an early adopter:

- Someone new to their post who is keen to 'do it differently'.

- Someone who is sick to death of banging on with command and control-led strategy and change leading to failed initiatives.

- Someone who is ham-strung by an executive team that has become tired and risk averse, but which they cannot change immediately.

- Activist managers or supervisors down the organization who need encouragement.

- Employees who need an outlet for their change ideas.

This chapter marks the end of the second part of the book dedicated to engagement interventions that deliver fast and sustainable results. The third and final part covers the challenges of grafting the spirit, values and practices of employee engagement into the culture of the organization.

PART III

Beyond the Intervention: The Engaged Organization

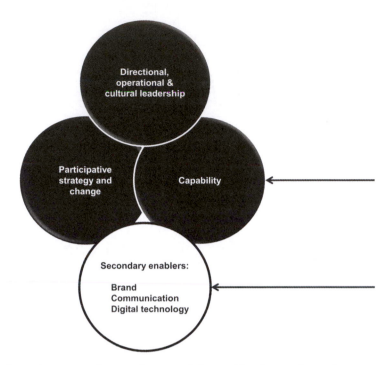

Figure III.1   The primary and secondary enablers of leader and employee engagement

The third part of this book focusses on the second lever of employee engagement – grafting the values, mindset and behaviours into the day-to-day rituals and experience of work. It also covers the three supporting enablers; brand, internal communication and digital technology.

Interventions can be a powerful stimulus, but ultimately it will be the engrained attitudes and supporting organizational systems that support sustained and effective engagement (see Figure III.1).

These chapters start with a review of Engage for Change's research into the factors which help to drive effective engagement so as to have a robust platform to explore the identified key drivers. In particular, we look in more depth at the role of leadership, with a particular emphasis on behaviours, technology and the role of brand.

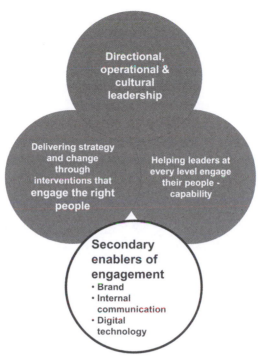

Figure III.2   The attitudes and systems that support engagement

10

The Evidence

Jerome Reback

This is the first of six chapters in the third and last part of the book. It was written by Jerome Reback, a long serving partner at Engage for Change.

In this chapter we review research completed by YouGov on behalf of Engage for Change which establishes important criteria to further develop effective leader and employee engagement. In particular, the research provides insight into the leadership characteristics and capabilities that are needed by leaders at every level in order to inspire and support effective engagement amongst others. These attributes are further reviewed and developed in the next chapter.

This chapter covers the following areas:

1.   About the research.

2.   Six benefits of employee engagement.

3.   Are employees engaged?

4.   Do employers engage their employees?

5.   The significance of power sharing.

6.   Inclusivity in decision making is the basis of power sharing.

7.   Other drivers of engagement.

8.   The critical role of the manager.

9.   Engaging leaders.

10.   Measurement is not helping.

11.   Boardroom support for employee engagement.

1) About the Research

Eager to underpin our work at Engage for Change with robust data, we commissioned YouGov, the UK-based global research agency, to analyse our assumptions through a UK-wide research programme. Around 2,064 interviews were undertaken online with a sample selected from the YouGov panel of employees. The sample was selected to be representative of the type of sector (public, private and voluntary sectors), the size of business (sole traders, micro, small, medium and large businesses), part-time and full-time working and gender. The sample was also weighted.

The research identified people who defined themselves as either being engaged with their work, not engaged or who felt that their organization worked to engage them to improve performance. The charts here make a distinction between the results based on these categories of respondents. Overall, 71% reported that they were engaged with their work and 12% stated that they were not engaged. Responding to a separate question, 41% claimed that their organization worked to engage them to drive performance and 34% reported that this was not the case.

The survey comprised a questionnaire which repeated many of the questions used in a similar survey conducted by YouGov in 2008. This enabled us to make comparisons between results where relevant and some of these are repeated here.

Results from the research are reported using net satisfaction and net agree scores. Net satisfaction scores have been derived by adding together the proportion who said they were very satisfied or satisfied and taking from this the proportion who said they were dissatisfied or very dissatisfied. The net agree scores have been derived by adding together those who strongly agreed and tended to agree and subtracting from this figure those who disagreed and tended to disagree. Net scores are used because they are a much more accurate indicator of the strength of feeling.

SUMMARY

1. Well-governed power sharing is the basis for effective employee engagement. The research illustrated that there is increased evidence that well-governed 'power sharing' is the primary driver for employee engagement. Improvement in the way in which change is managed can also substantially drive up levels of engagement. A total 83% of employees who felt engaged by their organization say they were satisfied with the extent to which they were empowered to make decisions. For those who said that their organization did not engage them, only 29% were satisfied.

2. Enabling effective engagement has dramatic implications for leadership. The research consistently supports the view that engagement is primarily brought about by the behaviour of leaders and managers. Where people were effectively engaged, they reported higher scores for employee engagement being a key responsibility of line management and of it being a visible priority for managers and supervisors. Well-engaged employees also believed senior management in their organization were doing a better job leading the organization (76%) than those who were not engaged (9%).

3. Considerable scope remains to build competitive advantage through improved employee engagement.

Other headlines include:

Enhanced service and brand advocacy

Engaged employees reported higher levels of customer service, financial returns, market advancement and comparative peer performance for their organizations than those who were not engaged. The survey also shows that effective engagement leads to substantial brand and product advocacy by employees, resulting in the attraction and retention of top talent and causing people to be more motivated, have higher levels of job satisfaction and to be more determined to 'go the extra mile'.

Better performance

Employee engagement is reported to be one of the top three contributors to driving performance, scoring more highly than having a differentiated brand or a compelling strategy.

Investing in the future

Investment in employee engagement is rising and remains a high priority in the Board Room. Despite this, only 41% of respondents say their employer manages to engage employees to perform well with 34% acknowledging that their employer does not engage them to perform well.

Overall, there is substantial opportunity to increase engagement and to secure a wide range of benefits as a result.

2) Six Benefits of Employee Engagement

The survey clearly shows that there are strong business benefits for strengthening employee engagement.

BENEFIT 1: GOING THE EXTRA MILE

- A very significant proportion of employees (80%) say that they go the extra mile to ensure a good result for their employer.

- The net scores for public sector employees and those in large firms are lower than average but are still very high.

  To what extent do you agree with the statement 'I tend to go the extra mile to ensure a good result for my organization'.

- Overall, those who say that they are engaged with their job have a net 'extra mile' score of 90 compared with just 12 for those who are not engaged (Figure 10.1).

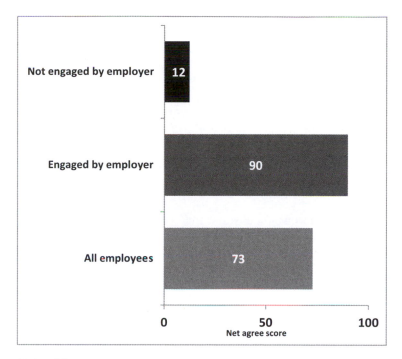

Figure 10.1   Net agree score

BENEFIT 2: MOTIVATION AND ENGAGEMENT

- Employees were more motivated in March 2010 than they were in 2008. In the earlier survey, 60% said that they felt motivated to perform well in their work. The more recent data showed a positive response of 68%. The net agree score increased by 16 points.

- There is a strong correlation between motivation and engagement.

- Respondents who say that their organization engages with their employees so that they perform well have a net motivation score of +87. Those who say that their employer does not engage have a score of -4.

In those organizations that did not engage their staff, a greater proportion were demotivated than motivated.

BENEFIT 3: JOB SATISFACTION

- A total of 62% were satisfied with their current job, but 21% were dissatisfied. This gives a net satisfaction score of +41.

- Satisfaction with job was inversely related to the size of the organization. The larger the organization, the less likely an employee was to be satisfied. Being your own boss provides the greatest job satisfaction and working for a FTSE 100 business the least (+21 net satisfaction score).

- Satisfaction was highest in the voluntary sector with public sector employees being least satisfied.

Satisfaction increased with seniority. Board members had a net satisfaction score of 76, senior managers had an above-average score of 44, but middle managers (32), junior managers (33) and people with no managerial responsibilities (34) had below-average scores.

The conclusions from the findings are clear: organizations that successfully engage with their employees are more likely to have staff who are motivated, are satisfied with their job and are prepared to go the extra mile to ensure good results.

BENEFIT 4: BUSINESS PERFORMANCE AND EMPLOYEE ENGAGEMENT

The research suggests a strong relationship between engagement and the perception among employees of stronger performance (see Table 10.1):

Table 10.1   Engagement and the perception of performance

Over the last 12 months, my organization has:	All	Engaged with my job	Employer engages
Performed well	39%	43%	53%
Performed better than its peer group	31%	34%	44%
Increased its market share	22%	23%	32%
Exceeded customer expectations	45%	42%	70%
Exceeded service delivery targets	43%	49%	63%
Exceeded financial targets	31%	33%	44%

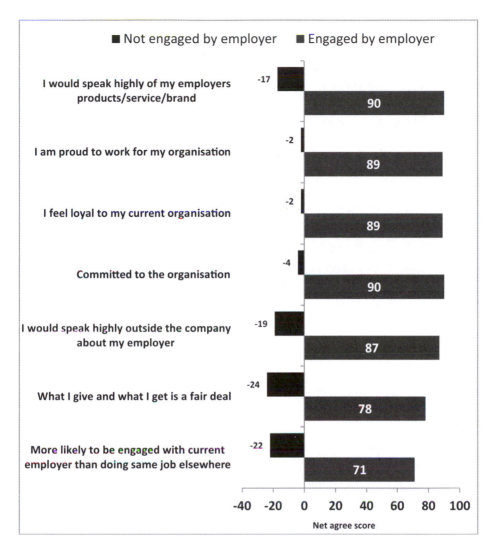

■ Not engaged by employer   ■ Engaged by employer

I would speak highly of my employers products/service/brand   -17   90

I am proud to work for my organisation   -2   89

I feel loyal to my current organisation   -2   89

Committed to the organisation   -4   90

I would speak highly outside the company about my employer   -19   87

What I give and what I get is a fair deal   -24   78

More likely to be engaged with current employer than doing same job elsewhere   -22   71

-40   -20   0   20   40   60   80   100

Net agree score

Figure 10.2   Are employees engaged?

- Employees who say that their organization engages with them are much more likely to report that their organization has performed well in the last 12 months, outstrips its peers and has increased market share.

- It is acknowledged that what is being reported is the perception of employees and that this might not be a true reflection of actual performance. However, there is good evidence for thinking that employees are correct in their views. Board members of those organizations where the employee said that the organization managed to engage them were much more likely to report positive performance than their board-level counterparts in businesses that did not engage.

BENEFIT 5: ENGAGEMENT AIDS ADVOCACY AND COMMITMENT

Employees who were engaged had higher net agree scores on a wide range of criteria (see Figure 10.2).

BENEFIT 6: WINNING THE WAR FOR TALENT

In the 2008 survey, 30% agreed that their organization attracted the best talent. In the 2010 survey, this figure was 29%, which means that nothing much had changed over that period. The overall net agree score of -6 was also unchanged. Board members had a highly positive view of the extent to which their organizations attracted top talent. Their net agree score in 2010 was +29. Senior and middle managers tended not to share the positive view of the board with a net agree score of -7 and -6 respectively. Large businesses and the public sector were least likely to agree that their organizations attracted the best talent. However, a very high proportion of employees (31%) neither agreed nor disagreed.

Regarding the war for talent, there were quite profound differences according to whether or not the employer engaged with employees. Employees who worked for organizations that did not engage with them strongly disagreed with the statement that their employer attracted the best talent. On the other hand, those who were engaged were in strong agreement with the statement (see Figure 10.3).

The same was true for staff retention. The net agree score for those businesses where employees believed that their organization did all it could to engage was significantly high. By contrast, those who said that their employer did not engage with staff had a net agree score of -70. The message is clear – greater employee engagement means better attraction and greater retention of talented staff.

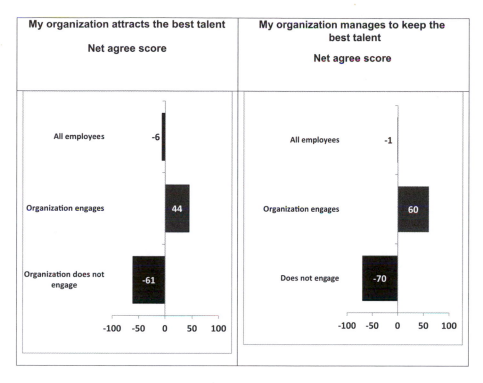

Figure 10.3   The implications for organizations that do and do not engage

3) Are Employees Engaged?

- The survey revealed a high level of engagement among employees with the work they do. A total of 7 out of 10 said that they are engaged, with only 12% stating the opposite (see Figure 10.4).

- Engagement fell the less managerial responsibility an employee possessed. A total of 79% of senior managers said they were engaged, but this fell to 65% of those without managerial responsibility.

- There was a good level of engagement across the private (71%), public (75%) and voluntary sectors (79%).

- Employees in large businesses were slightly less likely to be engaged compared with the average – 67% said they are engaged.

- Those aged over 55 were more likely to be engaged than younger people (those aged 16–24). A total of 77% of older people said they were engaged, compared with 69% of younger workers.

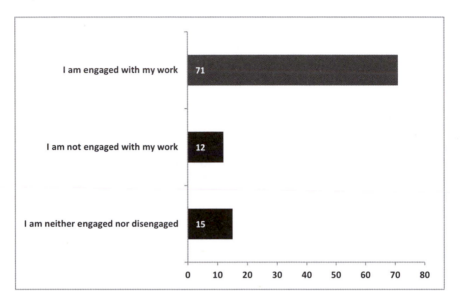

Figure 10.4   Are employees engaged with their work?

4) Do Employers Engage Their Employees?

- Although 71% of employees said that they were engaged in their work, only 41% said that their organization managed to engage their employees so that they could perform well (see Figure 10.5).

- Over one-third (34%) did not believe that their employer engaged them. The inference from these findings is that a substantial proportion of employees were engaged with their work despite the (limited) efforts of their employer.

- That said, the extent to which an organization managed to engage with its employees so that they would perform well increased over the period 2008 to 2010 by four percentage points. This is a small increase, but is statistically significant.

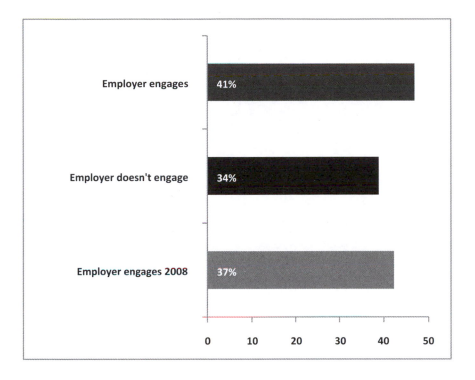

Figure 10.5   How the levels of employer engagement have changed

5) The Significance of Power Sharing

One of the key drivers of employee engagement is the extent to which staff are involved in decision making – whether big or strategic decisions or everyday ones. Engaged staff are far more likely to feel empowered to make and influence decisions. A total of 83% of employees who felt engaged by their organization said say they were satisfied with the extent to which they were empowered to make decisions. Of those who said their organization did not engage them, only 29% were satisfied – a remarkable contrast.

The graph in Figure 10.6 shows that the more power sharing that takes place, the greater the level of engagement that occurs. increases. This is evidenced by the decline in the 'not engaged' line as levels of consultation increase. We also note that as communication increases (between 'tell and sell'), this has a significant impact on reducing the level of those not engaged.

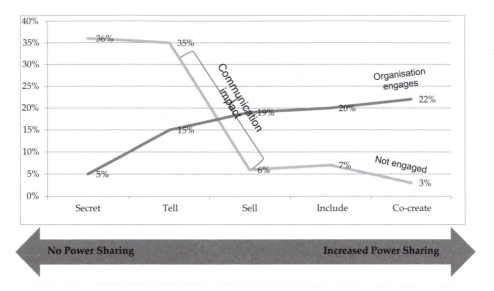

Figure 10.6   The correlation between power sharing and engagement

However, whilst engagement increases along the power sharing scale, there remains considerable potential to build higher levels of engagement beyond the reported 22%. This represents a substantial opportunity to reap the benefits of enhanced performance through improved employee engagement.

6) Inclusivity in Decision Making is the Basis of Power Sharing

Engaging with staff means being inclusive and empowering them to make and contribute to decisions (see Figure 10.7). An organization that engages is far less likely to make decisions behind closed doors and is much more likely to involve staff right from the outset.

- In the 2008 survey, a total of 44% said that big decisions were made behind closed doors and that they were either expected to catch up themselves with the decisions made or were instructed what to do as a result.

- The 2010 survey suggested that there was slightly more openness in decision making – the corresponding figure was 38%.

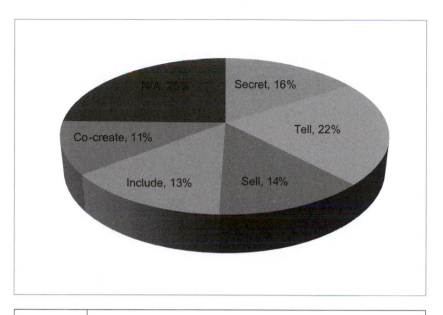

Secret	Big decisions are made behind closed doors and the organization expects me to catch on to what has been said
Tell	Big decisions are made behind closed doors and I am then instructed on what has been decided
Sell	Big decisions are made behind closed doors but the organization makes an effort to explain the decision to me
Include	Big decisions are made by others but the organization involves me in decided how those decisions are implemented
Co-create	The organization involves me from the outset in contributing to and shaping big decisions

Figure 10.7   Different forms and levels of involvement

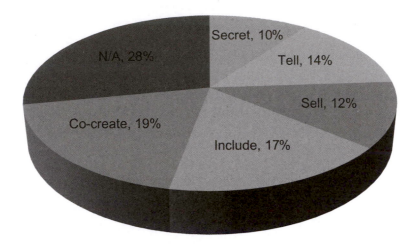

Figure 10.8   Employee involvement in everyday decisions

- Only 11% in the 2010 survey were involved from the outset in decision making, a figure that remained unchanged compared to the 2008 survey.

- While there was evidence of some openness in making the big decisions, this did not seem to extend to everyday decisions made by managers (see Figure 10.8).

- In the 2010 survey, 24% said that their managers made everyday decisions behind closed doors and expected them to catch up with the decision or would then tell them what to do. In the 2008 survey, the figure was 26%. The difference between the two figures is not statistically significant.

- One in five (19%) in the 2010 survey believed that their manager involved them from the outset in decision making. This was slightly down (although not statistically significant) on the 2008 figure (22%).

- As with the big decisions, those at a more senior level were less likely to say that they were not involved, while those at the more junior level were more likely to say they were not involved.

7) Other Drivers of Engagement

The research tested the following criteria and mapped the results against those who felt their organization engaged them to drive performance, those who stated they were engaged and those who stated they were not engaged:

4.   The extent to which I am empowered to take decisions.

5.   My understanding of how I contribute to my organization's strategy.

6.   The culture and values of the organization I work for.

7.   My work/life balance.

8.   Recognition I receive for the work I do.

9.   The way change is managed where I work.

10.   The training and career development opportunities available to me.

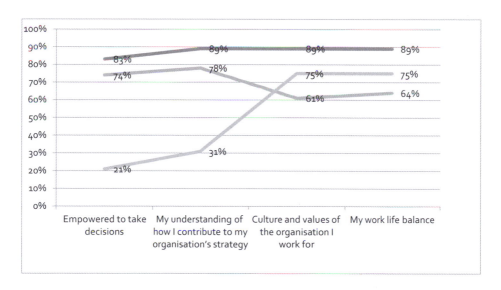

Figure 10.9   Work/life balance and engagement

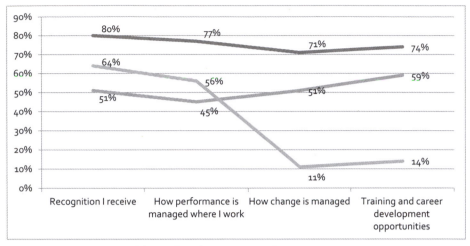

Figure 10.10   Recognition, development and engagement

- The recognition people receive for the work they do and the development opportunities available to them also rank highly as drivers of engagement (see Figure 10.10).

8) The Critical Role of the Manager

People who work in organizations which they report as being effective at engaging them to drive performance provide consistently high net agree scores to all of the following (across both the 2008 and 2013 studies):

- improving employee engagement is one of the key responsibilities of line management;

- employee engagement is a visible priority for line managers and supervisors in my organization (Figure 10.11);

- my manager is effective at engaging me in my work (Figure 10.12).

Not surprisingly, the opposite is true for those who are not engaged. Again, the evidence is clear – effective engagement rests critically on the role of the manager and the approach managers take to guide, support and involve their team. In the next chapter we unpack the specific capabilities that leaders, manager and supervisors.

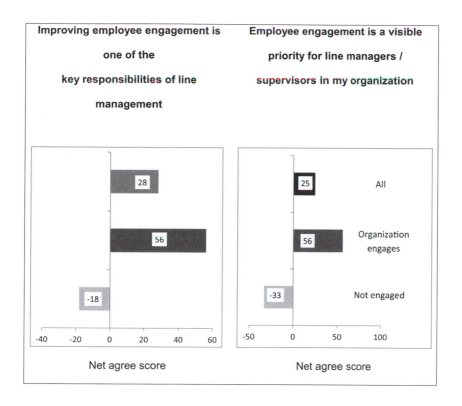

Figure 10.11   Is employee engagement a priority for managers?

The effectiveness of your manager at engaging you at your work

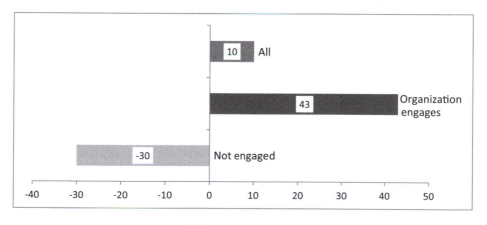

Figure 10.12   How effective are managers as engagers?

IMPACT OF SENIOR MANAGEMENT

As part of our research, we tested employee views on satisfaction with the effectiveness of leadership in their organization. Whilst there were compelling messages for leadership overall, it was clear that the most admired leaders were those whose organizations invested in employee engagement (Figure 10.13):

- 43% of employees expressed satisfaction with their senior management, with 35% expressing dissatisfaction.

- Dissatisfaction was greatest in the public sector (53% were dissatisfied) and within FTSE 100 organizations (41% were dissatisfied).

- Over three-quarters (76%) of employees who believed that their organization managed to engage with them were satisfied with their senior managers.

How satisfied are you with the way senior managers lead your organisation?

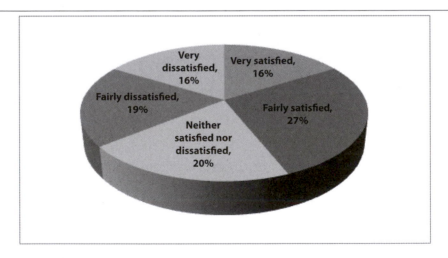

Figure 10.13   Satisfaction with senior managers

9) Engaging Leaders

Leaders, managers and supervisors have a significant impact on employee engagement. Following the 2008 survey, Engage for Change created a set of manager competences that appeared from the results of that survey to be the requirements needed to drive effective employee engagement. The competences, listed below in Table 10.2, were tested in the 2010 survey.

Table 10.2   Competences to drive employee engagement

Competences to drive employee engagement
Articulate: communicates clear messages about what needs to be done
Expert: has the knowledge needed to lead our team in the work we do
Authentic: provides personal insight and narrative to create a meaningful context
Empathetic: tailors the message and delivery style to best suit the audience
Open: accepts challenge and addresses questions
Coaches through change: helps members of the team to overcome resistance to change
Negotiation: gains agreement to extend involvement beyond those entitled to this by the hierarchy
Discernment: identifies the right people to contribute given the demands of different situations
Sharing power: creates value by engaging others
Balancing pace and pressure: creates space for teams and individuals to test and explore whilst ensuring that short-term demands are met
Facilitation: helps groups integrate different perspectives to create sustainable solutions

We will examine these qualities and their impact in more detail in the next chapter; however, the research results are startling and clear. The results are displayed below and display considerable difference in the delivery of these competencies by managers of those were not engaged compared to those who were engaged.

- The chart in Figure 10.14 shows a number of competencies that were identified as being vital to employee engagement. For each competency, the chart shows the proportion who strongly agreed and tended to agree separately for those who said their employer engaged them and those who said that their employer did not. The chart also shows the gap between each of these proportions.

- For each competency, there is a significant gap between those who were engaged and those who were not. For some of the competencies, the gap is greater than 50%. The smallest gap is 39% for the competency that the line manager has the knowledge needed to lead the team in the work they do.

- The chart clearly shows that the greater the competence of the line manager in each of the factors, the greater the level of employee engagement.

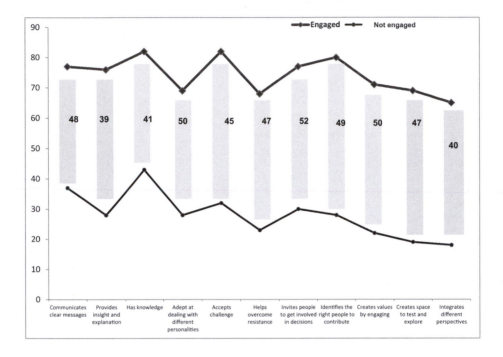

Figure 10.14   Competencies essential for employee engagement

10) Measurement is Not Helping

As the saying goes, 'if you can't measure it, you can't manage it'. In the case of employee engagement, it would appear that what gets measured is not necessarily the right thing and that the results generated do not lead to effective management of what is required to deliver enhanced engagement. The habit of regular measurement is in place, but analysis of the focus of the measurement and how to apply the results to make a difference needs much more work. We believe that surveys and measurement are often bolted on to corporate cultures because it is in vogue. We also suspect that resident cultures are far more ingrained than imagined and hence difficult to influence via survey processes, often resulting in little change to underlying culture brought about by surveys and post survey processes, despite the huge cost of undertaking them. This is an area ripe for inquiry.

Indeed in our 2010 YouGov UK inquiry workers who were engaged rated the impact of measuring employee engagement more highly than those who were not, but even this group felt the measurement approach was not helping as much as it might do to drive up levels of employee engagement (Figure 10.15).

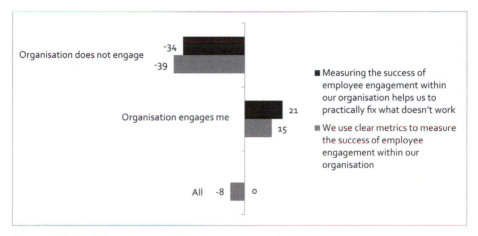

Figure 10.15   The impact of measuring employee engagement

What is needed is a rethink of what the measurement is there to do in the first place in terms of the following factors:

- The outcome being sought.

- What exactly is being measured.

- The questions being asked.

- How the results will be applied.

- What they will impact.

- The degree to which the measurement is likely to contribute to meaningful change.

- The readiness of leaders at every level to act on the results.

- The ability of the organization to monitor in a meaningful way the degree to which leaders at every level are adjusting their own behaviours to enable engagement to flourish.

11) Boardroom Support for Employee Engagement

In both the 2008 and the 2010 surveys, the extent to which board members felt investment in employee engagement was an important part of their agenda and also whether they expected investment to increase were both tested (Figure 10.16):

- In the 2008 survey, it was noted that employee engagement was quickly moving up the board agenda. Despite the recession, there is some evidence that advancement up the agenda might have stalled.

- In the 2010 survey, there was a slight decrease in the proportion of board-level staff who said that employee engagement was a visible priority, but the difference is only four percentage points compared to the 2008 survey and is not statistically significant. We will be very interested to see the results of the next round – will the ravages of recession have reversed the employee engagement movement or will it have shown resilience?

- However, the proportion who stated that employee engagement was considered a more important issue than 12 months ago and the proportion who considered it to be more of a strategic issue than 12 months ago fell significantly.

- From a wide range of possible factors impacting performance in their organization, senior leaders noted high employee engagement as the third most important factor, running slightly behind having a clear vision and having a strong focus on the customer (see Figure 10.17).

- In 2008 just under one-third (29%) stated that over the next 12 months, investment in employee engagement was planned to increase. In 2010, this figure had increased to 33% – over four times the proportion who said that investment in employee engagement was likely to decrease (Figure 10.18).

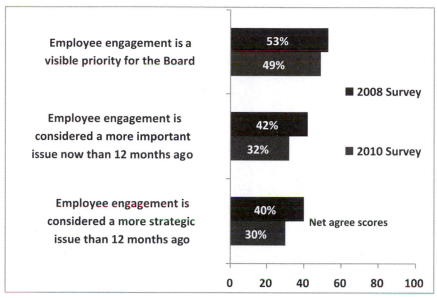

Figure 10.16   Board members' perception of engagement

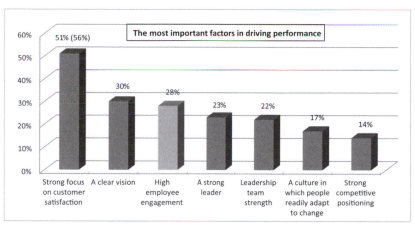

Over the next 12 months do you expect investment in engagement to increase, decrease, stay the same (Board members only)

Figure 10.17   Employee engagement as a factor in performance

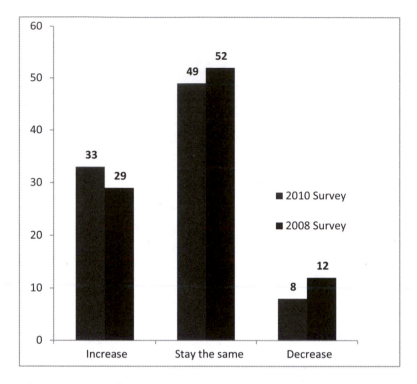

Over the next 12 months do you expect investment in engagement to increase, decrease, stay the same (Board members only)

Figure 10.18   Investment expectations in engagement

Summary: Conditions for Effective Employee Engagement

This research has highlighted three key conditions necessary for effective and sustainable employee engagement:

- A culture of distributed leadership.

- Driving value by inviting employees who deliver the end result to contribute to day-to-day decisions, strategy and change in a well-governed way.

- Leaders at every level who have the appetite and capability to engage people in the decision-making process.

These conditions are created by having the key drivers of engagement in place which, in summary, include the following.

LEADER'S FOOTPRINT

- Trust.

- Credibility/judgement.

- Absolute transparency all the time.

- Consistency of narrative and role model across executive teams and teams at all levels – healthy teams, like good personal relationships, involve open negotiation.

- Creating a role model of well-governed power sharing.

THE ORGANIZATION'S COMPASS

- Moral purpose.

- Distinct business purpose.

- Clear and compelling vision.

- Authentic and current values and beliefs.

- Believable brand.

- Line of sight between people's jobs and the organization's purpose.

THE INDIVIDUAL'S SPACE IN THE INSTITUTION

- My boss' role model of well-governed power sharing means I know that I am safe to challenge and contribute.

- My involvement with our communities.

- My connectivity with the resources of the organization, with people I need to collaborate with and the external world.

- Skills I can grow within the organization or take elsewhere.

When these various components combine in the right way, they create the environment, culture and work experience that will encourage employees to lend their talents and their energy to their work and their employer. The challenge to those hoping to enjoy the additional productivity and other benefits of engagement is to steer their organization, its leaders and their attitudes to a place where all of the components are balanced, distributed and delivered.

11

Helping Leaders at Every Level Engage their People – Capability

Jerome Reback

This chapter focuses on the second big lever of engagement – helping leaders at every level to enhance their capability to engage their people.

It covers:

1.   The drivers of leader and employee engagement.

2.   What support at every do leaders at every level need to be effective at engagement?

3.   The shifting nature of leadership – new model or last millennia HR practices.

4.   Leadership competences required for enabling effective employee engagement.

5.   The role of the HR department in supporting the development of a culture for sustainable employee engagement.

6.   A diagnostic tool to assess engagement skills capability.

1) The Drivers of Leader and Employee Engagement

Throughout the book we have attempted to support the thesis that the key enabler of engagement is a culture of distributed leadership based on leaders, managers and supervisors at every level in the organization who have the appetite and capability to engage those they work with in making decisions. This is a big ask, both for those who need to let go of control as well as those being asked to make more of a contribution. The distribution of decision making, particularly for those delegating their authority, requires skill, understanding and care.

2) What Support Do Leaders at Every Level Need to Be Effective at Engagement?

- Are clear about the behaviours they need to display and the examples they need to provide in order to create the right sort of environment and opportunity for people to contribute in the right way.

- Are coached and supported in delivering engaging behaviours.

- Are encouraged to deliver the behaviours through the example they experience via their own role model leaders and as a result of appropriately focused personal performance reviews and performance management systems.

3) The Shifting Nature of Leadership – New Model or Last Millennia HR Practices

We can observe a shift in leadership requirements over a number of years. Whereas 50 years ago, the focus was more on the individual at the helm, the interest now is more biased towards the impact of the top team overall and the ability of the CEO and leaders at every level to enable a collective process. Likewise, in the past, power was concentrated at the top of the organization, now it is more likely to be distributed more widely. In a bygone era which was more reflective of a 'decide and tell' leadership style, leaders were expected to be self-reliant, while nowadays the skill lies in engaging others to deliver performance with them. Finally there is a shift from knowledge and content-based leadership to capabilities that are based more on effective relationship building that leads to accessing the knowledge embedded in others throughout the organization.

Leadership for effective engagement needs to be collaborative and distributed, and leaders need to be effective at creating context and managing participation. Complexity demands new capabilities beyond the individual and this is driving the leadership requirement in an era where employee engagement is seen to be a route to personal and organizational success.

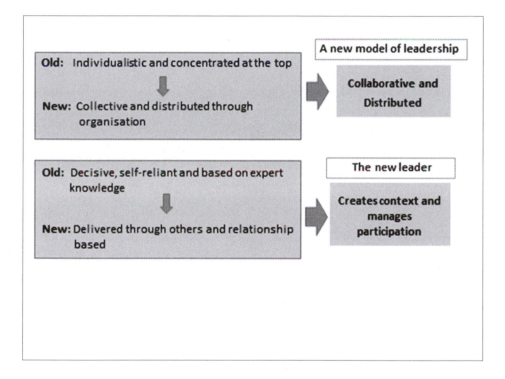

Figure 11.1   The shifting nature of leadership

This shift in leadership is set in the context of the evolution from a past millennia to a new model workplace (Figure 11.1).

Readers may want to reflect on the social processes to which their people are exposed and which shape the workplace experience, including recruitment, induction and development, and map these onto Figure 11.1. Clearly, if these HR processes seem to be more redolent of last millennia workplaces, there is work to be done to bring them up-to-date.

4) Leadership Competences Required for Enabling Effective Employee Engagement

We reported in the previous chapter on the research results when we tested the following leadership competences against those engaged by their organizations to perform well and those who did not feel engaged. The difference in the results was remarkable, with the engaged group illustrating that their managers and leaders delivered far more of each of the criteria below (Figure 11.2) in their relationship with them at work than those who were not engaged at work.

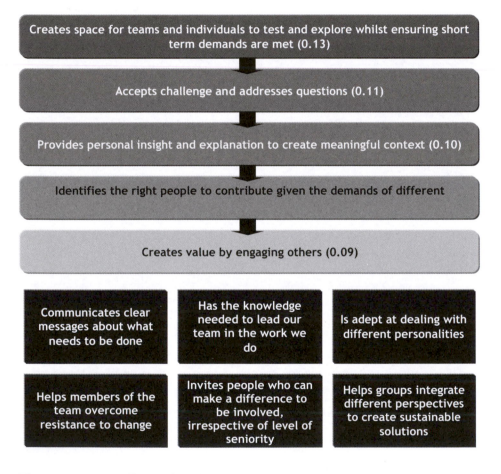

Figure 11.2   Attributes that drive engagement

The attributes in the boxes are those which drive engagement and performance most significantly. The higher the corresponding bracketed number, the greater the influence of the driver in enabling employee engagement.

Whilst some of the attributes are not statistically significant, that is not to say that they are not important in influencing effective engagement. They are important additional factors, but the analysis suggests that they do not exert a statistically significant influence.

Let's take a look at the driving factors in more detail. What exactly do they require, how can they be put into practice and how can leaders and managers improve their skills in delivering each of them (Table 11.1)?

Table 11.1   Competences that drive engagement

Competences to drive employee engagement
Balancing pace and pressure: creates space for teams and individuals to test and explore whilst ensuring short-term demands are met
Open: accepts challenge and addresses questions
Authentic: provides personal insight and explanation to create meaningful context
Discernment: identifies the right people to contribute given the demands of different situations
Sharing power: creates value by engaging others
Articulate: communicates clear messages about what needs to be done
Expert: has the knowledge needed to lead team in the work they do
Empathetic: tailors the message and delivery style to best suit the audience
Coaches through change: helps members of the team to overcome resistance to change
Negotiation: gains agreement to extend involvement beyond those entitled to this by the hierarchy
Facilitation: helps groups integrate different perspectives to create sustainable solutions

BALANCING PACE AND PRESSURE

In today's world, the demands to meet deadlines and deliver projected goals and targets can override everything. Clearly, an environment that demands output with no or little apparent concern for employees responsible for delivering that output will result in an instructional leadership style. As we have seen, this will not contribute to effective employee engagement and can cause an exodus of the most valued and most required talent.

A manager's ability to provide employees with space to test and explore is indicated as the most significant driving force in enabling their employees to feel that their organization engages with them and, as a result, perform well. This reinforces the importance of creating conditions in which people feel safe and rewarded to challenge and contribute. For example, the more employees are given, the more engaged they are. Similarly, the more independence they are given in developing themselves (i.e. through testing and exploring), the more likely they are to perform well and be more engaged.

The need is to get the balance right between 'pace' and 'pressure'. What does this mean? It means maintaining a focus on short-term targets and goals and delivering on these, whilst simultaneously creating the opportunity for people to test other ideas, to experiment with different options and to explore new ways of doing things. In practice, this means a manager who delivers on short-term operational goals but at the same time encourages his or her team to look up, look out and look ahead beyond the short term.

People want to improve, they want to build their skills, enhance their knowledge and be given the opportunity to do things beyond their current perceived boundaries. Helping people see and understand that their boundaries can be stretched and see that they have the opportunity to explore new ideas and experiment with new ways of doing things will enable people to bring the best out in themselves. The Total UK case study discussed earlier shows that even in times of deep organizational crisis, employees will rise to the occasion and contribute creative measures that will save their company and develop personal capability that will help individuals to thrive in harsh environments.

Rather than divert attention elsewhere, awareness of enhanced opportunities and the innovation experience inherent in experimenting with new ways of doing things will actually build confidence, drive hope and inspire enthusiasm. The determination to deliver in the short term will increase as people's views about potentially improved futures are enhanced.

The leader who is able to balance pace and pressure needs to be good at:

- maintaining focus on delivering short-term goals and delivering against these;

- creating space for people to experiment with new ideas;

- developing risk-free opportunities for people to challenge and explore options and alternatives;

- encouraging members of his or her team to stretch capabilities and opportunities;

- creating situations where team members can learn from their mistakes.

BEING OPEN

An often-heard mantra is that of the need for openness and honesty in the workplace, and particularly between leaders and managers and their teams. In fact, being open and honest is a prerequisite of effective engagement. If people feel they cannot trust their manager, if they do not believe what he or she says or if they feel information they need and should be aware of it being held from them, then the basis of an effective relationship is undermined. In these circumstances, engagement will always fail, however well motivated the people in question. If they experience a lack of openness over an extended period of time, team members are likely to seek roles elsewhere – either in other teams or in other organizations.

The dilemma for leaders is often what to be open about and to whom. It is not that people in more senior roles particularly want to be more secretive; rather, quite often, people with access to more privileged information feel it would either be inappropriate, unfair or commercially sensitive to share that information with wider groups. This is where some serious self-questioning is required. I can think of countless situations where, once challenged, leaders allowed themselves to be more comfortable sharing what previously was considered to be privileged information with wider groups and in all instances the following results can be noted:

- There were no negative consequences in sharing the information more widely.

- Concerns about commercial sensitivity, whilst understandable, were not an issue in practice.

- Recipients of the information responded positively and responsibly to the 'privileged' access.

- Rumours were quashed because the legitimate voice of leadership could now be heard.

- Recipients used the information to contribute positively to the issues that needed to be addressed.

- Levels of engagement were boosted.

Being open is not just about having a readiness to share information, it is also about being ready to accept and deal with challenges and being available to listen to and respond to questions. There is no hiding behind closed doors when it comes to enabling effective engagement.

Employees will respond enthusiastically to those who include them, address them as equals and respect them as people who have a contribution to make. Active and lively dialogue is the basis of effective interaction. This means a readiness to be challenged and either to effectively defend one's point of view and position or to shift perspective because facts, data and arguments presented by others are persuasive and correct. Arrogance or intransigence has no place for leadership or management if employee engagement is sought.

Of course, it is also quite possible, and often likely, that different perspectives can lead to different views – each equally plausible and seemingly justifiable – from different people. In this situation, the engaging leader needs to recognize the opinion of others, see things from their perspective, empathize with their situation but explain why a different course of action is nonetheless being pursued. People may not agree, but they will feel listened to, respected and understood. Respect for leadership will be enhanced and whilst engagement may not improve – although even in this situation it can – it should not be damaged.

The leader who is open is:

- able to articulate goals, tasks and actions clearly;

- comfortable at sharing potentially sensitive information with members of his or her team;

- ready to negotiate with peers and seniors the need to share more widely what might initially be viewed as potentially sensitive information;

- ready to be challenged and prepared to accept and respond to that challenge;

- sensitive to the needs of others and able to see things from their perspective;

- prepared to be flexible when a robust and sound alternative is proposed;

- able to promote and defend his or her agenda and approach with empathy for those around him or her whilst displaying understanding of the differing perspectives.

BEING AUTHENTIC

Authenticity is important. People respect authenticity even if they do not agree with the outcome. Authenticity provides the opportunity for leaders to let their personality shine and for more of their personal experience and confidence to pervade. It leads to authority being accepted, but authority of the right type. It is about leadership through respect, even in some cases as a result of admiration, but not through instruction. Being authentic leads to positive commitment to a leader who is seen to make the right judgements based on personal experience and good insight. People want to be part of a team that is led by a leader they can learn from and who they respect. Authenticity lends itself well to creating these conditions. Elsewhere in the book it is noted that effective engagement requires strong leadership (only) on the issues that the leader(s) has(/ve) concluded are givens. It is also noted that those will be far fewer in number than under command and control.

Leaders who are authentic tell stories about their previous experiences which help those around them to take confidence in them. They are able to provide a clear and accurate context for the conditions that the rest of the team is now facing or the challenge they are being asked to address, thereby helping people understand why they are being asked to do what needs to be done and to see that there is a route that will lead to success. People become more engaged when they have a clear line of sight between the work they are doing and what is ultimately delivered by the organization they work for to their customers, clients or the public. They want to have – indeed, they need to have – a sense of personal mission, worth and value.

Of course, it is important not to show off, not to be the type of leader who is so interested in their own background and advice that they become blind to the interests and needs of the members of their team. The need for authenticity is not an excuse for indulgent personal history or exaggerated references to previous circumstances that others might (but probably will not) take some insight from. The requirement is to get the balance right and to always think about the impact on those around you. Inspire with insight and guide with experience, but always be conscious of the needs of the situation and the members of the team. Maintain a conscious focus on helping them understand and deal with the current situation.

The leader who is authentic:

- provides regular context and explanation about the work under way so that employees understand why they are being asked to do what needs to be done and understands how and where their effort fits into the greater scheme of things;

- relays relevant stories from his or her own experience to help team members understand issues and options constructing meaning with metaphor, imagery and simile;

- builds confidence by enabling their team to make sense of the current experience and the forward journey;

- is conscious of the needs and expectations of members of their team and creates the opportunity for those needs and expectations to be acknowledged and respected.

BEING DISCERNING

In this context, 'being discerning' is the ability to identify the right people to help contribute to the task. Being discerning requires being able to determine who is best placed to contribute ideas for solutions. This may not be the expected or the obvious people and ideally involves reaching deep into the organization to license those who otherwise would normally not get a chance to have their voice heard and have a legitimate channel for making a contribution.

As we have seen, the basis of effective employee engagement that leads to enhanced performance is the opportunity people have to influence everyday and bigger-ticket decisions that impact them and which they can affect constructively. If people are to contribute, they need to be invited to do so and they need a well-governed process in which to participate. It is not about anarchy where everyone believes they have the right to make a choice and to impact any issue in a way they personally prefer, nor is it about absolute democracy. Effective engagement requires good process and good governance. It demands that those involved in impacting decisions, process or outcomes are clear about the invitation that has been provided to them and are clear about the boundaries into which their invitation to participation fits.

The discerning leader needs to be good at:

- finding the right people to;

- clarifying the nature of the invitation they are responding to;

- getting agreement, where necessary, from others who may be impacted by the outcome of the process;

- managing the process so that people have the freedom they need to operate but are clear about the areas beyond their remit;

- ensuring others who feel that they should have been invited to contribute to the process understand why they have not been and are comfortable that their interests are nonetheless well represented.

SHARING POWER

We have been arguing throughout this book that the basis of effective employee engagement is judicious power sharing. Sharing the opportunity to influence the way things are done, sharing opportunities to impact decision making and distributing power that otherwise might have remained at the very top of the organization.

A readiness and ability to share power is one of the key characteristics of leaders who are able to build sustainable performance cultures based on widespread and meaningful employee engagement.

In an environment where career success may well have been built with the belief that 'information is power' or where the inherent but not necessarily explicit prejudice is that greater command and control comes with greater levels of seniority, the concept of power sharing can be difficult to acknowledge and hard to execute. Power sharing does not mean losing prestige or letting go of personal accomplishments, it means using one's confidence and experience to invite a wider group of people to guide, advise, inform and solve. It means recognizing that the wisdom is in the crowd and that success in today's world comes from being a great team coach who inspires through guidance rather than being a god who is expected to have all the answers, to whom everyone feels answerable and from whom all are awaiting instruction and direction.

Sharing power can seem difficult. It may be viewed that others cannot be trusted to get it right because they do not have the wisdom, experience or access to take a wider perspective and make the right moves, or it might be that the view is that it is the role and responsibility of senior leaders to take the key decisions with everyone else liberated, not having to worry, so that they can simply get on and manage the execution of what needs to be done. Whilst these views may be held and whilst some may promote them robustly and with impact, it nonetheless remains that sticking to these paternalistic views will not deliver employee engagement or any of the positive outcomes that are possible as a consequence.

5) The Role of the HR Department in Supporting the Development of a Culture for Sustainable Employee Engagement

The HR department has a significant role to play in helping leaders develop the skills required to enable effective employee engagement:

- Leadership development programmes need to provide guidance in developing understanding and skills in the attributes listed and explained above.

- Remuneration and performance management approaches need to inquire about, monitor and reward the behaviours that lead to effective employee engagement.

- Career planning processes need to give credence to those who deliver effective employee engagement together with effective delivery of results and avoid promoting those who simply focus on the numbers.

- Recruitment and induction procedures need to reflect the values inherent in enabling an effective employee engagement culture and ensure that those who join the organization are both ready and inclined to exhibit the behaviours that enable effective engagement – from both the point of view of a participant and a leader.

- Measurement approaches need to ask the right questions, the questions which test the extent to which leaders around the organization exhibit and deliver the traits advocated here. Only through this route can organizations get a true gauge on what to address in order to drive up levels of engagement.

6) A Diagnostic Tool to Assess Engagement Skills Capability

Using the criteria listed in the behaviours outlined above, we have devised a quick diagnostic to help you gauge your leadership engagement skill in Table 11.2. Answer each of the questions under each competency area as honestly as possible; each question relates to a different behavioural trait that contributes to the delivery of the associated competence.

Table 11.2   Engagement capability – self-assessment test

Balancing pace and pressure	(Not at all) → (Extremely well)
	1 2 3 4 5 6 7 8 9 10
• Maintaining focus on short-term goals and delivering against these	□ □ □ □ □ □ □ □ □ □
• Creating space for people to experiment with new ideas	□ □ □ □ □ □ □ □ □ □
• Developing risk-free opportunities for people to explore options and alternatives	□ □ □ □ □ □ □ □ □ □
• Encouraging members of the team to stretch their capabilities and opportunities	□ □ □ □ □ □ □ □ □ □
• Creating situations where team members can learn from their mistakes	□ □ □ □ □ □ □ □ □ □
Being open	**(Not at all) → (Extremely well)**
	1 2 3 4 5 6 7 8 9 10
• Able to articulate goals, tasks and actions clearly	□ □ □ □ □ □ □ □ □ □
• Comfortable at sharing potentially sensitive information with members of the team	□ □ □ □ □ □ □ □ □ □
• Ready to negotiate with peers and seniors the need to share more widely what might initially be viewed as potentially sensitive information	□ □ □ □ □ □ □ □ □ □
• Ready to be challenged and prepared to accept and respond to that challenge	□ □ □ □ □ □ □ □ □ □
• Sensitive to the needs of others and able to see things from their perspective	□ □ □ □ □ □ □ □ □ □
• Prepared to be flexible when a robust and sound alternative is proposed	□ □ □ □ □ □ □ □ □ □
• Able to promote and defend your agenda and approach with empathy for those around you whilst displaying understanding of the differing perspectives	□ □ □ □ □ □ □ □ □ □

Table 11.2   Engagement capability – self-assessment test (*continued*)

Being authentic	(Not at all) → (Extremely well)
	1 2 3 4 5 6 7 8 9 10
• Providing regular context and explanations about the work under way so people understand why they are being asked to do what needs to be done and understand how and where their effort fits into the greater scheme of things	☐ ☐ ☐ ☐ ☐ ☐ ☐ ☐ ☐ ☐
• Relaying relevant stories from your own experience to help team members understand issues and options	☐ ☐ ☐ ☐ ☐ ☐ ☐ ☐ ☐ ☐
• Helping people to see the connection between their own work and the goals and outputs of the organization they work for	☐ ☐ ☐ ☐ ☐ ☐ ☐ ☐ ☐ ☐
• Building confidence by enabling your team to make sense of the current experience and the forward journey	☐ ☐ ☐ ☐ ☐ ☐ ☐ ☐ ☐ ☐
• Being conscious of the needs and expectations of members of your team and creating the opportunity for those needs and expectations to be acknowledged and respected	☐ ☐ ☐ ☐ ☐ ☐ ☐ ☐ ☐ ☐
Being discerning	**(Not at all) → (Extremely well)**
	1 2 3 4 5 6 7 8 9 10
• Finding the right people to ask to be involved	☐ ☐ ☐ ☐ ☐ ☐ ☐ ☐ ☐ ☐
• Clarifying the nature of the invitation they are responding to	☐ ☐ ☐ ☐ ☐ ☐ ☐ ☐ ☐ ☐
• Getting agreement, where necessary, from others who may be impacted by the outcome of the process	☐ ☐ ☐ ☐ ☐ ☐ ☐ ☐ ☐ ☐
• Managing the process so that people have the freedom they need to operate but are clear about the areas beyond their remit	☐ ☐ ☐ ☐ ☐ ☐ ☐ ☐ ☐ ☐
• Ensuring that others who feel that they should have been invited into the process understand why they have not been and are comfortable that their interests are nonetheless well represented	☐ ☐ ☐ ☐ ☐ ☐ ☐ ☐ ☐ ☐

Table 11.2   Engagement capability – self-assessment test (*continued*)

Being open	(Not at all) → (Extremely well)									
	1	2	3	4	5	6	7	8	9	10
• Being able to define the non-negotiables	□	□	□	□	□	□	□	□	□	□
• Being able to agree the non-negotiables	□	□	□	□	□	□	□	□	□	□
• Licensing others to deliver change	□	□	□	□	□	□	□	□	□	□
• Being ready to share key data and metrics	□	□	□	□	□	□	□	□	□	□
• Accepting criticism	□	□	□	□	□	□	□	□	□	□
• Open to others' points of view	□	□	□	□	□	□	□	□	□	□
Other attributes	(Not at all) → (Extremely well)									
	1	2	3	4	5	6	7	8	9	10
• **Articulate**: communicating clear messages about what needs to be done	□	□	□	□	□	□	□	□	□	□
• **Expert**: having the knowledge needed to lead the team in the work it does	□	□	□	□	□	□	□	□	□	□
• **Empathetic**: tailoring the message and delivery style to best suit the audience	□	□	□	□	□	□	□	□	□	□
• **Coaches through change**: helping members of the team overcome resistance to change	□	□	□	□	□	□	□	□	□	□
• **Negotiation**: gaining agreement to extend involvement beyond those entitled by hierarchy	□	□	□	□	□	□	□	□	□	□
• **Facilitation**: helping groups integrate different perspectives to create sustainable solutions	□	□	□	□	□	□	□	□	□	□

Note: Use a 1–10 scoring approach. Score a 1 for a poor score up to a 10 for an excellent score. Then ask someone you work with, ideally a member of the team who takes leadership from you, to provide their ratings about you for the same criteria. Use the following table to determine an appropriate course of action.

Table 11.3   Developing your employee engagement capability

Score for each trait within each competence	Your own scoring	Others scoring of you
Score of less than 5	A score of less than 5 suggests self-acknowledgement of the need to develop that trait more effectively. Seek opportunity through experience on the job and via development courses to strengthen this ability	The team can deliver more if it is more engaged. Where team members give you a score of less than 5 for any particular trait, they are providing important indicators of their perception of where you need to improve the engagement experience and opportunity you provide for them. Focus on these traits and discuss with the members of your team how they think you can better deliver what they need
Score of 6–8	A score of 6–8 suggests a need to strengthen your ability with regard to the trait. Do you best to make yourself more conscious of your impact on others when providing leadership and seek feedback and guidance from those around you on how you can improve the experience you give them in regard of this trait	The team holds you in good regard in respect of these traits. Consider what you have done to cause them to be enthusiastic about the experience you are giving them in this respect and aim to do more of the same. Try to improve their experience by discussing with the team how you could collectively improve the engagement experience
Score of 8 and above	This is a high score. Work to keep achieving high levels of engagement with those in your team. Regularly seek feedback and aim to be as conscious as possible about your delivery of the leadership engagement competencies	The team clearly thinks highly of you with regard to traits scored at this level. See what you can learn about the situations where the team has been highly engaged and where you have successfully managed to invert the hierarchy to drive performance. Do what you can to replicate these conditions elsewhere

DIFFERENCE IN SCORES BETWEEN YOUR OWN SCORING AND THAT OF MEMBERS OF YOUR TEAM

Ideally, you want to find yourself rating your ability in each trait along similar lines to the ratings provided by members of your team. Where there is divergence of more than three points, you need to find out why the team's view of your ability is different from that of your own.

Where the team, or any of its members, rates you more highly than you rate yourself, clearly you are providing a better engaging experience for them than you may have thought. Evidently, you believe you can inspire and encourage your team to be more engaged and more effective than it is even though its members are reasonably satisfied. Surprise them by stretching the boundaries further and doing more of what you have self-assessed you want to get better at. Seek opportunities to learn and practise the trait, and understand more about how you could strengthen it via feedback from members of your team as well as from peers who you believe deliver the trait well.

Where you rate yourself more highly than the team, clearly there is a credibility gap. The experience you are providing for your team members is not as energizing or as engaging as you may think. For each of the traits where the team has a perception gap of at least three points below your own score, pursue the same course of action as suggested in 'score of less than 5' above.

OVERALL COMPETENCY ASSESSMENT

Use the table below to gauge your overall engagement impact.

Table 11.4   Diagnosing your leadership engagement skills – three parts

260–330	Excellent score. You are great at motivating and engaging your team. Keep it up
200–259	Good score. The team feels licensed to contribute and is quite well engaged. Keep it up and see what you can do to move up to the top level
140–199	Reasonable score. The team is engaged to perform, but you could do more to drive better performance by improving your engagement approach. Read this book and see what you can apply
100–140	Poor score. You provide some effective engagement opportunity for your team, but not enough. Aim to more consciously consider when you can delegate your decision-making authority and see what you can do to improve your ability to deliver the leadership competencies proposed in this chapter
Below 100	Not good at all. Your team members are unlikely to be delivering anywhere near their best and some of your best people may well be looking to work for another leader or elsewhere

12

Brand Needs Engaged Employees to Deliver the Customer Promise

It's the people, stupid!

Most if not all good and bad stories about companies and institutions start out with a human story. The head of housekeeping at the Plaza Inn (on London's South Bank) who ransacked the hotel looking for a favourite shirt of mine, found it, cleaned it and returned it within 24 hours exemplified a brand promise that was delivered.

The positive stories often point to individuals going beyond the extra mile, maybe in contradiction of procedures and coming across as one human being talking to another. The fact that staff are doing so invariably means that it is safe for them to do so, and that is a good indicator that their boss provides them with leeway to act using their discretion and is an example of the effective behaviours covered in the last chapter. Negative stories often result when we come across people in organizations who are constrained by procedures, practices and systems that are dysfunctional and where they have little room for manoeuvre either because of the system, through fear of their boss or due to the existence of a 'a no can do' culture in their team. Walk into any corporate culture and you can get a sense very quickly if it is a speak-up or a dumb-down place to work. I would be prepared to guess that speak-up cultures are mostly attack brands; the ones out to knock bigger brands off their perches. And that the dumb-down cultures are typical of defender brands in which risk taking is discouraged.

No book on employee engagement could be complete without reference to the idea of brand and other stakeholder groups – the ultimate purpose of employee engagement is to improve the experience of these groups for mutual benefit (see Figure 12.1).

This chapter covers the following areas:

1.   What is brand?

2.   Dealing with the deficit between the brand promise and the stakeholders' experience.

3.   Bringing strategy to life through inside-out brand engagement.

Whilst the nature of the job, the local team and the local boss are the greatest influences over whether people are engaged, the big idea of the institution, its identity and its public standing also influence employee engagement.

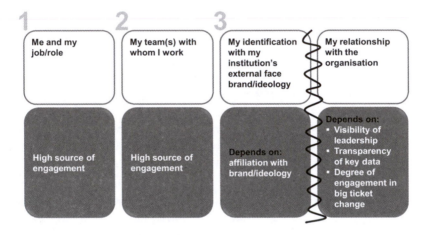

Figure 12.1   Brand – the third influence on an employee's relationship with the organization

1) What is Brand?

Brand is an investment by the institution designed to construct a consistent favourable impression amongst stakeholders which enables the institution to operate effectively. It is designed to influence the impression that individuals (inside and outside) form of an organization from all their experiences. The idea is to create consistency of message, behaviour, appearance and practices so that the organization is recognizable at every point of interaction that people have with it.

The relationship between a 'stakeholder' (including employees) and an institution is often described as the stakeholder journey around the institution. The journey consists of a number of key interactions or 'touch points', such as face-to-face contact, digital contact, hearsay and so on. These journeys can be mapped and influenced over the life of a relationship between an individual and an institution. Smart companies like the UK's supermarket group Tesco know a lot about consumer behaviour derived from their loyalty card programme. Even when the relationship between an individual and the institution fades, the ghost of the brand lingers in our memories and continues to influence other people's views when we share those brand memories.

Brand exists in the minds of stakeholders as a result of their interactions with it and whilst the institution can try and propagate a view of itself that is shared by many, absolute control is impossible as there are too many variables beyond the influence of the organization. However, there are many touch points over which the institution has influence and some which it can control.

The best organizations can hope for by investing in brand is an aspiration resulting in an approximate shared impression amongst stakeholders. The sum of these touch points is the stakeholder journey.

Touch points include the following:

- physically when we are present in a brand's premises, perhaps instore, and when we have direct interpersonal interactions with a brand's people;

- through electronic media – the online service experience;

- directly through the consumption of products and services;

- indirectly via the absorption of paid-for media, promotion, sponsorship and PR;

- indirectly through the experience of the identity and architecture of the brand;

- indirectly via gossip and hearsay and through services like TripAdvisor, which are other people's memories that may conflate with our own;

- through our own memories of previous interactions.

Touch points are moments of truth in which we re-enforce or change our view about a brand, be it a supermarket, airline, local restaurant or global corporation. The first three touch points above are where an organization's people are the key influence on relationships with stakeholders. Their attitudes, behaviours and capability all have a bearing on the brand experience and they are much more accessible and probably more inclined to be advocates if they are proud of what they do and feel able to add value. Brand can never be a monolithic impression shared by everyone simultaneously – each of us has a unique perspective about organizations we deal with.

Whilst organizations may try to create a universal brand journey, it will always be subject to everyone's individual experiences, which in turn are contextualized by what else is going on in our lives. Our mood on one day will cause us to view an organization with one impression which might be quite the reverse on another. These individual interpretations are completely beyond the influence of the organization and may well be unconscious to the individual. Organizations need to be careful to avoid the hubris that results if they believe that they can control the brand impression in individuals' heads and hearts. They can control the investment and the input, but not the outcome.

Brand could be said to be the language, personality, aspiration, ethics and spirit of an organization, community, tribe or country or federation of countries, the essence of which is remembered. Let's take a look at the ingredients of the organization which result in the brand impressions that form in people's minds about an organization using the diagram given in Figure 12.2.

Figure 12.2 tries to show the flow from left to right from the foundations of an organization (vision, values, mission, strategy and ethics) to its expression to stakeholders that it interacts with. Brand is a systemic concept aimed at delivering a coherent proposition that will enable commercial and community activity. Presenting it as a systemic concept poses a question about the degree to which it can be managed as a system.

Staff and external stakeholder's experience is the sum of all their interactions with the organization

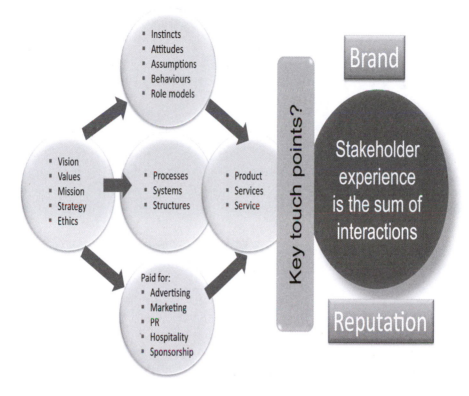

Figure 12.2   The relationship between interaction, experience and brand

Many successful organizations centralize control of the brand experience into one function, usually marketing or corporate communication, (with lots of input from HR) giving that function oversight over the stakeholder touch points that collectively deliver the desired brand experience. Famous and well-known brands are nearly all consumer brands where significant marketing spend keeps corporate brands like McDonald's and British Airways and product brands like Diageo's collection (Baileys etc.) in the public eye.

Managed or not, every institution has a brand image that is shared amongst its followers. And every institution has the opportunity to use the brand concept to reflect the outside world's views and experiences of it as the basis for a dialogue about change to its purpose, strategy, values and conduct of relationships. Brand lies at the core of most consumer companies, but it can also drive change at business-to-consumer and business-to-business companies too.

However, there is an issue with marketing- led brand cultures, which is the frequent gap between the brand promise and stakeholders' experience.

2) Dealing with the Deficit Between the Brand Promise and the Stakeholders' Experience

The employee experience of work spills over into external stakeholders' experience and whilst other ingredients of the brand journey covered earlier may be very influential, an institution's employees are the only ingredient of brand which thinks for itself and has emotions. (That said, artificial intelligence experienced through digital interaction will increasingly influence our perceptions about a brand's performance.)

Not surprisingly, I advocate the idea of 'brand from the inside out'. The power of marketing functions often outguns others like HR and communication and always outspends them, sometimes making brand promises that employees are ill-prepared to deliver on or are even unaware that there is a connection between the promises made to consumers and stakeholders and their role in delivering them. Whilst most employees are aware of the external promotion of brand promise before it hits the screens and the high street, their awareness of the message via an internal cascade is rarely enough to equip them to deliver on the brand promise.

The construction of brand essence by an internal elite, often supported by design and brand agencies, frequently excludes the people of the organization, who will have plenty of useful contributions to make to the brand experience of customers and other stakeholders, and thus to the essence or core content of the brand. And even where employees are involved it is usually in tell, sell mode rather than in co-creational mode. Putting it another way much has been pre-decided before employees are engaged. It is therefore usually an exercise in creating understanding, alignment and advocacy.

This is in marked contrast to the increasing trend to engage the organization's people in developing strategy, change and operational plans, hitherto the preserve of elites and 'strategy' consultants.

When it comes to brand, the custom and practice of some in marketing is to employ command and control as the decision-making model where a few decide and then tell and enroll the many – often entertainingly but with little room for challenge and contribution to the 'what' with, perhaps a wider invitation for employees to challenge and contribute to the 'how'. But even the latter exercises tend towards resembling a sheep dip.

As organizations are now inviting employees to 'co-create' strategy and change the logic follows that brand could and should be co-created with an organization's people and customers, clients and communities. If people have been part of devising the brand promise and have contributed to the stakeholder journey (of which they are a part), they will not only add value to its content but will also be more likely to be authentic advocates for it. Authenticity in this context means having been a partner in the process as opposed to a pupil who has learnt her lines.

Consider for a moment the business start-up. In the early days, everyone in a start-up gets involved in constructing brand promise, usually in an informal way, until the moment arrives when there are too many variations and it becomes time to bottle the magic of the organization so that it can focus on its core capabilities and grow. This is usually accompanied by a sense of relief that the ethereal has been marshalled and articulated. The tacit focus of the start-up becomes formalized and the beginnings of corporate behaviours emerge. The benefits of focus are a clear market position and a brand which attracts talent and customers and clients.

Mature organizations elevate responsibility for defining brand essence or what the company's purpose is to functional specialists and external experts. But there are attendant dangers of a top-down brand. The danger of the focusing effect of brand is the exclusion of possibilities that fall outside the boundaries imposed by purpose, vision, strategy and brand as the means of expression. Brand is designed to express and differentiate the organization, which involves focusing the scope of an institution's proposition. The ultimate danger of a strong brand is that it locks an organization into a set path whose time and value will be time-limited. IBM nearly strangled itself with its adherence to mainframes, changing course just in time to rebound back as a champion of laptops.

A glance at the FTSE 100, Forbes and Fortune 500 lists of companies shows that few survive more than a few decades before losing relevance. Companies, with some real exceptions (often in private hands), are short-lived, lasting for a few decades or less before being supplanted by a better idea, or a more agile competitor. Survival times in these lists declines every year. On the one hand this demonstrates the power of the market as attack brands pursue defender brands that try to hold their position at the top.

Other social phenomena like cities and social movements (for example religions and political systems) thrive for decades, and some for many centuries. Cities and movements are porous systems, a trait which enables them to innovate constantly. Corporations on the other hand seem to go to lengths to be much less porous to ideas which are perceived to be at odds with a carefully constructed singular view of purpose with brand acting as the border guards stopping internal divergence from purpose, and externally promoting the desired image or positioning.

Overly managed brand may actually be toxic to corporate health and longevity.

WHY IS (CORPORATE) BRAND STILL PREDOMINANTLY A TOP-DOWN PROCESS?

Marketing and branding specialists tend to distinguish between brand development (the what) and brand propagation (the how) in the same way that command and control strategists view strategy development (the what) and strategy implementation (the how) as consecutive phases in which an elite owns the development phase with communication and some broader engagement in implementation – a linear approach that all but precludes challenge and contribution from those nearest the marketplace.

Good employee engagement frames the 'what' and the 'how' as an integrated approach, with the right people, often in very large numbers, being engaged in front-end development. Presently this approach is anathema to traditional thinking in marketing and brand where an elitist role is more usual. If that is the problem, what is the solution?

In a nutshell, I think Part II of this book is the solution. Leader and employee engagement interventions are now being used to manage the inclusion of larger numbers of people to dramatically energize strategy formulation, change, service, values and operational effectiveness processes. I advocate that a co-creational approach to brand would build ownership and pride in the outcome.

3) Bringing Strategy to Life through Inside-Out Brand Engagement

The QBE (Australia's largest insurer) case in Chapter 6 describes the journey from strategy renewal to brand from the inside out. The lightbulb moment for the two most senior figures (one of whom is now group CEO) was the insight that an inside-out brand process was the vehicle to create momentum and delivery of the business strategy internally first and with external stakeholders second. A big external campaign was important, but it did not lead the process – it was led by it.

Similarly, when a client in a service industry decided it wanted to compete harder on service, it turned to its employees to help do the work. Drawing from rich industry comparative data, it was possible for competing teams of staff to visualize the end-to-end customer journey and to use their own experience of customers to suggest which key touch points were decisive in forming customer perceptions. The touch points are the parts of the customer journey that customers or clients most value and remember. The trouble is that there are hundreds of points of interaction, but only a few are deal makers and deal breakers. By getting staff to suggest their views about the identity of the critical (to purchase or renew) touch points, the company was using crowd sourcing techniques applied to a specific business opportunity. Having put forward their views as individual teams, the staff teams had to negotiate between themselves until they had whittled the list of core customer touch points down to a target list to focus on as part of a service strategy. Having completed their view, the members of the combined staff group were asked to compare their view with the external research – it tallied, but there was much richer material from the staff groups.

Staff are full-time anthropologists watching, listening to customer behaviour and storing quirky information and anecdotes. Most of the time, this reservoir of insight remains dormant until the company provides the safe, enjoyable conditions of an engagement intervention.

The customer journey in a business-to-business example with key touch points identified is given in Figure 12.3 and in a business-to-consumer context in Figure 12.4.

From the eyes of the customer

Figure 12.3   The customer journey in a business-to-business context

The leisure company customer journey around competing silos

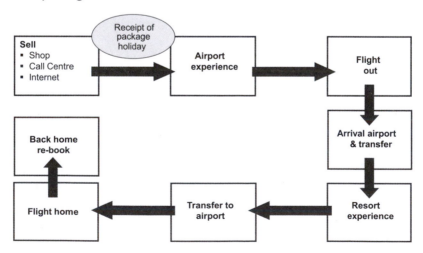

Figure 12.4   The consumer customer journey

In closing, let me take you back to the stories about experiences that people have about organizations. When you next find yourself considering the nature of the impact of the institution's brand, reflect on the trail of stories that you hope might form the dominant narrative amongst critical groups. What essence of experience might they have in common about the organization? And who better to add and contribute to this essence than the people in the organization who are closest to those stakeholders?

13

The Impact of Employee Engagement on Internal Communication

This chapter covers the following areas:

1.   Internal communication at a crossroads.

2.   What good internal communication looks like.

3.   The role of internal communication in balancing the top-down with the bottom-up.

4.   Implications of the rise of employee engagement on the capabilities of internal communicators.

1) Internal Communication at a Crossroads

Internal communication lies at a crossroads between being the radio station of the powerful, on the one hand and, on the other, being a contributor to sustaining a healthy workplace where expression and constructive challenging are encouraged and enabled. In this chapter I argue that internal communication should try to find the balance between the two roles. Presently many communication functions are being trammelled into being turbo-charged message boards.

Looking back, internal communication has been an adjunct of power since people organized themselves into groups. Every social group has structure of some kind and every structure needs social processes to negotiate the allocation of resources and responsibilities. Whether it is an authoritarian state, a local community, a non-governmental organization or a commercial enterprise, every group also needs to communicate about the process of negotiation and the outcomes of negotiation.

Note here the distinction between the role of communication in explaining the process of negotiation and its role in communicating the outcomes of negotiation. Think of the media's role in reporting on the election process and its subsequent role in reporting winners and losers. In an absolute dictatorship, the former (communicating the process of negotiation) may be almost non-existent. In more inclusive or democratic environments, providing information about the process of negotiation will be as significant as the role of communicating about outcomes of negotiations.

This text is aimed primarily at people in the workplace, but we will all have experienced communities and bosses or leaders that range from the despotic to the over-consensual who seem unable to close down any decisions. Neither is particularly functional, but it might be argued that the benevolent dictator is more productive than the hippy. Just look at Singapore for an example of the former which seems to work quite well – when the residents of Singapore are fed up, they can leave; not so for the residents of North Korea. Most of us at work can choose to leave despotic cultures, although in tough times we might put up with more bad behaviour than when there are more options elsewhere. When this downturn ends, plenty of bad employers will be punished and good ones will be rewarded by the retention of staff who have been treated fairly and involved in decisions that affect them and which they can affect constructively.

In organizations, formal internal communication grew up in the post-Second World War years with the realization that power could be better exerted if the powerful focused the efforts of employees on their agenda.

The internal communication discipline echoed the external communication process with the emphasis on articulating key messages and distributing them using increasingly engaging media embracing digital media.

Put simply, the purpose of communication was and often still is the alignment of the many with the intentions of a few powerful people. The traditional process of communicating to align comprises:

- elites deciding;

- message forming;

- message delivery;

- message impact;

- message reinforcement.

'Good' internal communication results in widespread understanding by employees of the big picture and clarity about the part that different employee groups have to play in delivering the goals of the enterprise. It also ought to echo the values of the enterprise, celebrate success and make transparent all the data which people need to do their jobs and see the impact they are having. Moreover, it can provide for feedback and challenge and the setting for innovation of product, service, working practices and community involvement.

This is a positive picture enjoyed by some, perhaps many employees. It is certainly a vision which communication should aspire to. And it is fair to say that the role and purpose of formal communication has developed more of a balance between the employer's agenda, which typically seeks alignment of efforts, whilst also meeting the needs of employees. Getting this balance right is a tough challenge, but it is possible to see that effective heads of communication should be advising both on the likely impacts on different stakeholder groups of decision options as well as on communication about decisions once they have been made.

However, too often, the decision-making process is a linear one in which communication is employed only after decisions have been made, by which time the influencing role, if invited at all, is too late and the task defaults to message articulation and delivery. As the need for speed ramps up in organizational decision making, especially in organizations where a crisis may submerge communicators, many find themselves in 'tell or sell' mode with inadequate front-end influence on the decisions themselves.

Linear decision making and tell and sell communication provide an appearance of speed, but also result in deluges of communicated decisions which recipients may ignore or become overwhelmed by. In these cases, more and more top-down communication simply adds to a sense of an enterprise being out of control and shooting from the hip. The symptoms are manic energy and a ferocious communication machine confusing quantity of messages for connection with the groups that need to internalize the communication and take action.

Internal communication seems to be at a crossroads between reverting to being solely a messenger (albeit an increasingly creative one) and being a contributor to sustaining a healthy workplace where expression and constructive challenging are encouraged and enabled.

2) What Good Internal Communication Looks Like

Good communication requires a balance between being an effective messenger and a positive influence on workplace culture. The role of internal communication has become a core part of decision making at the heart of the enterprise, advising the senior leadership team as an equal partner. Today the sophisticated internal communication function is doing four things well – advising and advocating, communicating effectively, providing feedback and enabling dialogue.

ADVISOR AND ADVOCATE

- Advising senior and local management on *staff expectations* and the appetite for organizational messages and information.

- *Influencing the substance of decision making* by providing views on the impact that each option might have on critical stakeholders.

- Providing *demographic insight* about how best to communicate with different internal groups, enabling the tailoring of the relationship with different groups.

- *Balancing hard messages and emotional impact* – in the midst of a crisis or any fast-moving agenda, it is easy to reduce communication to a message delivery service. Good communicators think about the emotional impact and seek to resonate with the emotional state of employees. In hard-nut negotiations, for example, unions will often appeal to the emotional needs much more effectively, whilst employers stick to perfectly rational but unemotional arguments which resonate less well with employees.

- Coaching and *guiding the C-suite on their own internal communication* role, helping them to improve relationships with their people by raising trust levels – proximity, visibility and credibility being the foundations of trust.

- *Integrating communication across business units/regions* and other structures by ensuring that each uses a common format for developing communication strategy/plans in which the commonalities (in message, approaches to commonly shared stakeholders, etc.) are identified.

- *Transferring* their skills as communicators to leaders so that the roles described above become a practice of leadership with less or no reliance on the communicator.

EFFECTIVE COMMUNICATOR

- Provider of *big-picture messages* about purpose, vision, strategy and other core 'content' on a broadcast or targeted basis.

- *Localizing* the big picture, perhaps within a business unit or geographical region.

- *Celebrating* corporate and individual success.

- Acknowledging corporate *failure.*

PROVIDER OF FEEDBACK

- Listening in order to assess *mood and motivation* and taking the necessary action to redress where possible.

- Listening to employees to detect *hot topics to guide decision making* via formal and informal means.

ENABLER OF DIALOGUE

- Providing opportunities for *dialogue* between the leaders and the led.

- *Equipping leaders* to communicate, perhaps in concert with learning and development and other HR colleagues.

- Providing opportunities for corporate *innovation and collaboration* where value may be derived.

These roles when viewed as a complete list might suggest a workplace culture that is quite compelling and 'engaging'. But I think that if an organization ticks all or many of the above roles as being representative of their communication practice, it should be reviewed again through the lens of the 'new model workplace' Figure 2.1.

What is the real underlying purpose of internal communication? If the reality is that the organization is comfortably on the left side, it is likely that the real purpose of the internal communication function is alignment and coercion, perhaps delivered with a paternal velvet glove. If the roles of good communication (above) are reviewed, it is quite possible that 'good' communication means good in the context of a predominantly command and control ethos. Many workplaces may be judged as good workplaces when seen in the context of other command and control cultures, but in these circumstances, communication may be an agent and enforcer of command and control.

As more and more inclusive workplaces emerge and people make choices between a command and control environment and one which involves them more in running the place, internal communication will need to adapt its purpose to balance the top down and the bottom up. I do not for a moment advocate a free-for-all; far from it.

3) The Role of Internal Communication in Balancing the Top-Down with the Bottom-Up

There will always be a role for top down 'tell/sell' internal communication to convey the non negotiables or givens that an executive team has negotiated – as I have commented previously, strong leadership is required to govern effective engagement.

Strong leadership means an executive team that has, as a team, negotiated and agreed:

- the *why* – the rationale for change, strategy, etc.;

- the *what* – the nature and extent of the changes to the structure, operating model, vision/purpose, customer-centric proposition, etc.;

- the *how* – the streams of work which are and will deliver the refreshed business and the behavioural role model required on the journey;

- the *invitation* to wider leadership teams and others to challenge and contribute to the *what* and the *how*.

However, it should be noted that strong leadership does not mean authoritarian or bossy behaviour.

By taking part in this negotiation, members of an executive team will also have developed a shared narrative about both content and the process of implementation. If they have not participated in this negotiation, the communicator will get a top-down communication brief which makes no process or time provision for engaging wider groups in decision making, regardless of the number of feedback loops.

In Figure 13.1, I try to illustrate the flows of communication when an organization has chosen to engage groups beyond an elite in decision making. It is a very different picture compared to communication in top-down mode. From left to right, the elite has negotiated on the why, the what, the how and the invitation, and has communicated this process via a range of face-to-face and indirect methods.

The process of engaging people in decision making provides a role for communicators to communicate about the process of engagement to make challenges and contributions visible to all. Earlier I used the metaphor of the media reporting on an election process, not just the final outcome.

The final outcome of the engagement occurs when the leadership team reviews to ideas that have been contributed and chooses which challenges and contributions to adopt.

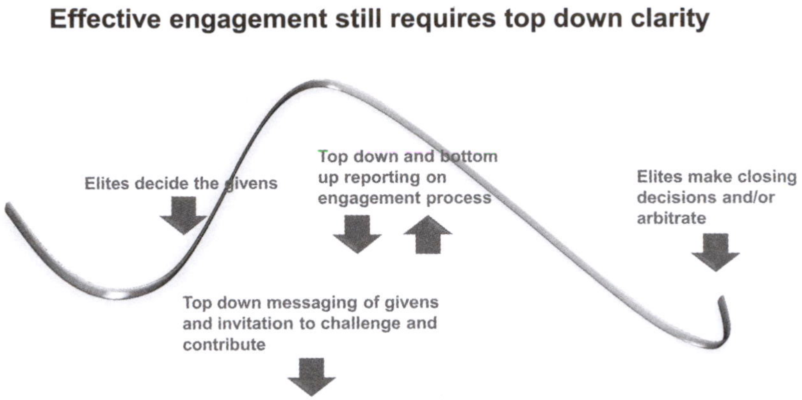

Effective engagement still requires top down clarity

Elites decide the givens

Top down and bottom up reporting on engagement process

Elites make closing decisions and/or arbitrate

Top down messaging of givens and invitation to challenge and contribute

Figure 13.1   The flows of communication in an engaged organization

Figure 13.1 tries to show that the original top down communication is valid but is now added to by the need to communicate about the process of engagement and the outcome of it. This is also true for individual leaders in their day-to-day dealings with employees.

The communicator that balances the top down with the bottom up has instincts, skills and a pain threshold that extend beyond the traditional top-down communicator's ability to articulate and communicate top down messaging.

In the following model, the what (decisions made by a few about purpose, vision, strategy, etc.) is pre-decided and the scope of invitation to others is confined to implementation: the how. If that is a deliberate and rational decision, it at least provides for some wider involvement.

When an organization starts to accommodate more inclusive approaches to decision making, the assumption that internal communication's primary role is messaging decisions made by elites must extend to setting the context for engaging people more widely, albeit in a disciplined way.

NEW ROLES OF COMMUNICATION IN A NEW MODEL ORGANIZATION

The roles of internal communication in the new model organization include:

- *Challenging patterns of automatic top-down* decision making (which otherwise must end in tell/sell communication) in the interests of

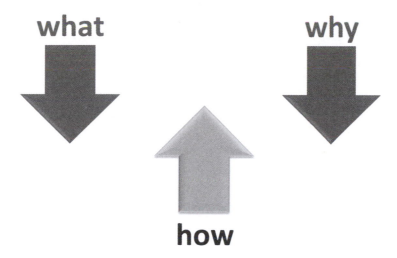

Figure 13.2   The what down, how up model

seeking a decision-making approach which adds the most value to the organization and its people.

- Helping the leadership team to articulate the *'top-down givens' and the scope of the invitation* to other levels to contribute to the content and delivery of strategy, change, etc.

- Being part of the team that *designs* leadership rituals and full-scale engagement interventions that genuinely engage chosen groups as opposed to entertaining them in an engaging way to 'make them feel engaged'.

- Building the 'engagement challenge' into *change and operational* improvement processes.

- Building *engagement capability* into training, development and performance management as an addition and complement to communication skills. Bear in mind that communication and engagement capability can be in direct conflict if the intention of communication training is primarily alignment.

Put these roles together with the earlier set for communication under command and control and communication has a powerful role to play in developing the new model organization.

When it comes to adopting the right approach to engagement, the communicators must of course take their cue from the leadership team, although they do have a role in facilitating debate about which approach to engagement will add value.

A REFLECTIVE EXERCISE WITH A PRACTICAL PURPOSE

Those responsible for corporate internal communication, change communication and leadership communication might benefit from reflecting on which roles communication is currently enacting and whether the current set of roles is in sync with the leadership, behind it or ahead of it. Use the diagram that follows (Table 13.1).

Table 13.1   A communicator's development plan

Advisor and advocate	Score yourself 1–5	Development required
Advising senior and local management on *staff expectations* and appetite for organizational messages and information		
Influencing the substance of decision making by providing views on the impact that each option might have on critical stakeholders		
Providing *demographic insight* about how best to communicate with different internal groups, enabling the tailoring of the relationship with different groups		
Balancing hard messages and emotional impact – in the midst of a crisis or any fast-moving agenda, it is easy to reduce communication to a message delivery service. Good communication thinks about the emotional impact and seeks to resonate with the emotional state of employees. In hard-nut negotiations, for example, unions will often appeal to the emotional needs much more effectively, whilst employers stick to perfectly rational but emotional arguments		
Coaching and *guiding the C-suite on their internal communication* role, helping them to improve relationships with their people by raising trust levels		
Transferring their skills as communicators to leaders so that the roles described above become a practice of leadership with less or no reliance on the communicator		

Table 13.1   A communicator's development plan (*continued*)

Advisor and advocate	Score yourself 1–5	Development required
Integrating communication across business units/ regions and other structures by ensuring that each uses a common format for developing communication strategy/plans in which the commonalities (in message, approaches to commonly shared stakeholders, etc.) are identified		
Effective communicator		
Provider of *big-picture messages* about purpose, vision, strategy and other core 'content' on a broadcast or targeted basis		
Localizing the big picture, perhaps within a business unit or geographical region		
Celebrating corporate and individual success		
Acknowledging corporate *failure*		
Feedback		
Listening in order to assess *mood and motivation* and taking the necessary action to redress where possible		
Listening to employees to detect *hot topics to guide decision making* via formal and informal means		
Enabler of dialogue		
Providing opportunities for *dialogue* between the leaders and the led		
Equipping leaders to communicate, perhaps in concert with learning and development and other HR colleagues		
Providing opportunities for corporate *innovation and collaboration* where value may be derived		
New roles for communicators in the new model organization		
Challenging patterns of automatic top-down decision making (which must end in tell/sell communication) in the interests of seeking a decision-making approach which adds the most value to the organization and its people		
Helping the leadership team to articulate the *'top-down givens' and the scope of the invitation* to other levels to contribute to the content and delivery of strategy, change, etc.		
Being part of the team that *designs* leadership rituals and full-scale engagement interventions that genuinely engage chosen groups as opposed to entertaining them in an engaging way to 'make them feel engaged'		
Ensuring that the wider leadership teams and all the organization's people understand their *role, responsibilities and rewards* in an organization which is reaching out to engage them		

Table 13.1   A communicator's development plan (*continued*)

Advisor and advocate	Score yourself 1–5	Development required
Building the 'engagement challenge' into *change and operational* improvement processes		
Building *engagement capability* into training, development and performance management as an addition and complement to communication development, whilst bearing in mind that the two can be in direct conflict if the intention of communication training is primarily alignment		

If the communication is lagging behind and needs to catch up, those responsible for communication may want to develop the capabilities of their professional communicators. If so the above development framework for communicators will be helpful.

4) Implications of the Rise of Employee Engagement on the Capabilities of Internal Communicators

Historically the primary capabilities of the internal communicator were rooted in the journalistic tradition of reporting on events and decisions taken by others. When working at its best, this mode requires a certain detachment from the 'establishment' on which it is reporting in order to maintain credibility with its readership. By and large, though, the reporter mode was superseded by the messenger mode, in which the communicator was charged with conveying the wishes, commands and messages of leadership.

The skills, capability and outlook necessary for the communicator today (to deliver on the roles above) are summarized in Table 13.2.

Table 13.2   The make-up of a skilled communicator

Attitudes, outlook, behaviours	Development required
Natural relationship/coalition builders	
Confident with internal customers at every level	
Resilient in pressurized, conflicting and ambiguous situations	
Good at focusing on the issues rather than responding emotionally	
Good at knowing when to polarize debate in order to articulate choices	
Ability to participate in meetings as both a participant and an observer of 'what is going on', enabling reframing or redirection	
Open-minded to new ideas, whatever the source	
Organizational, analytical and creative skills	
First-rate facilitation enabling the communicator to enact the advisor role	
Listening skills (of the good consultant) who lets a group talk itself out before attempting to close and move on	
Spirit and source of creativity by knowing what will surprise and engage different stakehol	
First-rate planning skills to turn content and creativity into a deliverable plan	
Creating a clear and well-governed contract with internal customers	
Technical skills	
Clear thinker and writer	
Knowledge of all media, though not necessarily expert in many of them	
Resource investigator	

I will close the chapter by providing a diagram in Figure 13.3 summarizing the complementary relationship between communication and engagement.

Communication and Engagement

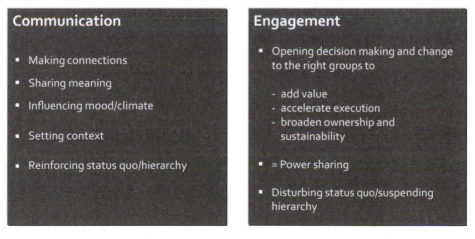

Figure 13.3   The correlation between communication and engagement

MINI CASE STUDY: XSTRATA – GLOBAL MINING COMPANY WHERE PEOPLE ARE ENGAGED WITH MAXIMUM DEVOLVEMENT

Xstrata was a tiny company when Mick Davis[1] became its CEO. It is now a major mining company by any standards. Mick is a driven individual and he has a very alternative way of leadership compared to the (very) traditional industry.

Devolved	Shared
☒ Leadership	☒ Purpose
☒ Accountability	☒ Vision
☒ Structures	☒ Big commercial risks
☒ Strategy	☒ Responsibility
☒ Processes	☒ Learning/information
☒ All operational decisions/risks	☒ Innovation

Figure 13.4   The tell-tale signs of the engaged organization

There follows two quotations, the first from Mick Davies and the second from Ian Pearce which convey a taste of their 'tight/loose' leadership philosophy:

> *Most of the other big players in mining are centralizing everything, creating huge monolithic, often inflexible institutions where decision making is slow.*

> *The best place to start with culture change is where there is no existing culture but where there is a strong existing culture you need powerful and visible forces of discontinuity which allow and require people to challenge the status quo in radical rather than incremental ways.*

---

1   Mick Davis recently left Xstrata but is already building a new start up in the industry.

Rather than (rigid rules) this we have 17 gold standards or principles which guide collective and individual decisions – each must pass through the standards.

The CEO's role in a devolved organization comprises the following areas:

- *Upholding the values;*
- *Upholder of ethos and ethics;*
- *Navigation of the headline strategy;*
- *Governor of devolvement – ensuring that the right accountabilities are devolved;*
- *Rewarding for risk taking;*
- *The 'sheriff' of performance.*

Of course there is a hierarchy – hierarchy channels the right decisions to the right place, but there is no hierarchy for information – nobody should ever have to go up the line to get information to do their work.

All operational risks are decentralized – net present value is much higher where the right risks are devolved.

Our advantage lies in decentralizing the right things and at the highest speed of post-merger integration – in 30 days we know who's in or out and 100n days we have grafted in Xstrata philosophy and the 17 standards/principles.

Ian Pearce of Xstrata Canada makes the following comments:

The devolved model is not just the CEO speaking, it's real – I get my wings to fly and I devolve as far down as possible. The centre never second-guesses the operating companies – everything is devolved to the lowest levels where there is absolute personal accountability and no ambiguity as in matrix organizations – there are 'no dogs relieving themselves on other dog's trees'.

Everyone has line of sight with local strategy – they know where and how they are contributing.

We have learnt that the 'God complex' (of supposed experts) is often less effective than people on the ground fixing things with trial and error. In the Dominican Republic, we had a problem [involving] a leak of carbon monoxide that all kinds of hired experts and universities could not fix. Then we handed it back to the local maintenance crew who, through patient trial and error, fixed it.

Absolute transparency is key to trusting relationships – when we negotiate with unions, they trust us as they know they have the same level of information as we do – we give it to them.

What happens is that any one of our businesses tackles a problem and shares it instantly with every other business – ours is a flat networking model, not a hierarchical centre-down model.

Like other companies with high levels of engagement, we engage with our local communities, usually around educational opportunities in remote communities.

Give people wings and they will fly.

Digital Technology Needs the Right Culture to be an Enabler of Engagement

John Smythe with Ben Hart and Max Waldron

This chapter has been written in collaboration with Ben Hart and Max Waldron. Ben has a rich history in the digital industry from pioneering the early coupling of interactivity with television broadcasts through to leading global digital strategy for blue-chip brands. Over the last 10 years, he has built two start-up digital marketing agencies. Today he is a consultant, trainer and an adjunct professor at Hult International Business School and is also growing his own e-commerce fashion retailer. Max recently completed his MA in International Relations at London's Kings College. He is currently at Bain & Company.

This chapter covers the following areas:

1. The social context.

2. The technology is in place, but the culture often is not.

3. From conscription to volunteering.

4. Examples of digital engagement.

1) The Social Context

It is self-evident that the social behaviours that we enjoy in the face-to-face world have found their way online. Digital brings immediacy of connection;

you don't have to wait for the phone or the face to face. The test is how much further the intimacy of human interaction will transfer from face-to-face to digital as experiences become richer and more interactive. Social media has also turned up the volume on the 'friendship capacity' that people can have. The old world's challenge is whether quality and social intimacy is traded for quantity. It is also a truism to note that content (ideas, debate, learning, etc.) circulates faster than at any time in history.

A product of the social media age is that people have an increasing propensity to share information with and disclose information to people they may hardly know in a way that they would be inhibited from doing face-to-face. People's reputations are out there in cyberspace, being modified in real time. Social media has also accelerated the emergence of new movements in ideas and political adventures, exemplified by open source software like Linux that would not exist were it not for the ability of people to network online around shared interests.

Social media is playing an important role in self-mobilizing people around other shared agendas, including the worldwide occupy movement and the Arab Spring. Many institutions are also playing catch-up with workforces that are already personally socially networked. And whilst some organizations have embraced it, many have not yet experienced the rewards of doing so. In friendship-led social networks, the reward is as simple as keeping in touch, being engaged with friends, knowing what is going on and being able to contribute. Organizations that have thrived through the adoption of social media have been rewarded with a flow of ideas and an enhanced sense of community that pre-adopters do not enjoy.

2) The Technology is in Place, But the Culture Often is Not

There has been much written about the liberalizing impact of digital technology for people in their social lives, and even more has been written on the technology itself. We won't attempt to add anything to either of those agendas; our focus here is on the potential for engaging large numbers of employees at work in consensus-building and decision-making online. This potential is being amplified as leaders who are digitally fluent outnumber the digital laggards. As they do so, there will be a shift towards negotiation 'online' from negotiation 'over the table'.

What do we mean by this? In the analogue world, issues are tabled and discussed in meetings. Some of these are on-the-fly affairs, while others are more formal. Some matters must be decided in meetings with due governance observed (boards/negotiations with third parties, etc.). Meetings start and stop and decisions are made, progressed or postponed. People have to be present to influence proceedings. By their nature, meetings are limited to the few people that have an interest in a topic, those who have the availability to attend and those who have power or are seeking to borrow power to make an initiative happen. Meetings are prone to invisibility. Often, those present will have little knowledge of who else either is or might be involved. In addition, meetings invariably mean that a few decide on behalf of the many. A lot of the time, this is efficient; focusing the right decisions on the right people is a prime function of a hierarchy. However, the downside of this is that decisions made in meetings mean that most of the time, very few people get a chance to challenge or contribute.

There will always be decisions made in meetings in the manner described above, but the digital era heralds the onset of wider involvement in decision making, enabling broader groups to get involved where value will be added. We already know from our client work in large-scale face-to-face strategy and change initiatives that the quality and quantity of breakthrough ideas gathered from large groups far exceeds the output from elites acting alone.

However, broad-scale face-to-face engagement interventions also have disadvantages. They incur high opportunity costs (for example, those involved in getting people together) and tend to be occasional. Occasional interventions can produce good ideas which, with robust delivery management, provide payback on the investment. Unfortunately, they are prone to 'volcanic eruption syndrome', in which there is a dramatic flurry of entertaining activity, but little 'lava flow' (payback). This contrasts with the organic flow of challenge and contribution on the Internet between self-organizing individuals and groups.

The goal in organizations is to achieve the same organic challenge and contribution in corporations and institutions that is achieved outside of work on social media in self-organizing communities. This aim, whilst exemplified by a few organizations, is hamstrung less by technology (for example, bandwidth) and more by the application of hierarchical attitudes hanging over from command and control ways of organizing institutions.

In short, the technology is in place, but a culture of distributed leadership often is not.

Moreover, corporations still put up defences to prevent employees using the company infrastructure for personal and social purposes, resulting in people going 'off the company grid' and using their own devices in company time. These same institutions, whilst denying access to external social media, use digital platforms for corporate purposes such as sharing procedures, providing access to information and enabling company-oriented dialogue. The employee experience of these corporate digital platforms is usually transactional and procedural in nature, with few of the benefits of free-flowing social media accruing to the organization. It is not much better than digitized paperwork In contrast, other institutions have embraced both the corporate and the social, reasoning that their people will subvert the spirit of denying them corporate access by using personal means. More significantly, these organizations argue that most people will act responsibly and will respect the company for its adult-to-adult attitude, and as such will be rewarded with better performance and employee advocacy. Peer-to-peer pressure also tends to kick in when a few try to mess it up for the many.

3) From Conscription to Volunteering

In its first phase, corporate technology successfully provided utilitarian functionality, such as access to standard operating procedures, HR facilities and opportunities for 'one to many' communication. People participate in this instrumental digital relationship because they have to, to do their job, to access benefits they want and to access information they need.

Intranets as a utilitarian aspect of a relationship between employer and employee are a must do. There is no reward for participation aside from survival. People are conscripts in this relationship, not volunteers. This coercive relationship rather colours people's attitudes to corporate technology. It often feels in stark contrast to their personal experience on the web. Intranet technology can also provide opportunities for dialogue, debate and engagement of targeted groups and whole populations in challenging the status quo and co-creating new futures. All we need to do is provide the kind of social rewards that will make participation attractive.

The stairway diagram given in Figure 14.1 below charts the progression in the functionality of corporate digital platforms from providing linear access to content provided in a top-down style, to more inclusive exchanges. Functionality becomes richer as the stairway ascends, and people are more likely to change from being a conscript to being a willing volunteer. The shift from conscript to volunteer depends on the perceptions employees have of the social rewards awaiting them when they engage in the higher-order activities at the top of the stairway.

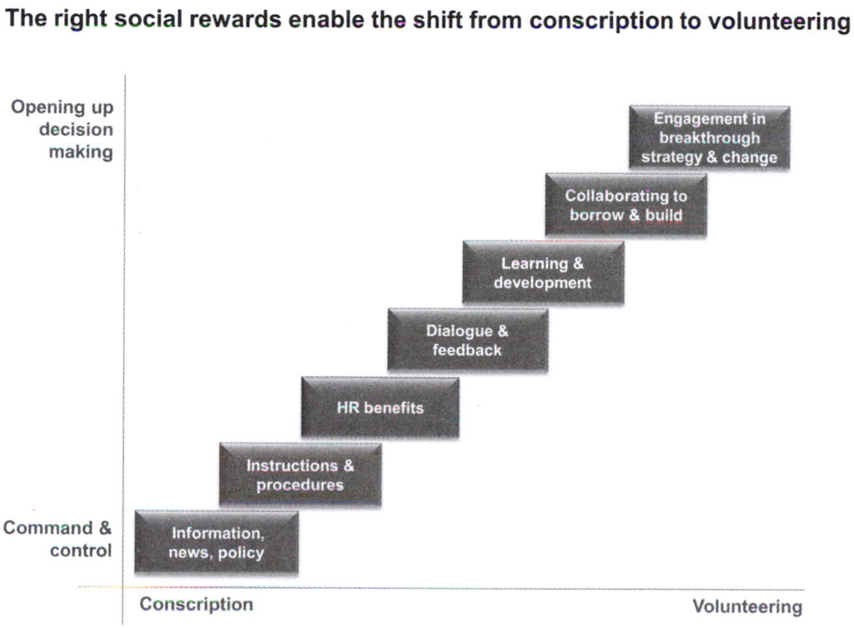

The right social rewards enable the shift from conscription to volunteering

Figure 14.1   The stairway diagram

Many corporate digital platforms do not escalate much beyond dialogue and feedback. Those that do extend to learning and development may still be under a culture of command and control which does not want or invite challenge or contribution to policy or strategy.

In order for organizations to benefit from the breakthrough ideas of their people, they must be willing to open up decision making to broader groups of leadership and all those who have a contribution to make. Opening up decision making requires three things:

- a culture in which people know and feel that it is safe to challenge and contribute;

- a digital platform that is technically accessible and engaging as a user experience;

- social rewards for participants that are similar to those that they enjoy in public social media.

In many corporations, there is scant reward for providing valuable breakthrough ideas and if there is no reward, people will decline to participate or will pay lip service if they are subtly coerced. Non-monetary social rewards which motivate people to participate at work are the same as in non-digital relationships. These include:

- the richness, challenge, excitement, risk, glamour, etc. of the (digital) experience itself;

- ease of access to the (digital) experience;

- professional curation of the process by the organization;

- acknowledgement of contributions made;

- feelings of belonging;

- being on the winning team – introducing friendly competition;

- learning from others;

- providing learning to others;

- being part of a successful endeavour where breakthroughs are achieved – think of the thousands of scientists participating in Europe's Hadron Collider, resulting in the Higgs particle being confirmed.

In this list of social rewards, we mention being on the winning team and competition as being a reward for engaging, drawing from the world of online gaming (such as *World of Warcraft* and online role-playing games) where complete strangers group together to compete. In online teams, people self-define their roles, learn how to contribute and amass skills and tools to ensure that their team wins. Competition to create superior ideas is an obvious reward. These social rewards act as a litmus test of the experience that employees have from their personal interactions with their corporate platforms. Architects of the online experience will need to be satisfied that rewards like these are built into the fabric of the digital experience.

We will end this collaborative chapter with a dozen or so examples of digitally enabled engagement collected by Max from publicly available sources.

4) Examples of Digital Engagement

A) GAS NATURAL: MANAGING CHANGE THROUGH EMOTIONAL AS WELL AS RATIONAL ENGAGEMENT[1]

In 2008 and 2009, the Spanish utility company Gas Natural acquired Unión Fenosa for €16.8 billion, making it the first company in Europe to offer both gas and electricity. The challenge was to portray the company as a united entity in the wake of a major change. Rather than bombard employees with details about the merger, Gas Natural decided to use social technology to generate a cohesive company culture.

A shared space called 'Our Energy' was created, with a number of separate areas. To begin with, the portal contained information presented in engaging 'capsules'. Each capsule focused on a discrete aspect of the company, including Gas Natural's strategic aspirations as well as its key business metrics. Next, a TV channel was used to display a series of videos from senior management. Instead of simply 'selling' to employees, however, many of the videos were produced with the direct participation of the workers themselves.

In addition, Our Energy facilitated direction participation. A space called 'Your Opinion' was set up to capture employees' feedback and suggestions. By answering questions on the portal itself, overlap could be avoided and best

---

1 *Communication Director* magazine, February 2010.

practice shared. Before long, 20,000 replies had been posted. A total of 34 focus groups were also initiated across four countries.

What makes Gas Natural's approach distinctive is the incentivizing of collaboration through emotional as well as rational aspects. In addition to providing information and the means to offer feedback, Our Energy appealed to the emotions of employees by involving them in a meaningful way. A photography competition, called 'The Company Seen From a New Angle', was launched and attracted almost 1,000 entries, with participants being awarded Our Energy merchandise. A photo shoot was also conducted with employees from both Gas Natural and Unión Fenosa to demonstrate cohesiveness.

Our Energy now provides both the communication capabilities of a multinational firm as well as a crucial hub for workers to feel engaged. On its first day, the portal received 50,000 visits. Just one year later, it had recorded as many as 1.7 million hits.

B) ALSTOM: DRIVING INNOVATION THROUGH COLLABORATION[2]

Alstom, a French multinational power company, has sales of over €20 billion and is responsible for the technology behind one in four lightbulbs worldwide. But its employee base spans over 70 countries, and multiple mergers and acquisitions have fragmented the workforce. The task was to leverage technology to coordinate and knowledge.

The digital strategy was founded on three pillars. First, the means were provided for collaboration. Forums were augmented with blogging and wiki capabilities. Importantly, every tool was combined into an integrated platform. Second, the culture was shifted to incentivize employees to use these capabilities. Collaboration was made into an explicit competency, and guides were put out to facilitate collaborative events and meetings. Third, the creation of communities was made simple by installing a toolkit that any employee could draw upon to start up a network with ease. Moreover, to avoid the problem of over-proliferation, the process was governed by a 'Community Lifecycle' process and explained through video on 'Alstom University Tube'.

The major barrier faced by Alstom was cultural: talk of 'social networks' was avoided. Yet the necessity and return on collaboration across 75,000 people

---

2   Dachis Group: 2.0 Adoption Council case study.

was also clear. In Alstom's case, the solution was to drive participation by democratizing accountability, as well as securing buy-in from key stakeholders. Each community was assigned a leader to stimulate activity. Alongside the leader, however, was a non-hierarchical position. Each group would have a 'sponsor' who would act as something of a co-creation advocate by promoting the community externally and providing resources.

These roles were supplemented by getting traditional networks on board. HR paid attention to employee participation and rewarded significant input, while IT was responsible for the build from the outset. Meanwhile, executive backing was secured from the outset. And in measuring success, 'Return on Experience' (ROE) replaced traditional key performance indicators by documenting effective groups through videos and posts on the corporate intranet.

The upshot of Alstom's technology intervention has been felt in a number of ways. Collaboration and innovation are both flourishing. New candidates have been attracted to the company. The company's carbon footprint has fallen due to the ease of virtual meetings. And the cultural importance of collaborative technology has been embedded by realigning the key skill set of managers along social behaviours as well as conventional functional expertise.

C) BT: BOTTOM-UP PARTICIPATION DRIVING VALUE THROUGH EFFECTIVE COLLABORATION[3]

BT, the global telecommunications company, operates in 170 countries and employs over 100,000 people. As a company specializing in communications, it goes to great lengths to facilitate collaboration amongst its workforce. Through a number of channels, it has replaced a traditional top-down approach with an innovative bottom-up communication culture driven by technology.

The first foray into E2.0 (Enterprise 2.0 came with 'BTpedia', which was a wiki-based application enabling any user to post and edit articles to share best practice. At the risk of the space being redundant and unused, BT accelerated participation in two key ways. First, BTpedia was configured to be necessary, rather than optional, by running key items such as monthly reports and corporate handbooks through it. Second, and more important, a platform called 'MyPages' was devised. This gave everyone a unique profile space with rich functionality: employees could upload and share photos, write blogs, set up calendars and

3   Digital Generation case study; Richard Dennison's blog.

create networks of 'friends'. MyPages was from the outset a genuinely bottom-up and user-driven device. It came about through the kind of creative turbulence characteristic of a right-brain approach to technology, having been adopted by employees rather than formally pushed by the IT department. This atmosphere generated widespread participation: 1,500 profile activations took place within a fortnight and BTpedia now boasts around 1,000 articles.

The notion of collaboration as a bottom-up phenomenon runs through other technology initiatives. Blogging is not simply another way for management to sell the corporate party line; instead, it is widely used for road-testing ideas and reporting back on meetings. Similarly, social networking functionality enables any employee to upload skills to his or her profile. By doing so, suitable collaborators are automatically suggested and a dedicated space can be created immediately without requiring the consent of managers. This attitude empowers a shared collaborate agenda.

By turning technological collaboration from a hypothetical business case into something easy and accessible, BT has brought colleagues together as never before, whilst making the whole process personally engaging and enjoyable. Demonstrating a concrete Return on Investment (ROI) is still a challenge, but even just the low cost of adoption would seem to demonstrate a worthwhile cause. Moreover, concerns over the misuse of the democratization of publication appear to be unsubstantiated, since so far employees seem sufficiently engaged not to abuse a network which has meaningful value for them.

D) INTRAWEST PLACEMAKING: FINDING A BALANCE BETWEEN THE SOCIAL AND BUSINESS AGENDAS[4]

Intrawest Placemaking is a real estate development company. In 2006, it became one of the earliest adopters of technology to drive internal collaboration and was adopted as a case study in Andrew McAfee's early book on E2.0 [see *Enterprise 2.0: New Collaborative Tools ...*]. Intrawest Placemaking adopted software from ThoughtFarmer which enabled every employee to be his or her own author on a wiki-style space named 'The Portal'.

The first major impact of 'The Portal' was to build the social personas of employees. In a similar approach to BT, a 'Place' functionality was set up to allow anyone to construct a profile. Each edit made to a wiki would

---

4   ThoughtFarmer case study.

link directly back to the employee's page. What Intrawest Placemaking found was that employees uploaded photos and amusing stories as well as documents and links. Humour and personality thereby became major contributors to developing trust and cohesiveness across the geographically dispersed workforce. This, in turn, boosted the recruitment and retention of 'Generation Y' workers who tend to expect a high level of social interaction through technology.

A key driver of participation in 'The Portal' has been its systemic aspect. Rather than acting as an optional storage space for information, it is a necessary tool for work. New ideas surface online as often as they do in meetings. And the authoring function runs deeply through core activities: the real estate development process, for example, is entirely editable by any user. In one case, a deeply embedded practice was challenged by a project manager, whose suggestion to reconfigure a tiling process saved $500,000 on a $2 million contract. Ten months after implementation, 'The Portal' was experiencing 10 times the use of the previous intranet system.

In order to solidify online participation, behaviours associated with 'The Portal' have been grafted on to the firm's core values. Technology does not sit alongside company culture, but is rather the main facilitator of key behaviours such as risk taking, open sharing and team spirit. What is more, misuse has been non-existent. As with BT, postings may not be anonymous, such that the democratization of authorship is matched by the proliferation of accountability.

E) IDEO: USING TECHNOLOGY TO FACILITATE HOW PEOPLE ACTUALLY WANT TO WORK[5]

Another adopter of ThoughtFarmer technology has been the design consultancy IDEO. With over 500 employees across multiple offices, the aim was to use technology to drive collaboration. But IDEO was conscious that its core value was innovation, not efficiency, so it used ThoughtFarmer to develop 'The Tube', an online space for cooperation.

IDEO's key insight was to use technology to facilitate participation rather than to impose a set of tools based on hypothetical 'best practices'. The Tube contained a wide range of functionality – blogs, wikis and collaboration spaces – but was made incredibly intuitive and easy to use. And to bolster the sense that technology was accelerating what employees already did well – innovate

---

5   IDEO's own website; interview with CTO.

– IDEO decided to keep the Tube in a persistent beta-like state. The team trials new features and incorporates bug fixes every Thursday, so that the system always meets what workers demand of it. Therefore, the focus was on playing to key behaviours rather than imposing an alien technology solution. By doing this, IDEO noticed that employees wanted to showcase their work. It also realized that, when collaborating with colleagues, employees focused on passion, experience and expertise, not instrumental skills, so profiles were engineered towards connecting people based on these aspects. As a result, over 95% of employees now take voluntary ownership of their own page. Meanwhile, participation elsewhere has been immense: over 10,000 wiki pages were created within 14 months.

By putting culture first, IDEO has created a platform not only for facilitating excellent work but also for connecting people on a personal level. Wiki pages cover travel recommendations as well as presentation guidelines. Blogs are written around sustainability and wellness projects as well as company-specific issues. And IDEO has never felt the need to formally evaluate the Tube. It has integrated so fluidly within the company's existing practices that measuring its financial utility would seem to miss the point.

F) BENNETT JONES: STREAMLINING INFORMATION FOR FASTER CLIENT SERVICE[6]

Bennett Jones is a Canadian law firm with around 1,000 employees based in six offices. The company's ambition was to create an online platform which harnessed technology in a more effective way than the legacy systems previously in place. Client service was inefficient because legal documents existed as static HTML pages on an unintuitive intranet.

The solution was to reorganize the library of legal precedents and research documents. A faceted search system was introduced so that each document could be associated with multiple classifications. Accessing key information became a straightforward process of 'online shopping'. As a result, the intranet – named 'BenNet' – was transformed into a mission-critical tool rather than an unintuitive archive of information. Streamlining day-to-day processes reduced overlapping work, facilitating faster client delivery. To further drive collaboration, BenNet was set up with functionality for employees to declare their skills and availability to work. In addition, offices were given unique

---

6   V51 case study and news; Bennett Jones announcement; Information Week.

profiles with organization charts and details of their location, boardroom facilities and other useful pieces of information.

Interestingly, unlike a number of other cases, Bennett Jones used technology purely to concentrate on work functions. The development of social personas, for example, was not put at the centre of the project. Bennett Jones managed to achieve high levels of online participation simply by putting core intranet functions at the heart of daily processes. Whatever the focus, the implementation has been tremendously successful: BenNet came first overall in the 2010 Intranet Innovation Awards and was recognized as one of the top 10 intranets of the year by Nielson Norman Group.

G) HCL TECHNOLOGIES: PUTTING THE EMPLOYEE FIRST TO DRIVE ENGAGEMENT, RETENTION AND PROFIT[7]

HCL Technologies is a global IT services company based in India. It operates across 26 countries and its revenues exceed $2 billion. Under the leadership of Vineet Nayar, HCL was realigned in 2005 along a philosophy of 'Employees First, Customers Second' (EFCS). The idea was to generate better performance for clients and a more satisfied workforce by turning conventional wisdom upside down. Instead of focusing on the demands of clients, Nayar prioritized the engagement of his employees.

Like other forward-thinking companies, HCL Technologies has used online tools to engender communication across the organization. A 'Smart Service Desk' addresses employees' queries, receiving over 30,000 tickets each month. A portal named 'i4excel' shares manager evaluations transparently with workers and a 'U&I' platform enables employees to put questions to the CEO, 90% of which Nayar answers himself.

However, HCL Technologies' approach goes much further. U&I has begun to work in reverse. In the 'My Problems' section, Nayar asked his own workforce for opinions on puzzles he was unable to crack himself. After receiving a wave of responses, he decided to engage in a continued dialogue with his employees over key issues. Now the leadership team posts policy initiatives online to elicit feedback. This mechanism works alongside other schemes which put power in the hands of employees. Weekly polls are conducted, with the results posted on the intranet. Meanwhile, 'Employee First Councils' help staff to design their

7   Slideshare presentation; Nayar's book.

own events around areas of common interest. In one year, over 1,500 such events were organized.

The case of HCL Technologies shows that technology really can be used to turn the hierarchy upside down in a global organization. The trick to achieving buy-in has been to lead from the front. Nayar was the first to post his own performance review online (practicality unheard of in western corporate cultures) , which quickly led to senior managers following suit. He eschews golf fixtures with clients in favour of putting in dedicated hours each week for internal communication.

As a result, Nayar demonstrates that the role of the CEO can be radically recast with E2.0. HCL Technologies' competitive advantage is linked to its culture and the technology that underpins it, rather than being grafted onto one particular CEO. The benefits of this philosophy are certainly paying off. Since the introduction of EFCS, the company has enjoyed a more engaged and loyal workforce, a lower attrition rate and ultimately a higher revenue per employee.

H) IBM: EMBRACING MASS DEMOCRATIZATION IN A LARGE-SCALE CORPORATE ENVIRONMENT[8]

IBM is a formidable enterprise. With revenues of $100 billion, 425,000 employees and one of the strongest corporate brands around, it wouldn't be unreasonable to expect the IT company to play on the conservative side. Yet IBM is responsible for some of the most innovative projects in business today. Despite the company's size, it has not been afraid to devolve responsibility and control right through the organization.

In the first place, technology has been used to drive a thoroughly decentralized approach to the brand. IBM has rejected the use of social media tools to reinforce the corporate identity through different channels, preferring to leave employees to construct the firm's culture. There is no corporate blog or Twitter ID; instead, there is simply a mass of internal social networks which acts as an aggregate of the internal culture. Thousands of employees have their own spaces on 'Blue Twit', which mimics Twitter. Over 50,000 IBM staff are on 'SocialBlue', a platform which acts like Facebook. And around 20,000 internal blogs are in use, whilst the internal wiki receives over a million views a day.

---

8   www.socialmediaexaminer.com; www.brandtechnews.net (accessed 2013).

The mass participation in social networks has enabled IBM to leverage its employees' ideas to extraordinary effect. Since 2003, the company has held 'jams' – collaborative sessions designed to encourage spontaneous innovation by crowdsourcing the combined talent of the workforce. Over the years, these events have given rise to a range of major ventures. One such example has been the 'Smarter Planet', which turns IBM's collective brainpower to issues as diverse as urban traffic and disaster response. These initiatives are successful because they are taken seriously. Jam projects are given millions of dollars in funding, while collaboration in general is allowed to proceed unrestrained from above. There are social media guidelines – but the employees write them.

The case of IBM proves that even the largest companies can benefit enormously from using technology to facilitate innovative forms of collaboration that go beyond traditional hierarchies. The lesson is that devolving power from the centre can have surprisingly positive effects – not only for the engagement of employees, but also for profit-generating ideas and the strength of a corporate brand.

I) LINUX: DRIVING INNOVATION BY USING DEEP COLLABORATION FROM THE OUTSET[9]

Linux is a computer operating system just like Microsoft Windows or Mac OS. But it has one crucial difference: it is entirely built on free and open source software. What this means is that anyone can edit the source code. Rather than waiting for updates to fix bugs or add features, Linux users are capable of editing their operating system whenever, and however, they like.

When Linux was conceived in 1992, it was way ahead of its time. Online collaboration has not been brought in to foster collaboration; instead, it lies at the very core of what makes the operating system distinctive. Moreover, the approach of Linux represents a break from more conventional uses of social technology. In many cases, organizations crowdsource their employees or customers to canvas multiple views, but the open source design of Linux does more than just democratize the input of ideas; it proliferates the benefits too. Every user can experience the return from his or her contribution. So ideas cannot simply dissipate out of the organization as they travel up towards leadership teams. In other words, Linux doesn't turn the hierarchy upside down – it removes it entirely.

---

9   Wikipedia; www.opensource.com (accessed 2013).

The culture of collaboration in Linux demonstrates some surprising insights. Users participate and give their time voluntarily. They are driven by the simple desire to make something work better (see the book *Drive* by Daniel Pink). Moreover, a strong community has developed around this idea. Local associations called 'Linux User Groups' hold meetings to discuss how Linux can function best for them. Similar networks exist online.

This bold approach has achieved impressive results. Linux is frequently favoured for server operation and powers the world's 10 fastest supercomputers. It has enjoyed widespread adoption by both personal and business users. And as software is increasingly rolled out with specific Linux capabilities, it seems that adoption rates will only increase as time goes on.

J) NEIGHBORLAND: HARNESSING CIVIC COMMUNITY FOR SOCIAL CHANGE[10]

Not all uses of technology have been focused on business. Neighborland is a crowdsourcing platform focused on improving urban environments. Currently in the alpha (early) development stage since June 2011, Neighborland is based on changing the face of New Orleans. It provides a platform for citizens to contribute their ideas on the businesses and services they want to see come about.

Neighborland enables users to post up their ideas freely with minimum fuss: 'I want the ability to recycle glass in New Orleans' or 'I want to recycle Food in Seventh Ward'. Others are able to rally around the idea by signalling their approval and commenting with their own thoughts. As with Linux, every participant is also a potential beneficiary. Based on initial buy-in, this seems to be an idea that people are willing to collaborate around. There is an explicitly social focus – Neighborland is free for users and free for cities. The success metric is simply the number of new sustainable businesses opened with the support of the site.

The process has been facilitated by 'hackathons', which are a little like IBM jams on a much smaller scale. Users come together in a physical space to contribute their ideas and the best are taken forward for implementation. There aren't millions of dollars to put behind the initiatives and designing

---

10   www.opensource.com; neighbourhood website (accessed 2013).

long-term projects is demanding, but that hasn't stopped the development of a vibrant and engaged community.

Neighborland is working closely with city leaders in New Orleans to turn visions into reality and is currently launching nationally to expand its influence. Securing angel investment is a key challenge, but the more a sense of civic community builds around the idea, the more it seems possible to generate meaningful change for a better living space.

K) OPEN SOURCE RELIGION: A DIFFERENT DIRECTION FOR COLLABORATION[11]

In addition to social change, online collaboration has been used in another, radically different sense. Building on the success of Linux, the idea of an 'open source religion' has appeared. The ambition is to construct a religion with a belief system that genuinely reflects the views of its adherents by bringing them into the conversation through democratized dialogue.

One such example is 'Yoism', which identifies itself as 'the world's first open source religion'. Yoism seeks to move beyond dogmatic religiosity by aggregating the experience and views of its members towards a more sustainable and fluid notion of 'Truth'. Adherents of Yoism collaborate online through discussion groups and Facebook pages. Their ambition is to continually build and refine 'The Book of Yo', which is available online for anyone to edit.

A similar endeavour has been undertaken by www.opensourcereligion. net, which enables any member to submit edits to a 'source code'. As a wiki-based platform, the source code encourages public deliberation and can be easily interfaced with similar tools such as Wikipedia to quickly build and organize a pool of articles. Furthermore, users will be able to subscribe openly to 'belief modules' in the source code.

It is a little unclear what the future of open source religions is. They encounter the obvious difficulty of having to decide whether everything is up for negotiation or whether a certain core remains intact with just those beliefs at the margins being re-evaluated Nevertheless, open source religion demonstrates the prevalence of online collaboration and the diverse ends to which it can be used.

---

11 Wikipedia; yoism site; www.opensourcereligion.net (accessed 2013).

15

Objections to Employee Engagement

There are objections to the concept of employee engagement which readers should be familiar with in order to both explore their own objections and to present a response to inform debate.

'It's an Expedient Method of Manipulating the Workforce'

The argument runs that bosses encourage 'discretionary effort' and bottom-up ideas using the kind of interventions described earlier which have the appearance of offering greater freedom of thought and decision making for the period of the exercise, but in reality are just another way to squeeze more discretionary effort from people at work.

We are at the beginning of the employee engagement movement and without apology we should use whatever wiles are available to show that the right kind of engagement interventions and behaviours create value for the institution and are enjoyed by participants.

Expediency has its place and the beginning of a movement is one such. We should highlight the selfish agenda for bosses who take the plunge because they will benefit and, having done so, are likely to reflect on how an experiment can become a way of working that is good for the business and good for employees.

A worse indictment of bosses lies at the feet of those that plough on with command and control as the template for leadership when they know there is the alternative of engagement which is now proven to deliver better, faster results than traditional top down strategy and change.

'Nothing New in It and It's All Common Sense Anyway'

I agree with those who express the sentiment that 'nothing is new'; however, what is new is the disintegration of the old workplace contract in which loyalty was traded by individuals for security with their employer. In the emerging workplace, there is no security and, in exchange, people demand flexibility, personal development and access to decision making. It's also common sense in that good managers and leaders should exercise leadership marked by courtesy, generosity of spirit and respect. But some managers are not blessed with natural courtesy and respect, and the imprint of command and control has been so strong that it has become their normal leadership mode.

The development of the engagement capability and skills (see Chapter 11) we have identified and validated across UK plc are a route to creating a workplace which is characterized by courtesy, generosity of spirit and respect. This is especially so in tough times when managers think they have no alternative to bullying their way to achieving performance. They need to be given, confronted even, with the choice and the skills to engage rather to coerce.

This is a valid role for HR and learning and development professionals but it will only be possible for them to act if top leadership provides a conscious role model.

What is new is the convergence of social movements on the national stage and on the corporate stage with citizens and employees demanding more say. This convergence is new and it may be enough to break the hold of authoritarian command and control styles of leadership in organizations in favour of more inclusive styles of leadership, management and supervision.

'Celebrity Companies Like Google and Facebook are Not Necessarily Role Models of Engagement'

Some iconic companies are great models of engagement, while others are not. Typically, though, the more authoritarian will be poor around strategy engagement, but considerably more open around innovation, where much greater discretion for disruption is encouraged. Most institutional environments are a mixture of authoritarian and liberal. And as I have said elsewhere, effective engagement can only take place within a context of strong leadership.

It's a question of striking the right balance. What is certain is that the pure top-down, command and control models of leadership will become less and less effective in creating a compelling place to work as more organizations model their decision making on more inclusive approaches. Equally, laissez-faire 'free-for-all' models of leadership will fail without strong leadership.

'Employee Engagement is Just Turbo-Charged Communication'

It should be recalled from Chapter 13 that the traditional role of communication under command and control is to present and report to the many on the decisions taken by the few. In this mode, corporate communication is the conduit of the 'state', however many feedback loops there are. This mode of internal communication is in direct conflict with the purpose of employee engagement which is about engaging people in influencing decisions that they are affected by and which they can affect.

New media does not change this either unless there is also an appetite to create a fundamental change to the leadership role model.

Yes it is the case that old style communication is being relabelled as engagement when the dynamic remains that of persuasion and coercion rather than inclusion. The critical test of communication is whether it is simply acting as the radio station of a powerful few rather than setting the stage for broader inclusion (see Chapter 13).

'Some Business Sectors Simply Can't Adopt It'

Up to a point, I agree that some sectors are constrained by essential rules than others. The demands of safety and regulation rightly remove room for discretion and inconsistency by individuals. Room for discretion is constrained in regulated sectors, in sectors where consistency of process, procedures and manufacture are essential, and sectors where tightly defined brand experiences govern appearance and behaviour. But care needs to be taken to prevent safety and regulation becoming an excuse to maintain absolute control.

The issue is that in these environments, there is sometimes a tendency for the instinct to control to infect every process in the business where some discretion could actually deliver more value. Thus, whilst a rail company will have a lot of inviolable practices and policies, when it comes to service and the customer journey, the staff have a terrific opportunity to contribute not just in the day-to-day delivery but also in refreshing the service proposition.

The role of leadership is to give strong leadership by clearly identifying which aspects of the business must be in compliance and which can be managed with more discretion provided to staff to create a safe operation as well as an attractive customer experience. I refer readers back to the peach analogy in Chapter 6 in which the stone represents the non-negotiable or givens decided by leadership, whilst the flesh represents the areas of operations or strategy which are open to challenge and contribution by others. Every business will have aspects of its operations which are inviolable. My advice is to methodologically go through the exercise of articulating which are inviolable (and why) and which are not. As a blanket objection, to assert that a sector is not able to adopt employee engagement is simply lazy thinking.

'Surely It's Mostly Driven by Personality?'

The personality of the CEO or change management sponsor will be key. Certainly a functional head who believes that they can 'do engagement' without the active sponsorship and visible leadership of the boss will be disappointed. The insight is to understand the personality profiles of potential sponsors with operational and strategic responsibilities and approach those who show a strong appetite for risk in terms of involving employees.

However, personality alone is not enough. One of my clients who had all the necessary personality traits simply did not realize that there were alternatives to devising and executing strategy top down. Given access to approaches to employee engagement, he understood that he had rational choices to make. He chose the perfect combination of a bottom-up approach to strategy governed by a framework of strong leadership.

'It's OK in Relatively Small Businesses But is Impractical in Large Ones'

Engagement can be tougher in large businesses, but there are some great examples out there, so anything is possible. Some huge companies are run every day according to the principles and practices of employee engagement.

The key response to this objection is to work out what the centre needs to do, perhaps in terms of desired objectives and the creation of a framework that ensures consistency, and what the businesses need to do in order to execute and signal back progress. Xstrata, the global miner, under Mick Davies was an exemplar.

Size is not a barrier – it just needs thought around sensible governance and trust.

'Why Would a CEO Bother When They Only Have Limited Tenure?'

A CEO will bother if he or she can see that an intervention will give him or her better performance. He or she will also bother if he or she knows that the company has a sufficient mandate for a turnaround because shareholder expectations have been set to expect that the engagement route will deliver sustainable results.

Internal advisors to the C suite often ask me how to raise the topic of engagement. A conversation about what legacy they would like to leave is the best route in – it makes the topic personal rather than transactional.

'Our Measures Tell Us That Our People are Engaged Already, So Why Do All This Stuff?'

I have touched upon this question earlier. There are two reasons to doubt internal measures of being engaged. The first is that many surveys don't actually measure engagement; most measure satisfaction with a twist. Lots of employees are satisfied as a spectator evaluating benefits, but they can also be simultaneously, very disengaged from the purpose of the business. The second is that many employees have little to compare their company with, especially if they have been there a while – I referred earlier to North Korea syndrome, in which the people know nothing else, so cannot rate their situation even if they were asked to do so.

This diagram in Figure 15.1 is drawn from our UK-wide research into the links between engagement and performance. In it, the vertical axis is a measure of satisfaction, while the horizontal axis is a measure of engagement.

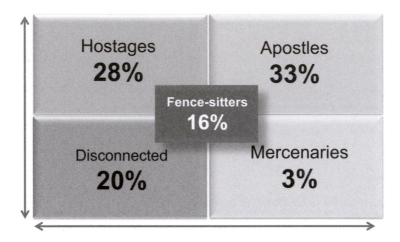

Figure 15.1   A breakdown of statistics on levels of engagement in the UK workforce

It says that just 33% of UK workers are engaged and are 'apostles' for the company. A total of 20% are disconnected and 28% are 'hostages' who are very satisfied but completely disengaged. Thus, in a company where there are enviable perks of the job, people may be very satisfied with their transactional relationship with the firm, but disengaged in its purpose and mission.

It would be instructive for readers to review what their research is really telling them. Satisfied workers who are disengaged are of little benefit to the firm and will probably be pretty disaffected and unhappy with their work.

16

Epilogue: Employee Engagement – Social Movement or Fleeting Fad?

This concluding chapter covers:

1. Employee engagement – social movement or fleeting fad?

2. Timing in life is everything.

3. Authoritarian or democratic capitalism?

4. Fair or unfair trade?

5. Values will become a standard measure of commercial and cultural performance.

6. Looking ahead – lighter, leaner organizations.

1) Employee Engagement – Social Movement or Fleeting Fad?

This book was researched and written between 2009 and 2013 in a world beset by economic woes, flights to democracy and the parallel rise of authoritarian capitalism in Russia, parts of the former Eastern Europe, Venezuela and of course China. Yet, despite very tough economic times, authentic employee engagement seems to be on the rise. Witness the publication in late 2012 of the UK government's second report (Engage for Success; Nailing the Evidence, David MacLeod & Nita Clarke 1012 www.engageforsuccess.org) on employee engagement, which shines a light on hundreds of excellent examples of employee engagement providing commercial and cultural value.

If the employee engagement movement is to gain traction, it must amount to more than a newish box of management tricks. It must have momentum as a social process in which people at work are invited to challenge and contribute for their own benefit and for the benefit of their organization.

There have been many false starts for employee engagement, the most recent being the so-called empowerment movement in the 1990s, which had similar rhetoric but was steamrollered by command and control. Earlier still, in the post-war years, the employee engagement movement did not take hold, despite the best efforts of Peter Drucker and other advocates at the time. Recall too the fervent anti-communist period in the 1950s and 1960s, especially in the USA, which, as the power house of the Western economy, was not then in a liberal state of mind.

The post-war period thus witnessed the rise of command and control as capital's way of harnessing the labour of people, an arrangement which workers were pretty happy with at the time following years of hunger and suffering. But in the years that followed the Second World War, nation states in the West gradually devolved responsibility for manufacture, production, infrastructure and transportation to the private sector via privatization, whereas in the communist diaspora, the state held on to power over production (etc.) until the momentous Gorbachev years.

In so doing the state also handed over responsibility to private enterprise for the nature of work. The straight jacket of state-inspired approaches to managing people gave way to innovation in managerial thinking.

Employee engagement is a further innovation in managerial and leadership thinking.

2) Timing in Life is Everything

It may be that the employee engagement movement is gaining traction now because people at work need to fill the vacuum left by the disappearance of the 'loyalty for security' contract which was the trade that command and control paid for employees' compliance. The security side of the deal of the 'loyalty for security' has all but lapsed and loyalty has, not surprisingly, waned. This is not universal. Family firms and some other enterprises have endeavoured to hold on to a collective security for loyalty deal. For the majority, though, work means people cutting their own deals and making choices about the values and cultures they want to work in. In tough times, many cannot do this, but smart employers know that soon enough people will be able to choose workplace cultures that will enable them to develop portable capabilities and a strong sense of personal responsibility.

The new relationship between employee and employer is transactional and one of the key transactions is the inclusion of employees in more of the decision-making process. The relationship is also structured more on the basis of adult to adult, rather than parent to child, with mutual respect as a cornerstone of modern organizational values.

Where authentic employee engagement sticks, it could also become a role model for turning old dictatorships into democratic regimes with democratic and mutual capitalism. If people experience it at work, perhaps they will see it on the bigger stage of the state.

3) Authoritarian or Democratic Capitalism?

Who knows whether these contrasting models will live side-by-side or whether one will grow to transcend the other? Democratic capitalism has had a long run, but is under fire for its failures in financial markets and other tests such as the viability of the euro. The rhetoric about the alleged benefits of a strong state is on the rise. Russia is eager to form an Eastern EU bloc and China is gradually weaving its economic tentacles into Africa and elsewhere. But as the Chinese middle classes emerge, will they start to view economic freedom as just the start? Once their garages, wardrobes and fridges are full, will they demand political freedom too? At the time of writing, this appeared to be the case. In South America, Venezuela seems to be trying to emulate old Cuba just as new Cuba may be emerging from its captivity under an authoritarian regime. South America is a continent to watch. It has tipped from Ealing comedy-style dictators to democracies and back again.

Multinational corporations have played a vital role as the ambassadors of democratic traditions and have a huge part to play in ensuring that democratic capitalism holds its place against autocratic capitalism. The danger is that giant corporations characterized by authoritarian capitalism will overshadow the democratic capitalist model. There is much at stake.

4) Fair or Unfair Trade?

The battlelines are also being drawn up between the interests of capital and labour, with daily reports of corporations putting the screws on suppliers and employees alike. Whether it is supermarket chains driving down their margins at the expense of farmers or Western and Eastern brands exploiting labourers who have no choice but to accept what they are given, exploitation has gone global. In contrast, there is the rise of mutuality between communities and corporations, with corporations competing to be partner of choice with their supply chains.

As employees become more critical of the values and ethics of their employer, policies of mutuality make sense if employers want to keep the best people. Some corporations will calculate that they only need to do this where employees have choices about where they work, whereas others will see it as part of their spirit of enterprise and their brand promise. In turn, corporations that conduct external relationships on the basis of mutuality will soon be under pressure to apply the same within. Of these, some will point to generous conditions which are important of course, but employees want to share more than money – they want a share of the decision making.

5) Values Will Become a Standard Measure of Commercial and Cultural Performance

Employee and external stakeholder engagement is and will become an integrated activity with one approach to many relationships. Internal and external relationships are conflating, not least due to digital technology. That means that organizational values, once considered to be an internal affair, are the yardstick by which all stakeholders are increasingly evaluating organizations. Too often today, values are still a charter for compartmentalizing internal and external relationships.

An integrated approach has implications for where the accountability lies for stakeholder engagement. Presently the often unseemly catfight between functions seems to exacerbate stakeholder silos along internal structural lines.

Better organizations see and manage internal and external relationships as two sides of the same coin.

MINI CASE STUDY: CEO OF WESTMINSTER COUNCIL IN LONDON – 'OWN THE WHOLE STREET'

As Mike More, CEO of London's Westminister council, said,

> it's hard turning around a culture of command and control that has persisted for a long time, and especially so when cuts have to be made in spending to square the books. And more especially so when residents within the 8.5 square-mile enclave rate services as already being very good. The shift has meant the need for "elective collaboration" rather than top-down collaboration.

> Elective collaboration is aimed at getting our people to see whole streets as their responsibility. It used to be the case that they would view their responsibility only through the lens of their own job (thrash or bin emptying for example). Now they see themselves as part of a wider team taking responsibility for the streets of London as a joined up experience for citizens and visitors alike. We call it elective collaboration which has required a similar change to the way we behave and engage internally between teams.

6) Looking Ahead – Lighter, Leaner Organizations

Power relationships between employees and their employers are changing fast. The deal under command and control required the employee to cede most power to the employer in exchange for some desirable benefits of an instrumental and social nature.

EMPLOYEES BECOME 'MEMBERS'

The new model deal (between employer and employee) recognizes a greater mutuality of power in which the employer gives much more say to its 'members' in the governance of the organization. In new model institutions, there is little rhetoric about familial care which was so familiar to values statements of the loyalty for security deal. That was the language of the parent-to-child relationship between employer and employee. The new deal is struck through negotiations about instrumental conditions and more particularly through the members' licence to influence. A greater say at work also requires employees to take responsibility for the licence they take. It requires generosity and discipline by both employer and employee. The generosity of leaders lies in sharing the power, while the generosity of employees lies in engaging themselves and in challenging and contributing.

Managerial discipline is required by leaders in governing a more inclusive relationship. Hierarchies may increasingly be confined to controlling the infrastructure of the organization, with less influence over the intellectual and emotional relationship with employees as the latter become more self-organizing.

Near where I live on the southern coast of Great Britain, there is an interesting example of self-organization in the workplace. Natures Way Foods packs salad in convenient bags for many of the UK's supermarket chains, including Morrisons, Tesco and Waitrose. Spread across three plants, about 1,000 employees work shifts in temperatures down to 5°C. It's a dynamic environment in which orders might arrive in the morning for collection within hours. The product needs to be shipped into the plants, sorted onto different product lines, bagged and shipped at the right time. Obviously, speed and quality assurance is of the essence. The employees are comprised of many national cultures and English is the main form of communication, but for many it is their second or third language. Most can speak enough to get by, but fewer can read fluently. Thus, essential standard operating procedures and inter-team negotiation are conveyed and conducted through self-organizing shop-floor negotiations. The key to self-organization according to the employees of Natures Way Foods is camaraderie and trust between teams that are also competing for time and resources.

LEANER AND LIGHTER PROCESSES OF SOCIAL CONTROL

This line of thought may also suggest that organizations will need fewer internal processes to manage relationships with their members as the latter become more self-organizing. This would mean a considerable shrinkage in managerial functions whose remit is underwritten by the assumption that large numbers of people need complex levels of social control.

And finally:

I have argued that engagement takes place both via organizational initiatives such as participative interventions that enfranchise many in strategy and change, normally the preserve of elites, and via the behaviour of leaders, managers, supervisors. I have not given air time to 'engagement programmes' as I believe that few add any value if participants are not working on real challenges and opportunities facing the organization. I have put the focus on interventions that are designed to solve strategic and operational challenges with widespread participation and on the day-to-day inclusion of employees by bosses that have equipped themselves to become more guide than god. If you are investing in driving performance through engagement I recommend that the focus should be on 'real work' interventions and capability that distributes decision making to those that can add value, rather than on adjacent engagement programmes.

Looking ahead to a possible next work I am reading as deeply as I can into the science behind what enables people to shift from incremental thinking to breakthrough thinking. Chapter 9 in this book starts to address this topic but I believe that as we learn more from neuroscience we will be able to make big leaps in the design of interventions and in the capability of managers, leaders and supervisors and thus in organizational and individual performance.

References

Arbinger Institute, *Leadership and Self Deception*. 2000. Beret Koehler.

Briggs, Asa, *A Social History of England*, 3rd edn. 1994. Weidenfeld & Nicolson.

Carter, Elizabeth, *The Good Food Guide 2013*. 2013. The Good Food Guide.

Cashman, Kevin, *Leadership from the Inside Out*. 2008. Cashman.

Donkin, Richard, *The History of Work*. 2010. Palgrave Macmillan.

Edelman, Gerald and Tonono, Giulio, *Consciousness*. Penguin.

Greenleaf, Robert and Spears, Larry, *Servant Leadership*. 2002. Paulist Press.

Harrison, Lawrence and Huntingdon, Samuel, *Culture Matters*. 2000. Basic Books.

Heifetz, Ronald, *Leadership without Easy Answers*. 2009. Belknap Press.

Hillman, James, *Kinds of Power*. 2012. Doubleday.

Jaworski, Joseph, *Synchronicity: The Inner Path of Leadership*. 2011. Berrett-Koehler.

Keller, Scott and Price, Colin, *Beyond Performance*. 2011. Wiley.

Kets de Vries, Manfred, *The Leader on the Couch*. 2006. Jossey-Bass.

MacLeod, David and Clarke, Nita, *Engaging for Success*. 2012. Department of Business, Innovation and Skills.

Marsh, Peter, *The New Industrial Revolution*. 2012. Yale University Press.

McAfee, Andrew, Enterprise 2.0: New collaborative tools.

McGregor, Douglas, *The Human Side of Enterprise*. 1960. McGraw Hill.

McIvor, Arthur, *A History of Work in Britain 1880–1950*. 2000. Palgrave Macmillan.

Miller, Peter, *Smart Swarm*. 2011. Collins.

Mlodinow, Leonard, *Subliminal*. 2013. Allen Lane.

Nayar Vineet, *Employees First, Customer Second*. 2010. Harvard Business Press.

Pennebaker, James, *The Secret Life of Pronouns: What Our Words Say About Us*. 2011. Bloomsbury.

Pfeffer, Jeffrey, *Power in Organizations*. 1981. Ballinger.

Pink, Daniel, *Drive*. 2011. Canongate Books.

Pinker, Steven, *How the Mind Works*. 1999. Penguin.

Schien, Edgar, *Organizational Culture and Leadership*. 2004. Jossey-Bass.

Selected Works of Robert Owen. 1930. William Pickering.

Shipman, Pat, *The Animal Connection*. 2011. W.W. Norton.

Surowiecki, James, *The Wisdom of Crowds*. 2005. Abacus.

Taylor, Frederick Winslow, *Taylorism, Principles of Scientific Management*. 1911. Dover Publications.

Wheatley, Margaret, *Leadership and the New Science*. 2012. Berrett-Koehler.

William Ouchi, *Theory Z: How American Management Can Meet the Japanese Challenge*. 1982. Avon.

Zak, Paul, *The Moral Molecule*. 2012. Bantam.

Index

accountability 37, 62, 86, 109, 251, 270
action 21, 25, 28, 32, 72, 97
Action for Recovery 141–4
adaptability 62
added value 34, 62, 76, 81, 86, 89, 93,
    118, 142
advisor 230, 236ff.
advocacy 23, 24, 28, 173, 177, 218, 220,
    230, 236ff
age 180
agreement 81, 93, 158, 178, 189, 201,
    207, 211, 212
airport operators 24, 87, 99, 129
alignment 2, 9, 12, 25, 75, 96, 97, 106,
    220, 228, 229, 232, 235
Alstom 250–51
alternatives 112, 202, 205, 210, 261, 264
ambassadors 64–5, 90, 96
Amsterdam 124, 126
anger 16
animals 109, 147
'apostles' 100, 266
appetite 24, 27, 46, 65, 133, 140, 194,
    230, 236, 263
    for risk 68, 69, 125, 264
appreciation 23
Arab Spring 1, 17, 244
arguments 58
arrogance 35, 136, 204
assigned groups 153–4
attitudes 49, 168, 169, 218, 239, 245,
    246

authenticity 205–6, 211, 221
authoritarianism 18, 19, 75, 110, 262,
    269, 270
awareness 28, 81, 82

BA 76–7
balance 201, 202, 227, 229, 232ff., 263
banks 17, 59
Barclays Bank 17
barriers 103, 107, 137, 157
Barron, Paul 44, 77, 78
BBC 61
behaviours 30, 41, 45, 64, 168, 192,
    209, 215, 218, 219, 221, 253, 254,
    261
    collaborative 147
    communicative 239
    of leaders 109–10, 198
    social 243, 251
beliefs 1, 23, 33, 45, 195, 208, 259
Bell, Bob 37, 38
benefits 20, 41, 119–20, 173, 174–9
Bennett Jones 254–5
bias 78
big companies 68, 179, 257, 264–5
'Big Difference' 96, 97
'big picture' 35, 231
'big-ticket' change 18, 23, 66
Bishoff, Sir W. 15
Blackberry 68
blockers 70, 103, 106–8
blogs 77–8, 144, 250ff., 256

blood 148, 149, 150, 158
board members 176, 177, 178, 192ff.
    see also executive team
body 26, 110, 148–9, 150, 158
Borrow, Build, Breakthrough method
    125, 144
bottom-up approach 46, 54–5, 99, 117,
    118, 141, 232ff.
    digital 251ff.
brain 148, 150
brainstorming 113, 149–50
brand 23, 30, 33, 42, 48–9, 54, 68, 97,
    168, 169, 195, 215–25
    advocacy 173, 220
    definition of 216–20
    experience 217ff.
    and inside-out process 223
    and markets 221–2
    memories 217, 218, 223
    promise 215, 220ff.
    and reputation 49
Brazil 3
breakthroughs 47, 51, 116, 122, 125,
    130, 143, 149ff., 156
Brompton Hospital 37–9
BT 251–2
bureaucracy 12, 17, 37
business case 1, 7, 35, 46, 58, 59, 95,
    252
business objectives 67
business purpose 23, 195
business scenarios 112–13ff.

Cadbury 60–63, 68
calendar 61, 251
call centre staff 129
candidates 49
capabilities 24, 27, 30, 41, 42, 47, 50,
    54, 62, 81, 97, 107, 125, 168, 169,
    171, 186, 194, 197ff., 238–9

and internal communication
    232–8
self-assessment test 210ff.
    see also competencies
capitalism 10, 11, 269–70
Carnegie, Andrew 10
cascading 32, 54, 64, 71, 74, 96, 118,
    220
catalysts 134
causes 15, 20ff., 185ff., 201
    three categories of 22–3
central planning 75
    see also command and control
CEO 7, 13, 31, 37, 38, 43, 44, 63, 64,
    136, 198, 241, 264, 265
    and forward plans 133
    online communication by 255–6
    persuasion of 58
    in role play 115, 116
    visibility of 78, 165
CEO, Chief Engagement Officer:
    Turning Hierarchy Upside
    Down to Drive Performance
    xiii, 2
challenge 9, 13, 14, 18, 23, 24, 26, 32,
    49, 64, 86, 92, 108, 110, 126, 127,
    200, 204, 234, 235
    readiness for 205
    space to 22, 149, 201–2
change 18, 20, 30ff., 39 , 54, 68, 96,
    108, 185, 235, 238
    cultural 45
    difficulty of 36, 64
charisma 24, 60, 118
Charlton, Bob 123, 124ff.
charm 37
Chartered Institute of Personnel and
    Development 20
chemical reactions 26
choices 13, 27, 32, 80, 109, 140, 154

Churchill, Winston 60
clarity 62, 67
Clarke, Nita xv, 15, 58, 267
clients 94, 96, 124
CMO 43
coaching 38, 135, 198, 231
coalitions 59
co-creation 8, 27, 28, 39, 55, 79, 83, 92
    and brand 220, 221, 222
coercion 2, 14, 16, 148, 232
collaboration 7, 11, 26, 32, 51, 94, 199,
        271
    in creative groups 147, 148
    digital 250, 252, 253ff., 257
    purposeful 62
colleagues 20, 31ff., 39, 64, 114ff., 134,
        142, 143, 232, 252, 254
command and control 1, 2, 9, 12, 13,
        14, 18, 36, 51, 73, 118, 140, 221,
        232, 245, 247, 261, 263, 268
    and operational leadership 43
    story of 58
    weakness of 75–6
    see also top-down approach
commitment 20, 177
communication 2, 54, 62, 63, 65, 125,
        142, 220, 235, 263
    concept of 88
    myth of 34
    and negotiation 228
    purpose of 228–9, 232
    see also internal communication
communicators 231, 233, 234, 236
    capabilities 238–9
communities 13, 22, 23, 60, 66, 140,
        195, 228, 242
    digital 250, 258, 259
    and workspace 72
companies 11, 12, 21, 24, 31, 35, 36,
        62ff., 68, 94, 95, 144, 162, 262
    and democracy 269–70

life-span of 221–2
    and mutuality 270
    and regulatory obstacles 263–4
    and social media 246
    size of 264–5
compassion 134
competences 189–90, 200–208, 210ff.
    assesment 214
competition 92, 113, 121, 139, 142,
        248, 249
    in creative groups 148, 153, 154
competitive advantage 173, 256
completer finishers 134
computers 257–8
    see also digital technology
conditions 24, 25, 41, 151, 202
conductors 157, 164
confidence 49, 55, 86, 90, 110, 111,
        116, 143, 202, 205, 206, 211, 224
connection 20, 21, 22, 58, 195, 254
conscious choices 80, 86
consensus 62
conservatism 64, 83, 137
consistency 22, 38, 44, 67, 95, 124, 139,
        142, 195, 216, 263, 265
constraints 263
consumer brands 219
consumers 10–11, 220, 224
content 8, 9, 71, 74, 75, 82, 83, 89, 101,
        104, 198, 244
    see also strategy
context 17, 20, 33, 51, 88, 162, 189,
        199, 200, 205, 206, 211, 218, 223,
        224, 239, 243
contract 137, 142
contribution 9, 13, 14, 23, 25, 64, 76,
        88, 92, 149
    clamour for 18
    increase of 20
control 9, 18, 109, 110, 217, 218, 219
conversations see discussions

conviction 134
convocations 60, 63
COO 43, 94, 96
costs 67, 94, 128, 252
courtesy 262
creativity 13, 24, 31, 34, 49, 93, 97,
        111ff., 202
    excessive 134
    and groups 147, 149
credibility 22, 35, 82, 120, 131, 195,
        231, 238
    -gap 214
crises 104, 141, 202, 229, 230
crowdsourcing 223, 257, 258
C-suite 21, 43, 46, 59, 231, 265
CTO 43
Cullinan, Rory 59, 134
cultural change 45
cultural leadership 41, 42, 44ff., 54
cultures 1, 16, 19, 24, 27, 62, 63, 94,
        185, 190, 215
    and digital technology 244–6, 250
current approach 19, 67, 71, 124, 265
    diagnosis of 78, 137
customer service 173
customers 22, 45, 67, 87, 90–91, 97,
        100, 128, 223, 224
    experience of 48, 49, 99
    and role play 116, 121

Davis, Mick 240
debate, clarity about 62
Deci, Edward 24
'decide and sell' 8, 9, 34, 57, 75, 76, 88,
        104, 151
'decide and tell' 8, 9, 34, 58–9, 75, 76,
        88, 104, 118
decision-making 8, 18, 22, 50, 83, 229,
        230
    circular 98, 99

and digital 245
everyday 23, 67, 181, 184, 194
four modes of 27
individuals and 80–82
involvement in 28, 66, 98
and research results 181
default approach 9, 46, 71, 72, 75, 88,
        138
defend or attack 68, 126
    teams 114, 122
deference 12, 19
delegation 111, 112, 198
delivery 38, 39, 82, 83, 89, 101, 202
    planning for 107
democracy 1, 12, 207, 228, 269
demographics 89–90, 122, 142, 230
design team 137, 138
despotism 18, 228
development 22, 23, 98, 185, 199, 208
devolved organization 240, 241
diagnostic exercises 78–9
dialogue 50, 51, 94, 99, 204, 231, 246,
        247
    online 255–6, 259
differences 204
difficulties 26, 204
digital technology 30, 42, 50–51, 93,
        112, 151, 159, 163, 168, 217, 220,
        228, 243–59, 270
    culture of 244–6, 248
    and decision-making 245, 248
    and dialogue 255–6, 259
    portals 252–3
    and social context 243–4, 247–8
directional leadership 41, 42, 43, 54
directors 32, 44, 81, 96, 106, 165
discernment 206–7, 211
discipline 1, 44, 63, 228, 272
discretion 15, 21, 129, 140, 215, 261,
        262, 263, 264

discussion 58, 95–6, 107
disengagement 35, 100, 164, 172, 180, 181, 189, 190, 200, 265, 266
disruption 43, 54–5, 108ff., 137
dissatisfaction 172, 176, 188
distance 72–3
distributed leadership 18, 19, 24, 27, 147, 194, 197–8, 199
diversity of opinion 148, 153, 154
DLA Piper 123–7, 139, 159
Donkin, Richard 11
drivers *see* causes
Drucker, Peter 2, 9, 13, 268
Dunne, Ronan 90
dynamics, creative 123, 149, 150, 152

E theory 7, 18, 19, 20
early adopters 20, 125, 165
Eastern European revolutions 1, 12, 17
EFCS 255, 256
efficiencies 32, 33, 54, 66, 67
ego 110
elites 1, 2, 31, 50, 54, 72, 74, 98, 106, 122, 151, 228, 233, 234
emotions 20, 21, 86, 220, 230, 250
empathy 121, 189, 201, 204, 205, 210, 212
employee engagement 1, 55
    approaches to 8–9
    definition of 15–16, 20, 21
    drivers of 15, 20–29
    myths about 2, 26, 33–7
    in research 7–8, 172–3ff., 179
employee engagement movement 1, 19, 261, 268
employees 1, 12, 13, 20, 34ff., 45, 59, 91ff., 105ff., 109, 141, 165, 179, 270
    active role of 28, 76
    and brand 48, 220, 223
    clusters of 89–90
    in customers' shoes 121
    and 'going extra mile' 174, 215
    and local workspace 72–3
    as members 271
    and new model 18ff.
    online dialogue 255
    online profiles 252
    and psychological barriers 107
    and problem relationship 29
    reluctant 164
    and role play 105–6, 116ff.
    and social media 244, 246
employer/employee relationship 12–13, 14, 18ff., 20, 141, 255, 269, 271
employers 1, 12, 13, 20, 23, 49, 125, 270
    and communication 229
    digital portals 253
    research results for 180–81
employment for life 11, 12
empowerment 12, 182, 185, 268
    movement 268
enablers, supporting 30, 41, 42, 47ff.
    primary 54, 168
    secondary 54, 168, 169
encouragement 13, 27, 41, 47, 50, 65, 82, 106, 139, 148, 165, 202, 227, 261
enfranchisement 109
Engage for Change xiii, 2, 93, 113, 124, 125, 131, 134, 149, 171ff.
Engage for Success (2012) 267
engagement 1, 41, 42ff., 66, 263, 267–8
    concept 2, 20, 21, 88
    by employers 180–81
    levels of 28–9, 266
    limited 132, 180
    measure of 265
        see also measurement

myths about 2
programmes 273
research results 172–3ff.
three dimensions of 21
Engaging for Success xv, 15, 58
enjoyment 24
Enterprise 2.0 (E2.0) 251, 252, 256
entertainment 131, 150, 152, 163, 235
entrepreneurs 63, 94
environment 20, 25, 136, 148, 151,
    160ff.
escalation 143
ethics 44, 49, 218, 241, 270
ethos 16, 17, 45, 241
Europe 94, 96, 97
evaluation 83
eventing 106, 150, 151
evidence 1, 15, 43, 47, 49, 58, 94, 123,
    173, 177, 186ff.
exam questions 162–3
execution 8, 9, 63, 71, 77, 83, 104, 119,
    120
executive team 22, 58–9, 63, 92, 93, 97,
    118–19, 120, 143
  and communication 233
  participation by 164–5
expectations 59, 92, 121, 136, 206, 230
expediency 261
experience 7, 9, 17, 31ff., 44, 45, 48, 49,
    55, 78, 112, 121, 152, 157
  of brands 217, 220ff.
  of leaders 205, 206
experimentation 202
experts 221
explanation 136, 141, 183, 200, 201,
    204, 206, 211
exploration 143, 149, 158, 162, 189,
    200, 202

Facebook 256, 259, 262

face-to-face scenarios 117, 118, 126,
    151, 217, 233, 244, 245
facilitators 62, 68, 69, 82, 96, 134, 151,
    158, 159, 165, 212, 236, 250ff.
failure 231
family firms 17, 269
fans 91
fashion retailer 91–3
fear 19, 33, 58, 109, 110, 215
feedback 25, 51, 64, 122, 142, 151, 214,
    229, 231, 247, 249, 250
fervour 63
fight or flight mode 148–9, 150, 156,
    157
Finance & Projects (F&P) 123, 124,
    125
financial services 120–21
first timer 132
flexibility 20
'flight plan' 156–7
follow through 131, 132
food sector 49
Ford, Henry 11
formality 62, 134
four-box model 79, 82, 83
framing 59–60, 61, 69, 95, 136
freedom 91
friendship 22, 244, 252
front-line staff 34
fun 119, 127
functions 15, 46, 50, 59, 70, 74, 79, 103,
    107, 152, 219, 220, 228, 246, 247,
    251ff.

Gas Natural 249–50
GDP 12
gender 172
generosity 22, 24, 262, 272
geography 89
Geraldine 31, 32–3

'givens' *see* non-negotiables
Globe Theatre, London 126
goals 16, 202, 245
    short-term 189, 202, 210
governance 31, 122, 207, 271
groups 7, 16, 35, 68, 88, 89–90
    behaviour 110
    digital 251
    exercises 69, 93, 123
    pre-assigned 153–4
    role play 113–14, 120
    self-organizing 33, 153, 154, 245
        membership of 154–5
    size of 143–4, 147, 151, 155–7ff.
    see also teams
growth 120–21
guidance 18, 47, 135, 208, 213
guidelines 136–7, 257

Harel, Didier 140–41, 144
Hart, Ben 51, 243
HCL Technologies 255–6
Heifetz, Ronald 43, 108, 109
hierarchy 1, 12, 19, 89, 91, 123, 245
        reversal of 33, 46, 111, 112–13,
        256
history 9ff., 45, 60, 71
hospitals 37–8
hostages 36, 100, 266
hotels 161
hot-house 112, 120–21, 157
HR Department 208–9, 219, 220, 232,
        251, 262
humour 61, 97, 109–10, 253

IBM 221, 256–7
ideas 34, 67, 71, 96, 97, 113, 119, 120,
        121, 125, 126, 143, 149
    breakthrough 149

and digital 244, 253, 258
    embedded 131
    exploring 202
identity 89, 112ff., 121, 156, 216, 217,
        223, 256
IDEO 253–4
Immelt, Jeff 43, 69, 108
implementation 234
improvement 20, 33, 173, 202
inclusion 8, 13, 27, 31, 39, 43, 44, 58,
        77, 79, 98, 109, 182ff.
incremental approach 2, 32, 68, 69, 79,
        100, 108, 111, 118, 137, 141, 149,
        155, 240
independence 37, 95, 202
    of spirit 148, 153, 154
individuals 2, 7, 16, 25, 59, 65, 77, 78,
        95, 138, 147, 195, 216, 217
    and decision-making 80–82
    dominant 71
    and group exercises 155
    judgement by 148, 153, 154
industrial organization 10, 11
inexperience 108
influence 16, 46, 105, 230
information 51, 136, 203–4, 247
    online 254
    sharing 203
    withholding of 35
initiative 11, 19
innovation 33, 37, 38, 66, 120, 121,
        232, 255, 256
insight 74, 82, 84, 87, 108, 148, 149,
        154, 200, 205, 206
instincts 45, 49, 86
institutions 33
    see also organizations
instruction 16, 18, 163, 183
integration 222, 231, 270

interactions 49, 81, 82, 118, 119, 217, 219, 249, 253
Intercontinental 49
internal communication 30, 42, 50, 97, 168, 169, 227–42, 263
  and capabilities 232–8ff.
  new model of 234–8
  purpose of 232
  top-down 227–9, 233, 234
Internet 159, 244, 245ff.
interventions 54, 62, 101, 123, 128–9, 150, 245
  design of 101, 103ff.
  occasional 245
  purpose of 101, 104
  stalling of 132–3
  types of 111–12ff.
  see also participative interventions
interviews 2, 172
intranets 246, 251, 253, 254, 255
Intrawest Placemaking 252–3
inversion 33, 46, 54–5, 112–13, 256
investment 174, 192, 194
invitation 31, 82, 88, 92, 124, 127, 207, 233, 234, 235
involvement 22, 23, 28, 76, 182–4, 255

jam projects 257
Japan 11, 19
job losses 55, 111, 134–5
job satisfaction 173, 176
judgements 7, 8, 16, 22, 28, 43, 61, 108, 148, 153, 154

Kang, Mo 73, 94
knowledge 90, 97, 114, 115, 125, 154, 198, 200
Kotter 95

labels 60–61

language 9, 272
large groups 147, 155, 156, 159, 245
law firms 111, 123–4, 254
Leadbetter, Charles 27
leaders 1, 2, 7, 57, 71, 81–2, 90, 95, 107, 109, 126, 138, 147, 192, 194–5
  capabilities of 22, 26, 27, 62, 108, 127, 197ff.
  and communication 231, 232, 234
  and digital 244, 251
  and emotional intelligence 22
  engagement by 189ff., 200–201
  helping for 41, 47, 197ff.
  myths about 33ff.
  and research results 189–90, 194
  and rhetoric 60
  see also capabilities
leadership 1, 24, 31, 90, 98, 108ff., 120, 168, 169, 171, 240
  capability interventions 62, 125
  competences 189–90, 200–208
  directional 41, 42, 43, 54
  new model of 18–19, 199
  operational 41, 42, 43, 54
  research results 173
  role model 22, 23, 28
  shift in 198–9
  strong 1, 16, 18, 92, 134, 205, 232, 233, 262, 263, 264
  visible 63–4
  see also cultural leadership; distributed leadership
league tables 137, 139
learning 51, 81, 154, 203, 232, 248
left-brained arguments 58
legacy 58, 69
legal documents 254
Leighton, Allan 87
LIFFE 110
light 160

line managers 186, 187, 190
'line of sight' 23, 38, 195
linear approach 9, 98, 222, 229
Linux 244, 257–8
listening 27, 73, 81, 204, 231
local leaders 23, 65
local needs 64
long-term approach 133
'loyalty for security' 2, 12, 13, 18, 35,
    268–9

McAfee, Andrew 252
McGregor, Douglas 11, 13, 18
McKinsey & Co. xiii, 7, 21, 70
MacLeod, David xvi, 15, 58, 267
management 2, 43, 65, 141, 143, 173
   and communication 230
   and job satisfaction 176
managers 135, 173, 176, 178, 186–7ff.,
    198, 251
Manchester Airport 24, 99–100
manipulation 261
marketing 219, 220, 221
markets 68, 111, 222
Marks & Spencer 75, 133
Mars 17
meaning 88, 206
measurement 21, 35, 36, 97, 122–3,
    137, 190–92, 209, 265
   digital 251
media reports 69–70
meetings 78, 106, 124ff., 139, 159,
    161ff., 245
   virtual 251
media 217, 228
memories 217, 218, 223
mergers 104, 110, 111, 249, 250
message boards 50, 227
message delivery 98, 229, 230
message impact 229

message reinforcement 229
messenger 230
metaphors 9, 60, 61, 206
Miller, Peter 147, 148
mind 149
mission 17, 38, 39, 49, 63, 218
mistakes 90, 100, 203
models 1, 2, 18–20, 21, 22, 89, 199
monitoring 192, 209
mood 88, 231
moral purpose 23, 61, 195
More, Mike 271
motivation 13, 16, 20, 21, 111, 173,
    175, 231, 248
motor racing 73
mutuality 10, 12, 37, 126, 215, 269,
    270, 271
MyPages 251–2
myths 2, 26, 33–7

National School of Government 20
nation-states 17–18, 268
NATS 44, 76–7
natural work teams 152, 154
Natures Way Foods 272
Nayar, Vineet 49, 255, 256
NEDs 165
negotiation 68, 81, 85–90ff., 93, 120,
    126, 158, 204, 272
   and communication 228
   online 244
Neighborland 258–9
net agree scores 172, 175, 178, 186
net promoter scores 28
net satisfaction scores 172, 176
networking 123
neuroscience 110, 149
new leaders 107, 109, 136
new model 12, 17, 18–20, 47, 197, 199,
    232, 234ff., 271

new organizations 45
New Orleans 258–9
news 51, 70, 142, 247
NHS 37, 38, 39, 77
Nokia 68
non-negotiables 82, 85, 86, 88, 92, 96,
        118, 120, 122, 143
North Korea 228, 265

objections 33, 83, 106, 107, 119, 136,
        261–6
online forums 249, 250
online gaming 249
online networks 244, 249ff.
open source software 244, 257–8
openness 19, 144, 203–5, 210, 212
operational refinement 66
opportunities 20, 96, 123, 128, 156,
        185, 186, 202, 203, 210, 231, 232,
        237, 246
    leaders and 108
    sharing 207
opposition 65
organizations 1, 9, 10, 16, 18ff., 23, 45,
        108, 150, 172, 195, 234–5, 270,
        271
    and brand 221
    culture of 133
    and job satisfaction scores 176
    relationship with 29, 72
others 24, 86, 92, 105, 109, 114, 149,
        199, 200, 204, 205, 207, 248
O2 90–91, 135
Ouchi, William 13, 19
outcomes 2, 8, 9, 15, 20, 21, 26, 27, 46,
        64, 122, 144, 152, 153, 162, 208
    as causes 20
    financial 32
    and communication 228, 233, 234

    parallel 67
    unintended 107
outsourcing 96, 97, 129
ownership 8, 9, 31, 34, 55, 59, 63, 88,
        107, 119, 222, 239, 254
    syndicating 137, 128
oxygen 148, 150, 158
oxytocin 26, 149

pace 201, 202, 210
pairs 69, 143, 156
parent-child relationship 14, 34, 75,
        136
Paris 124, 140
Parker, John 77
participation 19, 77, 164–5, 249, 251,
        253, 255, 258
participative interventions 30ff., 41,
        42, 46–7, 55, 103–4ff., 108, 273
    creative 105, 111ff., 147ff.
    stalling of 132–3
    sustainability of 131, 133ff.
    and value 137–40
passion 254
past practice 58, 71, 75, 82–3, 108
pause 25–6, 87
pay 49
peach metaphor 85, 88–9ff., 118, 122,
        143, 264
Pearce, Ian 241
people 1, 11, 12, 27, 33, 38, 43, 82, 89,
        100, 112, 195, 207
    and brand 220ff.
    self-engaging 23, 24, 47, 67
    self-organizing 15–16, 26
perceptions 176, 177, 193, 213, 214,
        220, 223, 247
performance 11, 20, 23, 58, 78, 109,
        111, 174

cultural 44
data 141
levels of 150
management 29
research results 176–8
performance reviews 139, 198
online 256
permission 19, 22, 62, 90
persona exercise 89–90
personal disruption 55
personal growth 23
personal interaction 81, 82
personal limits 26
personality 205, 218, 253, 264
persuasion 58
philosophy 31, 73, 240, 256
photos 250, 251, 253
Pink, Daniel 258
plan 55, 67, 68, 97, 125, 131, 132
portals 252–3
positive aggression 62
positive attitude 20
positive energy 149, 150
post-intervention period 132
post-merger teams 154
power, balance of 107
Powerpoint 32, 115, 119, 161
power-sharing 8, 24, 25, 37, 66, 81, 97,
    171, 173, 181–2, 189, 195, 201,
    207–8
Predator concept 113–14ff., 121
predictability 152
preferences 154
pressure 201, 202, 210
Pret a Manger 49
pride 25
primary levers 30, 41, 43–7
private equity firms 44, 45, 113, 165
private sector 11, 12, 21, 172, 179, 268

problematic relationship 29
process 20, 32, 38, 46, 55, 63, 66, 79,
    81, 82, 118, 133–4, 207, 228, 233
professional groups 35, 38, 39, 89,
    123ff.
profit 10, 11, 37, 39, 120
progress 126, 140
psychological blockers 106–8
psychology 59, 101, 109, 110
public sector 11, 12, 77, 174, 179, 188
purpose 16, 17, 23, 61, 75, 195

QBE 61, 73, 90, 94–8, 165, 223
questionnaire 172
questions 58, 162–3, 191, 200, 204
    online 255

radicals 92
random groups 153, 154
RAPIC 23
rational approach 11, 16, 21, 80, 82,
    86, 234
rationale 85, 86, 122, 136, 141, 233
RBS 59, 134–5
real work 122
Reback, Jerome 171
recognition 185, 186
recovery 59, 60
recruitment 199, 209, 253
reflection 148, 149, 156, 236
regulation 263, 264
relationships 12, 20, 23, 29, 72, 75, 77,
    199, 217
Relevance 124, 125
religions 60, 222
    open-source 259
renewal 61
reputation 17, 49
research 2, 21, 36, 58, 76, 171ff., 265

methodology 172
    summary 173, 194–5
resilience 20, 239
respect 23, 204, 205, 262
responsibility-taking 26
retail sector 49, 90, 118
retention 23, 59, 178, 253
Return on Experience (ROE) 251
reviews 139, 142
rewards 25, 28, 43, 202, 209, 241, 246,
    247ff.
rhetoric 60
ripeness 95
risk 20, 26, 31, 39, 109, 113, 132
    appetite 68, 69
risk aversion 12, 165
rituals 29, 45, 61, 63, 151, 168, 235
roadshows 77
role model 22, 23, 44, 65, 195, 198
role play 112–13ff.
Ronson, Gerald 144
Rose, Sir Stuart 75, 133
Ruby 31–2
Russia 267, 269

safe to challenge 19, 141, 149, 202, 248
safety 25, 135, 136, 202
SAM 32
satire 61, 109–10
satisfaction 35, 172, 173, 188, 265, 266
    see also net satisfaction scores
scenarios 111, 112ff., 150
scepticism 65, 125, 127
security 268–9
self-assessment test 210–14
self-definition 172
self-engagement 23–4, 47, 67, 150,
    172, 173ff.
self-organization 15, 16, 26, 33, 147,
    153, 154, 245, 272

'sell' mode 8, 9, 79
    see also 'decide and sell'
sell offs 59
Semmler, Ricardo 3
senior managers 178, 230, 256
    employee views of 188
    engagement scores 179
services 32, 33, 38, 57, 94, 100, 104,
    115ff., 121, 123, 128, 152, 162,
    173, 176, 217, 222, 223, 229, 254,
    258, 264, 271
shadow strategy 111
shared narrative 68, 81, 93, 99, 120,
    233
shared purpose 16, 17
shareholders 111
Sharepoint 112
sharing 88, 98, 145, 203, 204, 210, 239
    online 246, 251ff.
    see also power-sharing
shock 33, 132, 140
short-term approach 133
showboating 96
simulations 114
skills 18, 38, 41, 124, 195, 202, 231,
    234, 236, 238ff., 249, 254, 262
    leadership 30, 47, 197, 201, 208
        diagnostic test 47, 209, 214
    digital 251
small businesses 264
small groups 147, 151, 155, 156, 157,
    164
small spaces 71, 72
smart groups 148
'Smarter Planet' 257
Smythe, John xiii
SmytheDorwardLambert xiii, 80, 113
social case 1, 2, 4, 10
social context 17, 243–4
social control 272

social identity theory 156
social media 244, 245, 247
  see also social networking
social movements 1, 9, 12, 17–18, 244, 267–8
social networking 159, 244
  in-house 249–50ff., 256
social processes 199, 222
social psychology 110
social rewards 247, 248–9
South America 269
space 22, 161, 162, 201
spectators 33, 34, 35, 118, 150, 151, 164
speed 46, 76, 79, 84, 93, 110, 120, 124, 142, 157, 229, 241, 272
sponsor team 57–8, 60, 63–4, 92, 93, 134
  and blockages 106
  and delegation 112
  and narrative 68
  participation of 164–5
  and Strategy Safari 118–19
staff turnover 74
stairway diagram 247
stakeholders 22, 45, 216, 217, 219, 251
start-ups 17, 221
state 11–12, 17–18, 268, 269
status quo 20
Stitzer, Todd 60, 61ff.
store managers 91, 93
stories 58, 63, 68, 69, 81, 119, 120, 165, 205, 206, 215, 223, 225
  online 253
strangers' roles 105–6
strategy 1, 2, 3, 8, 30ff., 54, 125, 142ff.
  attack 68
  defensive 68
  disruptive 54–5
  implementation 222
  lack of 75

  see also content
Strategy Safari 32, 93, 112, 117–20, 127, 143, 159
streams 79, 91, 92, 233
strikes 11
success 69, 70, 117, 122, 229, 231
supermarkets 217, 218, 270, 272
supervision 23, 26
supervisors 71, 72, 165, 186, 198
support 22, 168, 169, 171, 198
surprise 97, 122
surveys 15, 17, 21, 24, 172ff., 265
  efficiency of 190
sustainability 107, 131–44, 254
symbols 63, 160
systems 38, 72, 121, 168, 169, 198, 215, 222, 253, 254
  and brand 218, 219

tactics 137
take-overs 110–11, 115
talent 178, 257
targets 39
Taylorism 11, 13
Team Size Escalation 143–4, 155–7
teams 11, 22, 59, 64, 73, 86, 90, 91, 92, 98, 99, 124ff., 138, 195, 206, 213, 223, 235
  and blockages 106, 107
    failure to deal with 108
  composition of 152, 158
  exercises 69
  natural or unusual 152
  online 249
  and 'peach' exercise 93
  relationship with 29
  and role play 114, 115, 116, 120, 121
  size of 158
  see also groups; sponsor team

technology 38, 43, 112, 158–9
    see also digital technology
TED 27
television 249
'tell or sell' mode 8, 27, 79
terminology 59
tests 24, 122–3
texting 159
theories 11, 13, 18, 19
'thinking outside the box' 62, 92
time 2, 34, 44, 61, 69, 119, 133, 137,
        142, 151, 221
    framing 59, 133
    limits 132
    management 156
tools 21, 29, 47, 60, 74, 197, 249ff., 253,
        255
top-down approach 1, 2, 9, 12, 18, 33,
        34, 43, 44, 54, 57, 123, 144, 150,
        151
    and brand 221, 222
    and internal communication
        227–9, 233, 234, 235
Total UK 59, 136, 139–41, 202
'touch-points' 217–18, 223
Towers Watson 21
trade unions 11, 78, 106, 230, 242
training 96, 185, 235
transactions 47, 75, 110, 157, 246, 265,
        266, 269
transformation 62, 63, 66, 79, 86, 91,
        92, 104, 120, 121
transparency 22, 31, 50, 134, 135, 136,
        142, 195, 229, 242
trial and error 63–4, 113, 149, 242
trust 11, 19, 22, 31, 35, 91, 135, 136,
        148, 149, 150, 195, 231, 242
truth 110, 259
turbulence, creative 96, 111, 132, 153,
        252
Twitter 159

UK xv, 2, 7, 9–10, 11, 12, 14, 49, 61,
        109, 140, 172, 266
uncertainty 135, 137
unconscious mind 110
understanding 28, 82, 127, 185, 198,
        205, 206, 220
universality 36
USA 2, 10, 11, 63, 95, 268

values 11, 17, 23, 44, 45, 49, 165, 185,
        195, 218, 229, 241, 253, 270
Velvet Revolution 1, 9, 12, 17–18
venues 161
verbal announcements 163
videos 251
visibility 8, 29, 38, 48, 57, 63, 92, 98,
        109, 110, 127, 132, 134, 137, 139,
        144, 173, 186, 192, 216, 231, 233,
        240, 264
vision 17, 23, 38, 39, 49, 61, 63, 75, 77,
        91, 124, 125, 195, 218, 229
'volcanic eruption syndrome' 133,
        245
voluntary sector 179
volunteers 28, 51, 96, 246, 247, 258
Volvo 11

Waldron, Max 51, 243, 249
webcams 159
websites 43
Westminster City Council 271
wikis 139, 142, 144, 250, 251ff., 256,
        259
Williams, Andy 127
Williams F1 Team 73–4
wireless technology 93, 158
work 11, 34, 253, 255
work/life balance 185
workers 1, 9, 10, 24, 55, 78, 144, 180,
        253, 266, 270
    demands by 18

initiative of 11
participation of 249, 251, 253, 255
and satire 109–10
workplace, 71, 72, 199
architecture of 160–62
new model for 18–20
revolution in 17–18
workshops 32, 44
written instructions 163–4
Wulf, Gabriel 24

X theory 11, 20

Xstrata 240–41, 265

Y generation 36, 253
Y theory 11, 13, 18, 19
Yo! Sushi 49
YouGov 2, 24, 58, 171, 172ff.
2008 Survey 172, 178, 182, 186, 192
2010 Survey 172, 178, 182, 184,
191, 192

Z theory 13, 19
Zak, Paul 110, 149
Zurich Financial Services 28, 161–2

If you have found this book useful you may be interested in other titles from Gower

Changing Organizations from Within
Roles, Risks and Consultancy Relationships
Edited by Susan Rosina Whittle and Robin C. Stevens
Hardback: 978-1-4094-4968-3
e-book PDF: 978-1-4094-4969-0
e-book ePUB: 978-1-4094-7472-2

Choosing Leaders and Choosing to Lead
Science, Politics and Intuition in Executive Selection
Douglas Board
Hardback: 978-1-4094-3648-5
e-book PDF: 978-1-4094-3649-2
e-book ePUB: 978-1-4094-8701-2

Employee Communication During Mergers and Acquisitions
Jenny Davenport and Simon Barrow
Hardback: 978-0-566-08638-0
e-book PDF: 978-0-7546-8141-0
e-book ePUB: 978-1-4094-5864-7

Gower Handbook of Internal Communication
Edited by Marc Wright
Hardback: 978-0-566-08689-2
e-book PDF: 978-0-7546-9097-9
e-book ePUB: 978-1-4094-5851-7

Human Resources or Human Capital?
Managing People as Assets
Andrew Mayo
Hardback: 978-1-4094-2285-3
e-book PDF: 978-1-4094-2286-0
e-book ePUB: 978-1-4094-5933-0

GOWER

Making the Connections
Using Internal Communication to Turn Strategy into Action
Bill Quirke
Paperback: 978-0-566-08780-6
e-book PDF: 978-1-4094-0516-0
e-book ePUB: 978-1-4094-6061-9

Smart Working
Creating the Next Wave
Anne Marie McEwan
Hardback: 978-1-4094-0456-9
e-book PDF: 978-1-4094-0457-6
e-book ePUB: 978-1-4094-6014-5

The CEO: Chief Engagement Officer
Turning Hierarchy Upside Down to Drive Performance
John Smythe
Paperback: 978-0-566-08561-1
e-book PDF: 978-0-7546-8180-9
e-book ePUB: 978-1-4094-6051-0

The Culture Builders
Leadership Strategies for Employee Performance
Jane Sparrow
Paperback: 978-1-4094-3724-6
e-book PDF: 978-1-4094-3725-3
e-book ePUB: 978-1-4094-8392-2

Visit **www.gowerpublishing.com** and

- search the entire catalogue of Gower books in print
- order titles online at 10% discount
- take advantage of special offers
- sign up for our monthly e-mail update service
- download free sample chapters from all recent titles
- download or order our catalogue

Hay Library
Western Wyoming Community College